Praise for
Winning Management:
6 Fail-Safe Strategies for Building High-Performance Organizations

"When your employees are satisfied, so are your customers. Rinke's strategies provide invaluable guidance."
—J.W. Marriott, Jr., Chairman of the Board and President, Marriott International, Inc.

"Cutting edge! The wisdom and inspiration of Tom Peters, Ken Blanchard, and Stephen Covey all rolled into one. Truly a must read."
—Ellyn Luros, President, Computrition

"Wolf Rinke provides you with the foundation for business success. Anyone who wants to become a more successful manager or leader should read this book."
—Tom Phillips, President, Phillips Publishing International, Inc.

"Winning Management is a dynamic, comprehensive, 'real world' approach to managing in today's chaotic business environment. Wolf Rinke has formulated a common sense management philosophy that will transcend an organization that adopts his principles. I know, our organization has grown 260% since we began utilizing Wolf's consulting services."
—Daniel Cohen, CFO, AquaGuard Waterproofing Corp.

"Wolf Rinke writes from experiences he has had with other organizations. If anyone can teach you how to win in the game of management, he can."
—Lou Holtz, Head Football Coach, University of Notre Dame

"Buy this book! But don't quit there, READ it! It will help you transform the way you manage people. Guaranteed!"
—Joseph Wolinsky, President, Chesapeake Resources, Inc.

"Ready to reengineer? Read this book first. It will save you lots of time, money, grief, and aggravation!"
—Martin Edelston, President, Boardroom Inc.

"Wolf Rinke has created a game plan for winning in the tough arena of management and leadership."
—Alan Weiss, Ph.D., Author, *Million Dollar Consulting*

"Practice what Wolf teaches you, and you will be on the road to achieving quantum leaps in performance, productivity, and profitability."
—Gary Gunderson, Corporate Manager, International Operations and New Business Development, Food Works Management Services

"Hard hitting advice that you can put to work tomorrow and make your company grow, FASTER!"
—Nido R. Qubein, Chairman, Creative Services, Inc.

"Don't buy this book, unless you're ready to have your employees perform at levels you had never thought possible!"
—Robert E. Frey, President, Cin-Made Corp.

"This book teaches you six fail-safe strategies that you need to master if you want to thrive in today's brave new downsized corporate world."
—Peter B. Petersen, Professor of Management and Organization Theory, Johns Hopkins University

"A real meat-eater's book: focused tightly with lists, quizzes and illustrations."
—T. Scott Gross, Author, *Positively Outrageous Service*

"I've witnessed the power and enthusiasm of Wolf in person. This book has the same dynamic approach and powerful information. A must read, for managers into the 90s and beyond."
  —Daniel P. Royce, Regional Manager, Michelin American Truck Tire Corp.

"If you want to not only reengineer your approach but re-invent it—read this book first. Wolf has it all together."
  —Thomas J. Winninger, CEO, Winninger Institute for Market Strategy

"Managing change in a changing corporate world requires a total new performance mindset throughout the organization. Wolf shows us how to develop that."
  —Neil S. Reyer, VP Corporate Dining Services, Chase Manhattan Bank

"This book provides leaders and managers of mid-sized companies with the ABCs of required actions which will enable their companies to thrive in today's competitive, global economy."
  —Ben T. Austin III, President & CEO, PACER International, Inc.

"This cutting edge book by seminal thinker Wolf Rinke is just superb. Read it again and again!"
  —Joe Batten, Chairman, Joe Batten Associates

"If you want to turn your business around, give all of your managers a copy of Wolf's book and then use it as the basis for communicating sound business principles."
  —Ronald G. Moyer, CEO, Advanced Medical Products, Inc., Chairman, BIOTEL International

"Some books tell you what you need to do to be an effective manager. Others tell you what it takes to become a visionary leader. This book teaches you both—how to become a Winning Manager."
  —Thomas S. Monaghan, President, Domino's Pizza, Inc.

Winning Management

Also by Wolf J. Rinke:

The Winning Foodservice Manager: Strategies for Doing More with Less
Make It a Winning Life: Success Strategies for Life, Love and Business
The 6 Success Strategies for Winning at Life, Love and Business

Winning Management

6 Fail-Safe Strategies for Building
High-Performance
Organizations

Wolf J. Rinke, PhD

ACHIEVEMENT PUBLISHERS
Clarksville, Maryland

Winning Management:
6 Fail-Safe Strategies for Building High-Performance Organizations

Published by:

Achievement Publishers
P.O. Box 350
Clarksville, MD 21029
USA

© 1997 by Wolf J. Rinke
Printed in the United States of America
1 2 3 4 5 6 7 8 9 10

Publisher's Cataloging in Publication
Rinke, Wolf J.
Winning Management:
6 Fail-Safe Strategies for Building High-Performance Organizations
p.cm.
Includes bibliographical references and index.
ISBN 0-9627913-7-7
1. Management. 2. Leadership. 3. Organizational Effectiveness I. Title.
HD30.17   R56 1997   658.4   95-083088
QB195-20657

HD
30.17
. R56
1997
Dec. 1998

Generous bulk discounts for *Winning Management: 6 Fail-Safe Strategies for
Building High-Performance Organizations* are available for sales promotions,
premiums, fund raising, education use, or other programs.

For details regarding quantity purchases, contact:

Achievement Publishers
P.O. Box 350
Clarksville, MD 21029
USA

(800) 828-9653

(410) 531-9280

Dedicated to my parents,
Horst and Anna Rinke,
who instilled the discipline in me that
made writing this book possible.

Table of Contents

Management is a journey... travel it.

Management is a game... play it.

Management is a challenge... accept it.

Management is a commitment... make it.

Management is a privilege... cherish it.

Management is a sacrifice... offer it.

Management is trust... give lots of it.

Management is love... love it!

—Wolf J. Rinke

Acknowledgments

First, I would like to thank all the unnamed heroes in my life: clients, students, mentors, and others who have helped shape my beliefs about how we must manage if we want to achieve dramatic improvements in this rapidly changing world. Since there are too many to name individually, and since undoubtedly I would omit several important people, I would like to have you find yourself in these pages. Although you may not find your name, I know that you will find your influence and the wisdom that you have shared so generously with me over the years.

However, I would like to name several people who continue to influence me in a big way and to whom I owe an incredible debt of gratitude:

Marcela, my wife and Superwoman, who is everything a man could wish for and more, much more!

My parents, Horst and Anna, whose wisdom I've learned to respect and appreciate more and more with every passing year.

My oldest daughter, Jeselle, who after dedicating herself to improving the quality of life of "throwaway" children for the past eighteen months, has recently entered the exciting field of sales. Thank you, Jeselle, for giving so much of yourself in your quest to make this world a better place.

My youngest daughter, Nicole, who has moved from being "a rebel without a cause" to firmly planting herself in the driver's seat of her life. Thank you, Nicole, for keeping me on my toes and for making me proud.

Gail, my right and left hands. Thanks for reading this manuscript more often than you cared to and for being such a dedicated team member, super customer service champion, and patient editor.

My friends, Dan Cohen of AquaGuard and Gary Gunderson of Motorola Food Works, who were kind enough to critique an early version of this manuscript.

First Things First

Management interventions do not work! Just look at what happened to management by objectives (MBO), participative management (PM), total quality management (TQM), all the other derivatives of the quality movement, downsizing, rightsizing, and reengineering. According to Michael Hammer, the co-author of *Reengineering the Corporation* and most ardent advocate of this latest management intervention, 70 percent of all reengineering projects fail to deliver the results that management expected! These outcomes are probably very similar to all the other management approaches that have preceded reengineering. Why? Because managers are ill-informed? Because consultants don't know what they are doing? Because employees don't care? I believe the answer to all of these is a resounding *no!* I believe, based on what I have learned from my clients, that all of these interventions provide disappointing results for two major reasons.

The first, and this is the big one, is because managers have not built a solid *foundation.* Let me explain. Let's say you want to build your dream house. Since this is going to be your dream house, you buy the best of everything—the best lumber, the best bricks, the best roof, and so on. Then you proceed to build your dream house on quicksand. Will it last? Does it matter that you bought the best of everything? Of course not! However, that is how most managers go about implementing changes in their organization. They buy the best, or at least the latest, of everything and begin the implementation without a solid foundation, without getting their own heads screwed on right, without changing their basic belief system (especially as it relates to people), without clearly defining their philosophy and core values, and without changing the organizational culture. As a result, just like the dream house built on quicksand, the interventions will work for a while, but then they will crumble or even implode. The result is that instead of effecting a positive change, a change that will help build high-performance organizations, employees feel used or even abused; they become cynical and strengthen their basic defense mechanisms so that they can remain sane. The outcome is lowered performance and productivity and resistant employees who have mastered the art of playing the "let's pretend" game, who have hardened their protective shells just a little bit more so that they can survive the next management "solution" that will be coming along very soon.

The second reason that management interventions fail is that U.S. managers are too impatient. (That's an understatement.) They want results *now!* Actually, most of the time they want results yesterday. It reminds me of the person who has been overeating for thirty years and one day steps on the scale only to realize: "I'm fat." He immediately begins his search for a magical diet and, having found it, goes on it right away. And if that diet does not work in thirty days, the diet is "no good"! Effective long-term changes in weight can only come about as a result of a change in *behavior!* And changing one's behavior, as any mental health professional will tell you, takes time, lots of time. Changing the behavior of many people, which is what organizational interventions are all about, takes even longer—at least three to eight years. Of course, during that time several "new" management (dare I say the *F* word?) "fads" come along, which cause managers to jump ship. After all, it's tough to stick with an "outdated" management model when all your colleagues and competitors are doing the "in thing."

In short, what I'm saying is that just about any management paradigm works *if* you build a strong foundation and *if* you have the guts to *stick with it over the long term!* Perhaps the following reality check can serve to reinforce my point! I must confess it is one of my favorites because it is so "with it." (Be sure to note the date!)

Reality Check *

We trained hard... but it seemed that every time we were beginning to form up into teams we would be reorganized.... I was to learn later in life that we tend to meet any new situation by reorganizing; and a wonderful method it can be for creating the illusion of progress while producing confusion, inefficiency, and demoralization.

—Petronius Arbiter (1st century A.D.)

---

*I've inserted "Reality Checks" throughout this book to provide you with an occasional wake-up call and help you put things in perspective.

This book will address these challenges. It will help you build a high-performance organization, an organization that will achieve dramatic improvements in performance, productivity, and profitability. The second challenge, applying what you have learned and sticking with it over the long term, is up to you!

I am excited to have the opportunity to help you master the art of practicing *winning management* and am honored that you are reading this book.

If you have questions or suggestions, please feel free to contact me:

Wolf J. Rinke
c/o Achievement Publishers
P.O. Box 350
Clarksville, MD 21029
Phone: (410) 531-9280 Fax: (410) 531-9282
e-mail: wolfrinke@aol.com or 74267, 3703@compuserv.com

Mastering *winning management* is a journey. Enjoy traveling the journey!

Winning Action Step *

Get excited about the business you are in, and be sure to spread that excitement to all your team members and customers. If you can't get excited about the business you are in, make a plan to get out of it now! You'll never be excellent at it, nor will it be profitable!

---

*I've inserted "Winning Action Steps" throughout this book to help you translate knowledge into practice

Let's Get Started

1

To increase your power—give it away.

—Wolf J. Rinke

Welcome to a brave new world! A world dominated by globalization, information technologies, and dismantled hierarchies. A world fraught with seemingly overwhelming challenges and opportunities. As managers, we can perceive these challenges as crises and problems, or we can see them as opportunities—opportunities that will enable us to go beyond survival and help us thrive now and in the next millennium. To make that goal a reality, we must learn to harness the power of our employees—the people I like to refer to as *team members*. That paradigm shift, or transformation, starts with empowering ourselves first by maximizing our personal and professional potential.[1] Once we have mastered that, we are ready to cross the bridge from being an autocratic or traditional manager to becoming a *winning manager,* a manager who has mastered the art of empowering team members so that they can help build high-performance organizations and achieve dramatic improvements in performance, productivity, and profitability. That's what this book will help you do.

PREVIEW OF COMING ATTRACTIONS

To help you figure out where we are going, I will begin each chapter with a brief overview, a sort of preview of coming attractions. So let's get started by finding out what you are going to learn in this chapter. First, I'll provide you with a compelling reason why it is imperative that you adopt a new management paradigm. Then you'll get a chance to differentiate between leadership and management. Next you'll have an opportunity to find out what, specifically, I mean by *winning management,* assess your own readiness for implementing this new management paradigm, find out what it takes to learn how to become a *winning manager,* and assess your team members' readiness for a management transformation. I will also provide you with an overview of what's to come in the rest of this book, which will help you become a *winning manager.*

Reality Check
There is nothing permanent except change.
—Heraclitus (540–475 B.C.)

MANAGEMENT TRANSFORMATION: WHY BOTHER?

Good question! Why bother? Perhaps you don't feel a need to change anything. You might be saying to yourself, things are just fine the way they are. The short answer is one you may have heard before: "If it ain't broke, fix it anyway!" The longer answer comes from Jeffrey Pfeffer, who analyzed the data of the best performing companies, i.e., the companies that provided the greatest return to stockholders during 1972–1992. According to Pfeffer, the top five stocks and their percentage returns were: Southwest Airlines (21,775 percent), Wal-Mart (19,807 percent), Tyson Foods (18,118 percent), Circuit City (16,410 percent), and Plenum Publishing (15,689 percent).[2] What Pfeffer found startling was that these companies, which basically represented four different industries (airlines, retailing, food processing, and publishing), had few of the competitive advantages that one typically attributes to such super performers. Just the opposite was true. Instead they "were characterized by massive competition, and horrendous losses, widespread bankruptcy, virtually no barriers to entry (for airlines after 1978), little unique or proprietary technology, and many substitute products or services."[3] So what did they have in common? All of these firms achieved their competitive success through people—by empowering people, instead of replacing them, and by seeing people as a source of strategic advantage, not as a cost to be minimized.

Similar findings were reported by Huselid,[4] who studied a national sample of nearly one thousand firms that adopted what he called *high-performance work practices* (including incentive compensation, performance management systems, extensive employee involvement, and training). His findings confirmed that investments in *high-performance work practices* are "associated with lower employee turnover and greater productivity and corporate financial performance."[5] Such improvements, according to this research, were substantial. "A one-standard-deviation increase in such practices is associated with a relative 7.05 percent decrease in turnover and, on a per employee basis, $27,044 more in sales and $18,641 and $3,814 more in market value and profits, respectively."[6]

Reality Check
"…[companies] can do the right thing and make money."
—President Bill Clinton[7]

The ability to do right by people *and* make money has been achieved by such mega corporations as Corning, Cummings Engine, Johnson and Johnson, United Airlines, Kellogg, and Republic Engineered Steels.[8] But, you protest, we just don't have the kind of resources these big guys do! I hear you. So let me give you examples of several small to midsize companies that have achieved the same kind of benefits from building a kinder, gentler organization.[9]

Let's start with Cin-Made, a Cincinnati-based $6 million manufacturer of cardboard cans and boxes. Hardly what you would call a glamour industry. President Bob Frey encourages his employees to take advantage of continuing education and training opportunities (the kind you'll be learning more about in chapter 5) by paying 75 percent of all employee education expenses. The result? An increase in on-time delivery from 74 percent to 98 percent during 1990–1995, and a 100 percent increase in sales during the same period! Not too bad, would you say?

How about Phillips Publishing International, a privately owned publisher of over one hundred information sources, including newsletters, magazines, and directories, based in Potomac, Maryland. Tom Phillips, the founder and president, is passionate about investing in his most important resource—his people—and building an incredibly positive organizational climate (which you'll learn about in chapter 3). In addition, he goes to extraordinary lengths to transform his employees into what he calls *business builders,* by providing them with numerous continuing education and training opportunities and by promoting from within. Has it paid off? Well, I'll let you be the judge. The company has grown from an initial investment of one thousand dollars in 1974 to sales of $227 million in 1996. The average annual growth during this period was 38 percent, with sales doubling during each of the last three years.

Fel-Pro is a family owned automotive supply company in Skokie, Illinois, with $390 million in sales in 1995. Fel-Pro, under the able leadership of President Paul Lederer, does not just do right by their employees, they even worry about their families. For example, new parents receive a one thousand dollar savings bond and a pair of bronzed baby shoes. What does Fel-Pro get out of it? Incredible employee loyalty with an unheard of low employee turnover rate of less than 1 percent.

And then there is superstar, and darling of Wall Street, Starbucks, the specialty coffee company from Seattle with $465 million in sales. Another employer, albeit a bit larger, who believes in creating a kinder, gentler workplace. CEO Howard Schultz has done what is virtually unheard of in the retail world. He offers generous health benefits as well as equity in the form of stock options to all employees who work at least twenty hours a week. Why? Because he likes to waste his money? No! Because he found that above average employees with relatively high education levels consider health benefits a powerful draw. And it is these kinds of people who have helped Starbucks sustain a 700 percent sales growth during 1991–1995.

In short, all of these companies, small and large, unleash the power of their people by investing in them. They provide you with compelling reasons to change your management style: *because you want to thrive, not just survive, in this brave new business world.* And the easiest way to achieve that is to master *winning management.* Let's begin by clarifying some basic terminology.

Winning Action Step

Just say *yes* whenever new empowerment opportunities present themselves to you.

Leadership Versus Management: Is There a Difference?

I guess the best way to find out whether there is a difference between management and leadership is to begin with a definition. So I did my homework and consulted several classic textbooks. That was really confusing! There were almost as many definitions as there are authors. In any event, here are two that I thought represented the majority. Kreitner defined *management* as the "process of working with and through others to achieve organizational objectives in a changing environment."[10] Hellriegel and Slocum, on the other hand, defined *leadership* as the "ability to influence, motivate and direct others in order to attain desired objectives."[11] Are those really different, or are we splitting hairs? To answer that, I really had to get "into it." As a result of my extensive research, I came to the conclusion that even though the definitions may be very similar, what managers and leaders do *is* different.

Once I delineated the differences between management and leadership, it became evident that meeting the challenges of today's new business environment demands the process skills of a manager and, even more important, the vision and people orientation of a leader. In other words, even though leadership is currently "in" and management is "out" (Doubt it? Check the bookstores and see how many recent books there are on leadership versus management), I maintain that *we need both!* What I'm saying is that if you want to win in this brave new world, you must go beyond the traditional skills you were taught as a manager and develop or fine tune your leadership skills. One without the other might enable you to survive in today's rapidly changing business environment, but if you want to thrive and win in the game of management, you must not only do things right, at the same time you must also do the right things. In short, *winning managers* must master management skills *and* leadership skills and consistently *do the right things right.*(See Exhibit 1-1.)

Exhibit 1-1: Management Versus Leadership[12]

Management	Leadership
Doing things right	Doing the right things
Administration	Innovation
Maintenance	Development
Structure/system	People
Control	Trust
Direct	Inspire
Strategies	Vision
Power	Empowering

Winning Action Step

Get yourself a current management or leadership book, or better yet audiotape album. (There are several listed in the "For Your Continuing Learning" section of this book.) Study and listen. Now repeat this process so that you read or listen to at least one new management or leadership book every six months.

Winning Management: A Definition

At this point you're probably asking: "Okay, so what then is *winning management?*" I'm glad you asked, because that means you're with me and I like that. Here is my definition: *Winning management* is the art and science of empowering others to help them get the job done. My colleagues, who are pushing leadership as *the* skill to master for the next millennium, are partially missing the boat. We must adopt a new paradigm, one that encompasses both management and leadership, if we want to thrive in this rapidly changing and highly competitive world. (You know that a paradigm is a pair of dimes, don't you? Just kidding! The word *paradigm* comes from the Greek *paradeigma* and refers to a way of interpreting the world around you.)

So what is your management reality or road map? To find out, check yourself by reviewing Exhibit 1-2, which describes two different ways of looking at management.

Exhibit 1-2: What Kind of Manager Are You?

Traditional Manager	**Winning Manager**
Thinks of self as a cop or boss	Thinks of self as a coach or team leader
Thinks of employees as subordinates	Thinks of employees as team members
Follows the chain of command	Utilizes anyone to get the job done
Works within an organizational structure	Changes the organizational structure in response to market changes
Makes most decisions alone	Utilizes group decision-making
Hoards information	Shares information
Masters one major discipline (e.g., finance)	Masters many disciplines
Demands long hours	Demands results
Assumes that the company will do career planning	Assumes responsibility for own career career planning
Resists change and chaos	Thrives on change and chaos

Winning Action Step

Whenever you get a chance to practice *winning management*, do it. Make a mental or written note of what worked and what didn't. Remember, the ideal is to build on the concepts in this book, so that you end up with a paradigm that is uniquely yours.

Nature Versus Nurture

But, you protest: "I've been at this too long; I'm not ready for all this change. Besides, you can't teach an old dog new tricks." I certainly don't agree with that, but I suppose I'd better address the perennial nature-versus-nurture argument. In other words, can *winning management* be learned, or are we born with it? Since we know that we can learn to be managers, the next question is: Can we learn to be leaders and *winning managers?* Noted management guru Peter Drucker[13] maintains that leadership cannot be created or promoted, taught or learned. Indeed, if we review the leadership literature, we can find some empirical evidence to support his position. For example, Kouzes and Posner[14] reported on an AT&T study that followed the managerial careers of 422 recruits for thirty years. Using a series of instruments, the Managerial Progress Study (MPS) concluded that the skills and motivational patterns needed to predict managerial success were for the most part exhibited by the recruits in the first year and did not appear to result from developmental activities throughout their careers.

Fortunately, for every study supporting the nature theory, there appears to be about twice as many supporting the nurture paradigm. For example, after studying sixty CEOs and thirty leaders in the corporate and public sector, Bennis and Nanus[15] concluded that leadership can be learned and taught to anyone. Similarly, after studying five hundred middle- and senior-level managers, Kouzes and Posner[16] concluded that leadership involves basic practices and specific behaviors, all of which can be learned by managers at all levels. Covey[17] has popularized learning to lead with his best-selling book, *Principle-Centered Leadership,* and Bennis and Goldsmith[18] dedicated an entire book to teaching you how to become a leader.

Personally, I support the idea that there are certain innate abilities that will give you a higher probability of becoming an effective leader. They include such things as your level of intelligence (however that is measured or whatever that means), your emotional quotient (EQ),[19] how you look, your aptitude for language, and the family you were born into. Since you really can't control any of these, except your EQ, it is a waste of time to worry about them. More importantly, even if you possess all of these factors, no one can guarantee you that you will become an effective leader.

By the same token, it is possible to become an effective leader even if you possess none of these factors. The history books are full of the exceptions: Golda Meir, Winston Churchill, Martin Luther King, and the list goes on. In short, there simply are no scientifically reliable leadership predictors. Beyond that, my own experience confirms that people who are properly guided and taught have the ability to improve their leadership skills. Of course, the bottom line for me is that I'm a very different leader today than I was twenty short years ago. Given this conclusion, the next question is, are you ready for this paradigm shift?

Reality Check

Insignificant earthquakes, like incremental change in organizations, may cause rumblings, but often do little or nothing to relieve the pressure.

—Rhonda K. Reger

ARE YOU READY FOR THE TRANSFORMATION?

Now that you have a better idea of what I mean by *winning management* and have become convinced that you can master these skills, let's find out if you and your organization are ready for this transformation. After all, it is embarrassing to hold a revolution and have no one show or, worse, to try to have a revolution without leaders and followers. To find out if you are ready for the transformation, complete Exhibit 1-3 now. It outlines the twelve skills you must possess (or at least have the willingness to develop) to ensure that your transformation will be successful.

Learning How to Become a *Winning Manager*

To learn how to become a *winning manager,* you must start with *you*. It's the old saw that got its start with Socrates when he said, "The unexamined life is not worth living." (At least I think it was Socrates who said that; I just can't remember that far back.) And so it is with becoming a *winning manager.* To get good at it, you have to know yourself, understand where you are coming from, what's important to you, and where you are going. In other words, you have to be very clear about your values and your beliefs because they will be your guiding light on your *winning management* travels. Without having them clearly defined, you will be like the proverbial ship without a rudder, or the chameleon who changes his style with every new management fad that comes along.

Exhibit 1-3: *Winning Management* Self-Assessment Instrument

Instructions: Answer each question with a *Yes* if you are currently practicing what the statement describes, or if it applies to you. Answer *No* if it does not apply to you.

		Yes	No
1.	I know what I want my organization to be when it grows up, i.e., I have a compelling vision.	___	___
2.	I trust every team member.	___	___
3.	I am in the habit of giving my power away.	___	___
4.	My employees see me as a coach instead of a cop.	___	___
5.	I focus most of my efforts on service and quality, not on cost cutting.	___	___
6.	I consistently demonstrate a willingness to change *everything.*	___	___
7.	I invest in team members to help them become the best they can be.	___	___
8.	I provide team members with the opportunity to make mistakes and solve problems.	___	___
9.	I let team members make changes they suggest.	___	___
10.	I reward team members for improving the way they serve our customers.	___	___
11.	I tell team members more than they want to know about *all* aspects of our business.	___	___
12.	I spend the greatest proportion of my time with team members and customers.	___	___
	TOTAL:	___	___

Now, count how many *Yes* and how many *No* responses you have. If you have all Yes responses, you are already practicing *winning management* and have perhaps bought this book for reinforcement. If you have one or two *No* responses, you need to pay close attention to those areas that represent your areas for improvement. If you have more than two *No* responses, you will want to pay very close attention to this entire book.

This is the other reason why I'm firmly convinced that practicing *winning management* is a combination of nature and nurture, with the greatest emphasis on the latter. Speaking for myself, I had heard the admonition to "Know thyself" thousands of times. But for whatever reason, although it had registered cognitively, I did not really internalize it until several years ago. What turned things around for me was the realization that all people are different, that there is no perfection in the universe, and that everyone has a set of strengths and weaknesses, including me. This final realization led me to accept myself for what I am, instead of what someone else, such as parents and bosses, thought I *ought* to be. From that realization, as basic as it may sound, I derived all kinds of powerful outcomes. For example, once I began to like, respect, and love myself as I am, I began to be at peace with myself. That sense of peace led to a feeling of security that provided me the ability to like, love, and respect the diversity in other people. As a result, I began to see people's strengths, instead of their weaknesses. Once I was able to see people's strengths, I was able to build on them, for the most part forgetting about their weaknesses. (You don't see things unless you look for them.) In other words, it allowed me to see people as unique in their own right, instead of attempting to restructure or clone them in my own image. Even though this sounds simplistic, it took me more than twenty years of management and leadership experience to internalize it. I also know that my effectiveness has increased proportionately with my ability to become the "captain of my own ship." (If you'd like help traveling this journey, consult the "For Your Continuing Learning" section at the end of this book).

Winning Action Step

Next time you meet someone new—a new employee, customer, colleague, etc.—stop and analyze your initial attitude toward that person. If you tend to view the newcomer in negative terms, make a commitment to revise your attitude by assuming that every stranger you meet is okay in every respect until he proves you wrong.

In addition to getting to know yourself, you can also enhance your leadership skills by learning from:

1. *Mentors.* Mentoring is one of the best ways to grow leaders. A mentor can be anyone who will take an interest in you and tell it to you straight. If your boss fills this bill, consider yourself lucky. You will have hit the jackpot, especially if she* is also a winner and a mover and shaker. Be sure to understudy that type of mentor as long as possible, since she literally will be your ticket to success. Your lessons should come from observations of your mentor in action and being open to her feedback, both good and bad. So, when your mentor tells it like it is, listen up and don't be defensive, even if it hurts. A good mentor will also help you make valuable connections and give you every opportunity to practice your *winning management* skills. In other words, good mentors will give you more responsibilities than you can handle. They will also be willing to take risks by putting you in positions which initially may be over your head. Take advantage of those opportunities. If you are less fortunate and work mostly with autocratic managers, remember that you can learn from both good and bad behavior. Just be sure *not* to do what the autocratic managers do!

Winning Action Step

Find a mentor. Ideally it should be someone senior to you in your organization. Develop and nurture your relationship carefully so that the two of you establish a bond of trust. Be aggressive about learning everything you possibly can learn from your mentor, and be sure to provide your mentor with positive feedback whenever possible.

2. *On-the-job training.* Another effective strategy is to learn how to lead by trial and error. In other words, take the leadership initiative at every opportunity you have. You must, however, evaluate your efforts carefully so that you can learn from your successes but—equally important—also from your mistakes.

---

*To deal with the gender issue, I've elected to randomize male and female roles throughout the book instead of resorting to the cumbersome he/she him/her designations.

3. *Formal training and education.* Kouzes and Posner,[20] in their study of five hundred leaders, reported that educational activities are less important as a source of developing leadership skills than either mentors or trial and error. They estimated that formal training accounts for approximately 10 to 20 percent of the lessons of leadership. However, that is an important source for attaining *winning management* skills, especially since you will not always be fortunate enough to have an effective mentor.

4. *Self-directed learning.* Bennis and Goldsmith[21] maintain that being willing to become a lifelong learner is an important attribute of leaders. Senge[22] goes one step further and convinces us that becoming a "learning organization" is *the* competitive edge in today's marketplace. To become a voracious self-directed learner, I recommend that you read autobiographies of effective leaders, listen to audiotapes instead of being unproductive while in your car, and attend seminars and other continuing education activities on an ongoing basis. Going through Bennis and Goldman's workbook[23] will also enable you to develop *winning management* skills, while at the same time help you figure out what makes you tick. To make sure that you are able to thrive in this brave new world, I recommend that you spend 2 to 5 percent of your income on personal and professional self-development activities.

Winning Action Step

Schedule a minimum of two continuing education activities per year for yourself. If your organization won't pay for them, negotiate for time off and pay for it yourself. You are making an investment in your own future, which is the best investment you can possibly make.

Are Your Team Members Ready for the Transformation?

Assuming you are ready for this paradigm shift, let's see if your team members are ready for your new management paradigm. We know that virtually all of your success as a manager depends on your team members. If they are not ready for this new way of managing, then the transformation is not likely to succeed. Another way to say this is that leaders are only as good as their followers, and *winning managers* are only as good as their team members. So before you make any changes, let's start by finding out how well your employees are performing as part of a group or team.

Research tells us that every group, whether it is a social or work group, goes through four specific stages. The characteristics of each of these stages, which Tuckman[24] referred to as *forming, storming, norming,* and *performing,* are summarized in Exhibit 1-4.

Exhibit 1-4: Stages of Team Development[25]

- **FORMING**
  - The members of the team are concerned with testing boundaries of appropriate behavior.
- **STORMING**
  - Conflict occurs around interpersonal and task issues.
  - Team members seek personal recognition and their own spheres of influence.
- **NORMING**
  - The climate becomes one of compromise and harmony as shared attitudes and values develop along with clearer role expectations, a division of labor, and standard modes of behavior.
  - Personal feelings are subordinated to the team interest.
- **PERFORMING**
  - Structural and interpersonal issues have been resolved.
  - Team members get on with the task.

Research in group formation and team building has demonstrated that teams increase their effectiveness as they become more mature. (See Exhibit 1-5.)

Although every team must pass through each stage before it can get to the next, only a few are able to reach maturity and become a truly efficient and effective team. Of course, your transformation is significantly expedited if you are able to "travel" with a relatively mature team. So take a moment to complete Exhibit 1-6 to assess the level of maturity of your team members.

Exhibit 1-5: Stages of Team Development

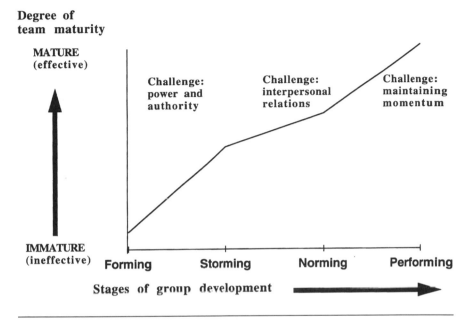

Exhibit 1-6: Team Member Effectiveness Scale[26]

Instructions: Using the following scale, circle the number that corresponds to your level of disagreement or agreement with each statement. *Please ignore the numerical values* when making a decision. (For purposes of this instrument, "team members" are the people you work with or who report to you.)

SCALE:	Strongly Disagree	Disagree	Neutral	Agree	Strongly Agree
	SD	D	N	A	SA

	SD	D	N	A	SA
Trust					
1. Members of this team trust each other very much.	1	2	3	4	5
2. Team members are playing roles in this team and are not being themselves.	5	4	3	2	1
3. Some members are afraid of the team.	5	4	3	2	1
4. The team treats everyone on the team as an important member.	1	2	3	4	5

5. Members seem to care very much for each other as individuals.	1	2	3	4	5

Openness

6. Members of this team are not really interested in what other team members have to say.	5	4	3	2	1
7. Members of this team tell it like it is.	1	2	3	4	5
8. Members often express feelings and opinions outside of the team different from those they express inside the team.	5	4	3	2	1
9. Team members are afraid to be open and honest with each other.	5	4	3	2	1
10. Team members don't keep secrets from each other.	1	2	3	4	5

Freedom

11. Members do what is required of them out of a personal sense of responsibility to the team.	1	2	3	4	5
12. The team puts excessive pressure on each member to work toward team goals.	5	4	3	2	1
13. When decisions are being made, members of the team express their thoughts freely.	1	2	3	4	5
14. The team spends a lot of energy trying to get members to do things they really don't want to do.	5	4	3	2	1
15. Members of the team are growing and changing all the time.	1	2	3	4	5

Interdependence

16. Everyone on the team does his or her own thing with little thought for other members of the team.	5	4	3	2	1
17. People on the team depend on each other to get the work done.	1	2	3	4	5
18. You need lots of control to keep the team on track.	5	4	3	2	1
19. There is little destructive competition on the team.	1	2	3	4	5
20. You really need to have some type of power to get anything done on the team.	5	4	3	2	1

TOTAL: _____

Adapted from *The 1977 Annual Handbook for Group Facilitators* by J.E. Jones and J.W Pfeiffer (eds.).©1977 by Pfeiffer, an imprint of Jossey-Bass, Inc., Publishers, San Francisco, CA. Used with permission.

Scoring Instructions: Total the numbers you have circled in the space provided.

Team Member Effectiveness: What Your Score Means

95–100   Lucky you! You have a highly efficient and effective mature team that is chomping at the bit and can't wait to perform! I can assume that you are already practicing *winning management* and can't wait to learn more about it. Remember, *winning managers* are voracious lifelong learners.

85–94   Smile, your group is just about at the performing stage. Your team members are ready to help you achieve the transformation. They may require some additional coaching and/or education and training to resolve *minor* structural and interpersonal issues. All in all, they are ready to get on with it! So what are you waiting for?

75–84   Your group is probably norming and will require additional coaching, education, and training to get to the next stage. Having a common vision and being task focused may, especially with the right guidance, help to get your group to the next stage. Go ahead and proceed with caution.

65–74   Storming describes your group. That means you must get your group involved in various trust and team-building exercises that will help minimize conflict and build a team spirit. Practicing *winning management* is exactly what the doctor ordered for your team! It also means that you must proceed slowly and cautiously with the transformation.

<65   Quit! I'm just kidding, but your team and other managers need more than *winning management.* I would suggest that you engage a consultant with team-building experience to coach you and your management team and to provide your team members with education and training to improve the maturity of your group. (The organizational transformation process (OTP) described in chapter 7 provides an excellent framework for such an intervention.)

Winning Action Step

Reflect on the findings from the assessments in this chapter. Find one behavior, attribute, or skill you want to change. Implement this change consistently for twenty-one days or until it becomes a new habit. Now repeat this process until you have created powerful habits that will enable you to win in the game of management.

THE SIX Cs: KEYS TO *WINNING MANAGEMENT*

Now that you have assessed yourself and your team, you're ready to reinvent yourself and your organization so that you can move from a machine economy to a chip economy. Exhibit 1-7 outlines what it will take for you to make this happen. It also shows you that a massive barrier will stand in your way.

Exhibit 1-7: How to Reinvent Yourself[27]

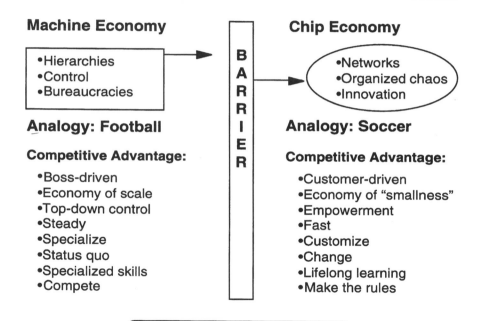

Machine Economy

- Hierarchies
- Control
- Bureaucracies

Analogy: Football

Competitive Advantage:

- Boss-driven
- Economy of scale
- Top-down control
- Steady
- Specialize
- Status quo
- Specialized skills
- Compete

BARRIER

Chip Economy

- Networks
- Organized chaos
- Innovation

Analogy: Soccer

Competitive Advantage:

- Customer-driven
- Economy of "smallness"
- Empowerment
- Fast
- Customize
- Change
- Lifelong learning
- Make the rules

Barrier Busters: The Six *C*s

- Creating a philosophy
- Climate-building
- Coaching
- Communicating
- Customer focused
- Change-driven

This barrier can be overcome by mastering the six critical *winning management* strategies, which I refer to as the six Cs:

- Creating an organizational philosophy
- Climate-building
- Coaching and empowering
- Communicating
- Customer focused
- Change-driven

Mastering these strategies will enable you to empower today's employee—an employee who is increasingly expecting and, in some cases, demanding a job that provides satisfaction, recognition, participation, and achievement. Mastering these *six Cs* will enable you to build a high-performance organization, an organization that will thrive in a rapidly changing, global, and highly competitive world.

SUMMARY

- A sustainable competitive advantage can best be achieved through the effective management of people.
- There is a difference between what effective managers, leaders, and *winning managers* do. Managers do things right, leaders do the right things, and *winning managers* do the *right things right*.
- *Winning management* is the art and science of empowering others to help them get the job done.
- You must learn to master *winning management* skills if you want to thrive in today's highly competitive and rapidly changing world.
- Becoming a *winning manager* must begin with *you*.
- *Winning management* skills can best be learned from:
  — Mentors
  — On-the-job training
  — Formal training and education
  — Self-directed learning
- Every team goes through four stages of development: forming, storming, norming, and performing.
- Only mature teams are able to maximize effectiveness and productivity and support a management paradigm shift.

- The six critical *winning management* strategies that will enable you to build a high-performance organization are:
  — Creating an organizational philosophy
  — Climate-building
  — Coaching
  — Communicating
  — Customer focused
  — Change-driven

Reality Check
Your organization is only as good as your people.

—Wolf J. Rinke

NOTES

1. W. J. Rinke, *The 6 Success Strategies for Winning at Life, Love and Business* (Deerfield Beach, FL: Health Communications, Inc., 1996).
2. J. Pfeffer, "Producing Sustainable Competitive Advantage through the Effective Management of People," *Academy of Management Executive* 9, no. 1 (1995): 55–72.
3. Ibid., 56.
4. M. A. Huselid, "The Impact of Human Resource Management Practices on Turnover, Productivity, and Corporate Financial Performance," *Academy of Management Journal* 38, no. 3 (1995): 635–672.
5. Ibid., 667.
6. Ibid.
7. J. Calmes, "'Corporate Citizens' Get Clintonian Nod as Good Workers," *Wall Street Journal*, 17 May 1996, p. B-3.
8. Ibid.
9. C. Chandler and S. Pearlstein, "All the President's Paragons?" *Washington Post*, 16 May 1996, pp. D-11, D-12.
10. R. Kreitner, *Management*, 5th ed. (Boston: Houghton Mifflin Co., 1992), p. 8.
11. D. Hellriegel and J. W. Slocum Jr., *Management*, 6th ed. (Reading, MA: Addison-Wesley Publishing Co., 1992), p. 467.
12. W. J. Rinke, *The Winning Foodservice Manager:* Strategies for Doing More with Less, 2nd ed. (Clarksville, MD: Achievement Publishers, division of Wolf Rinke Associates, Inc., 1990), p. 153.
13. P. Drucker, *The Practice of Management* (New York: Harper and Brothers, 1954).
14. J. M. Kouzes and B. Z. Posner, *The Leadership Challenge* (San Francisco: Jossey-Bass, Inc., Publishers, 1987).

15. W. Bennis and B. Nanus, Leaders: *The Strategies for Taking Charge* (New York: Harper and Row, Publishers, 1985).
16. Kouzes and Posner, *The Leadership Challenge.*
17. S. R. Covey, *Principle-Centered Leadership* (New York: Simon and Schuster, 1991).
18. W. Bennis and J. Goldsmith, *Learning to Lead* (Reading, MA: Addison-Wesley Publishing Co., 1994).
19. D. Goleman, *Emotional Intelligence* (New York: Bantam Books, 1995).
20. Kouzes and Posner, *The Leadership Challenge.*
21. Bennis and Goldsmith, *Learning to Lead.*
22. P. M. Senge, "The Leader's New Work: Building Learning Organizations," *Sloan Management Review* (Fall 1990): 7–23.
23. Bennis and Goldsmith, *Learning to Lead.*
24. B. W. Tuckman, "Developmental Sequences in Small Groups," *Psychology Bulletin* 63 (1965): 384–99.
25. B. W. Tuckman and M. A. C. Jensen, "Stages of Small Group Development Revisited," *Group and Organization Studies* 2 (1977): 419–427.
26. Adapted from J. R. Gibb, "TORI Group Self-Diagnosis Scale," in J. W. Pfeiffer and J. E. Jones (eds.), *The 1977 Annual Handbook for Group Facilitators* (San Diego, CA: University Associates, Inc., 1977).
27. Adapted from N. Tichy and S. Sherman, *Control Your Destiny or Someone Else Will* (New York: Currency Doubleday, 1993), p. 314.

Winning Action Step

Want to get promoted faster? Find out what your boss does not like to do, and do more of it.

Creating an
Organizational Philosophy

2

Senior managers… must move beyond strategy, structure and systems to a framework built on purpose, process and people.
—Christopher A. Bartlett and Sumantra Ghoshal

An organization can be like the proverbial ship without a rudder, not having any idea where it is going. (You know that if you don't know where you're going, the last thing you want to do is get there any faster.) As a result, people basically feel listless, discouraged, and unmotivated, never quite sure what the organization stands for, where it is headed, what it is passionate about, and what role and responsibility each individual plays to help it get there. Such an organization is one where people are majoring in minors and are occupied with stress-relieving activities instead of goal achieving tasks. On the other hand, you can create an organization where people have a clear sense of what the organization stands for, what its purpose is, where the organization is headed, how it plans to get there, and the specific role and responsibility each individual must perform to make sure the organization stays on track. In such organizations, people become committed, have a sense of pride, are motivated, feel valued, and become energized.

PREVIEW OF COMING ATTRACTIONS

In the previous chapter, I convinced you that there is a difference between management, leadership, and *winning management,* and

I'm sure you've become sensitive to the need of becoming a *winning manager.* In this chapter, you'll have an opportunity to better understand the importance of an organizational mission, vision, and values, as well as better understand exactly what those terms mean. You'll also learn to identify the six steps you need to follow to create and disseminate an empowering organizational philosophy—a philosophy that will serve as the driving force for the organization, empower team members, and lead to the attainment of organizational goals and objectives.

Reality Check
Where there is no vision, the people perish.

—Proverbs 29:18

PHILOSOPHY-BUILDING SKILLS: A QUICK SELF-DIAGNOSIS

Wait! Before you get into this chapter, you should complete the brief self-diagnosis instrument on the following pages. This will tell you how well you are equipped to help your team members "sing from the same sheet of music." Please take time now to complete Exhibit 2-1.

Exhibit 2-1: Philosophy-Building Skills: A Self-Analysis[1]

Instructions: Using the following scale, circle the number that corresponds to your level of disagreement or agreement with each statement. (People have different preferences and opinions; therefore, there are no right or wrong answers.)

SCALE: Strongly Disagree   Disagree   Neutral   Agree   Strongly Agree
            SD   D   N   A   SA

	SD	D	N	A	SA
1. I know why we are in business.	1	2	3	4	5
2. I am able to express my own value system.	1	2	3	4	5
3. An organizational philosophy has little impact on the bottom line.	1	2	3	4	5

4. My value system has little to do with how well I manage.   1 2 3 4 5

5. "Knowing myself" is one of the best ways to help me improve my *winning management* skills.   1 2 3 4 5

6. Every one of my team members knows our organizational philosophy by heart.   1 2 3 4 5

7. I believe that my team members basically want the same things for the organization as I do.   1 2 3 4 5

8. One of the most important responsibilities of a *winning manager* is to communicate the philosophy of the organization.   1 2 3 4 5

9. Managers need to know the philosophy of the organization more than anyone else.   1 2 3 4 5

10. Translating the philosophy into a slogan adds to information overload.   1 2 3 4 5

TOTAL: _____

Scoring Instructions: Score each item in accordance with the number you have circled, *except items 3, 4, 9, and 10,* which have to be scored by reversing the scale, so that 1 = 5, 2 = 4, 3 = 3, 4 = 2, 5 = 1. Then total the scores in the space provided.

Examples:

1. I know why we are .... 1 2 3 ④ 5 = 4
2. I am able to express my own............................... ① 2 3 4 5 = 1
3. An organizational philosophy............................. 1 ② 3 4 5 = 4

Philosophy-Building Skills: What Your Score Means

47–50   *Philosophy-building is your bag.* That means that practicing *winning management* should be like second nature to you. Give yourself an A+, and be sure to mentor others who are not as talented as you are.

43–46   *Excellent*—you really know how to get people to "sing from the same sheet of music."

39–42   *Very good*—you are on the right track.

35–38   *Good*—but you can do better. However, you know that already. After all, that's why you are reading this powerful book.

31–34   *Okay*—but you have not even begun to scratch your winning management potential. Get ready, get set... to learn and apply!

<31   *Time to pay attention.* Yes, you are definitely going to get your money's worth from this book.

PHILOSOPHY: WHO CARES?

The foregoing assessment will have provided you with an insight of just how important an organizational philosophy is to you. But what are the implications for your management effectiveness? Perhaps this philosophy stuff is just all a bunch of fluff. Not according to a study by Larwood et al., who investigated chief executives in 250 companies.[2] The researchers found that those executives who emphasized long-term strategy, extensive communication, and acceptance of their vision by their team members "are most likely to be successful in creating change within their organizations."[3]

Okay, so it's important to managers, but what about team members? Are you thinking that they really don't care? You're right. They *don't* care if they haven't been involved, if it doesn't add value, or worse, if the management team does not "walk its talk." According to Stewart: "There's a technical term for values that look good on a wall but don't add value to the business. The term is 'bullshit,' and even an MBA can smell it."[4] On the other hand, a sense of mission and purpose can be the single most important long-term motivator for employees. (See Exhibit 2-2.)

Exhibit 2-2:

What Is the Single Most Important Long-Term Motivator for Employees?[5]

Sense of mission and purpose	35%
Feedback and communication	21%
Raises and salaries	16%
Percentage of ownership	8%
Performance bonuses	8%
Profit sharing	7%

The importance of having a clear sense of where you're going was driven home to me during a tour my Superwoman and I took while on a recent Alaskan cruise. While in Anchorage, we visited a camp that trains dogs for the world-famous annual Iditarod Trail Sled Dog Race. One of the dog trainers, a very colorful chap with a long beard, wind-swept hair, wrinkled face, and overall rugged appearance and disposition, explained the rigors of dog sled racing to us. He emphasized the importance of the lead dog's leadership responsibilities and of teamwork to ensure that the sled reaches its destination. According to our guide, the role of the lead dog is to keep the dog sled moving no matter what the consequences. In other words, even in a blinding snowstorm, the lead dog must communicate to the other dogs that it has a clear vision of the path and an equally clear sense of direction and final destination. The reason this is critical, our guide explained, is that the lead dog's life literally depends on it. Here is why. If for any reason the lead dog hesitates or demonstrates to the other dogs that it is unclear about where it is going (or worse that it is lost), the other dogs will stop pulling the sled. As a result, the dogs end up strangling the lead dog, who has been trained to keep on pulling no matter what the obstacles.[6] Although perhaps not as cruel, your team members, too, will likely not follow you if they sense that you have no idea of where you're going.

At this point you are probably saying: "Okay, coach, you've got me convinced. Now, just show me how I can create such an organization." I'm glad you are getting excited, and I'm anxious to show you exactly how you can build a turned-on, tuned-in organization. But before we get going with the how, let's first make sure we use the same language, so that we can be productive.

Winning Action Step

Find out what is important to your team members by spending at least 40 percent of your time with them.

MISSION, VISION, VALUES, SLOGAN, AND PHILOSOPHY

As a consultant and seminar leader, I'm always amazed by how frequently these terms are mixed up, even by managers who have been in the business for a long time. So here are my definitive clarifications that will enable you to remember what these terms mean, once and for all.

Mission: What We Get Paid For

Peter Drucker[7] admonishes us that the most important question any-one in any business should be able to answer is: What business am I in? This is also referred to as your *overarching purpose* or *mission*. It is the reason you and every one of your team members comes to work and gets paid. Obviously, it is critical that you and your team members know what your mission is because if you don't know your rea-son for coming to work, sooner or later—actually sooner—you and your organization will cease to exist. At this point you may be saying: "Give me a break! What are you talking about? Of course I know why I come to work!" Do you? Quick, tell me what your mission is. If you are like the participants in my seminars and *fun*shops,* you may have just a bit of trouble with this. Usually, only 30–60 percent of the managers can tell me their mission. But then comes the more impor-tant question. What about your team members? One of your clerks, for example. Usually, only 1–5 percent of the participants are sure that *everyone* in their organization can tell me what the mission is! Let me say it again: If your people do not know why they come to work and what they are there to do when they get there, they (and you) will be *out of business very soon!* One of my seminar attendees told me that his employees come to work for a good cause—"cause" they need the money! (Are you chuckling? Are you with me? Are you having fun yet? If not, perhaps it's time for you to take a quick break.)

The other problem I frequently encounter is mission statements that are too long and lack passion. Here is an example from a tech-nology company of a mission statement that falls into that category:

XYZ Company will invest its resources in the research, development, manufacturing, and marketing of projects and services of competi-tively superior quality used in the life sciences for scientific research and in bioproduction worldwide. While the majority of our prod-ucts will be internally generated, we will expand our offering wher-ever possible through selected acquisitions complementary to our core businesses. Our ability to succeed depends upon recognizing and encouraging full use of the abilities of our employees. We are

*I prefer to call my workshops *fun*shops. To me, learning ought to be fun, because what's fun, gets done.

committed to the development of an empowered work force. As a result, we will maximize stockholder value by maintaining minimum annual long-term growth rates in sales and earnings of 20–30 percent.

I'm sure after reading this mission statement you are totally confused. Of course employees in this company have absolutely no idea what their purpose is. To ensure that your mission statement positively influences the direction of your organization, it is important that it is concise and memorable, and provides answers to the following questions:

- What products or services do we provide?
- Who are our customers?
- What do our products and/or services do for our customers?
- What makes us unique?

Reality Check
Vision is the art of seeing things invisible.
—Jonathan Swift

Vision: What We Want to Be When We Grow Up

It is hard to find consensus in the management and leadership literature regarding what sets leaders apart from managers, with one exception. There is virtually unanimous agreement that visioning is the one skill that all effective leaders have mastered. Study after study clearly demonstrates that leaders and *winning managers* have the ability to identify an organizational vision and generate the commitment to get all team members to move in the direction of the vision. In short, "There can be no leadership [or *winning management*] without vision."[8]

At this point you are probably saying: "Sounds good, but what is a vision anyway?" It is a dream that defines the future for your organization, or as someone once said in one of my programs: "It is a dream with a deadline." It is the ability to imagine a different and better situation or outcome and ways to achieve it. It is former President Kennedy seeing an American walk on the moon by the end of the decade. It is Lee Iacocca creating mental images of Chrysler as a quality-driven highly successful automobile company, when it was virtually bankrupt. It is Martin Luther King having a dream of a land where all people are provided the same opportunities. These are examples of what I mean by a vision.

To be effective, a vision must have meaning for all of your team members and customers, and it must be memorable, readily internalized, short and passionate, so that all of your team members can easily commit it to memory. (See Exhibit 2-3.)

Exhibit 2-3: Characteristics of an Effective Vision Statement

An effective organizational vision must:
- Describe the desired future
- Engage people's emotions
- Describe something worth going for
- Provide meaning to work

In addition, effective vision statements are also:
- Somewhat nebulous
- Simple
- Passionate
- Memorable
- Ideally descriptive of the journey, not the destination

Values: What's Important Around Here

Your value system helps you to decide what is good or bad and what is important to you in your everyday life. Beyond that, however, your values also determine how you manage and lead others. According to McCoy,[9] author of *Management of Values,* your value system helps determine how you:
- View others
- Perceive situations and problems
- Solve problems
- Decide what is right, wrong, or ethical
- Deal with and treat people
- Structure organizational tasks

The important thing to remember about values is that each individual has a unique value system. Although trite, you as a *winning manager* must have a handle on your own value system, i.e., know thyself. This perhaps was best expressed by Bartlett and Ghoshall: "Before senior managers can realign behavior and beliefs throughout the corporation they need to change their own priorities and ways of thinking."[10] This is particularly important because each of us tends to evaluate others based upon our own value system. In other words, we tend to use ourselves as the gold standard.

The case that comes to mind is a new secretary I hired a few years ago. In looking around, I found a young lady in another part of the organization who was the ideal candidate. She possessed all the right skills and was extremely sharp. In addition, the job with me would have given her everything she wanted plus a promotion. To me it was obvious that she would take the job. Well, I was wrong. Why? Because I used my own value system as the gold standard. To me, getting a job that offers you everything you want plus a promotion is an obvious choice. This woman, however, felt loyalty toward her boss, plus she had a number of personal concerns that never even entered my thoughts. In short, I didn't take enough time to figure out what made her tick.

The other important thing to remember about values is that every organization has a value system; I like to refer to these as the organization's *core values*. These values are unique to each organization and literally tend to drive the organization.

Winning Action Step

Randomly select about 10 percent of the team members who work with you. (Note, people work *with* you—not *for* you! More about that later.) Make sure you select at least one individual from each department, section, or unit. Visit each team member during the next month and ask him what your organization's mission, vision, and core values are. If 95 percent or more of the team members can describe them in their own words, you are doing super. If not, make up an action plan to remedy this *now!*

Slogan: Saying More with Less

A slogan is a short and memorable phrase, or even series of letters, that conveys the sense of what the organization is all about. Why is a slogan necessary? Because most humans have difficulty remembering more than seven chunks of information. This simply means that neither your team members nor your customers will likely remember your entire mission, vision, and core values statement, but they may remember your slogan.

An ideal slogan is one that is a mnemonic, acronym, or short sentence that has meaning to the team members and to the customers. For example, what if I asked you to complete the following: At _____ , quality is _____ _____ . Most of my *fun*shop participants know the answer, which is: *At Ford, quality is job one.* The reason we know the answer is that Ford has used their slogan very effectively to communicate both to their customers and their team members that quality is their number one priority. Other effective slogans include: Federal Express's "If it absolutely, positively has to be there overnight," Ritz Carlton's "We are ladies and gentlemen serving ladies and gentlemen," L. L. Bean's "100% satisfaction in every way," and United Airlines's "Come fly *our* friendly skies." All of these slogans tell us what is important to the company and what we, the customer, can expect.

Philosophy: The Whole Ball of Wax

At this point you're probably saying, "Enough, already. I didn't want to know that much," just like my daughter Nicole when she was little and full of questions. Whenever Marcela, my wife and superwoman, was too busy, she would say to Nicole, "Go ask Dad." And Nicole would reply, "But I don't want to know that much." Please stay with me, because we are almost ready to benefit from all this wonderful new knowledge you've been acquiring.

To me, an organizational philosophy consists of the mission, vision, and core values all rolled into one. I've taken this extra step because *philosophy,* as defined by Webster, means "the most general beliefs, concepts and attitudes of an individual or group." (All right, I admit it is only one of many definitions in Webster.) I searched for an all-inclusive term because, in working with a variety of organizations,

I have found that meaningful nomenclature and consensus is hard to come by. Even though mission, vision, and values all have very distinct meanings, some organizations use the term *mission* to refer to their philosophy, others use *vision,* and yet others, like Johnson and Johnson, use *credo.*

Later in this book I will share a comprehensive and effective philosophy statement from one of my clients. At this point, let me emphasize that in order to be effective your philosophy statement needs to contain at least four critical elements.

An effective philosophy defines our commitment to:

- Employees (after all, they are the ones who get the job done)
- Customers (I mean really taking care of them, not just providing lip service)
- Quality (doing what you do with excellence)
- Innovation (because without it you will not survive)

"Okay, coach, I've got a good handle on what an effective organizational philosophy is. Now tell me why knowing all this theoretical stuff is important to me. All I want to do is run a winning company." Great, that is exactly what I wanted to hear. The reason is that running such a company requires you to figure out what your organizational mission, vision, and values are, or should be, and then translating them into a philosophy that everyone can identify with and, even more important, take ownership of. Now, before we get into the how-to, let's first look at why you should even be concerned about going through all this trouble.

Winning Action Step

Tomorrow, walk into your organization as if it were for the first time and as if you were a customer. Count the number of times you see the philosophy statement before a customer gets to her destination. If it is fewer than three times, get your philosophy statement printed on laminated posters and post them in high traffic areas throughout your organization. The following day, repeat the process, but this time walk in the shoes of one of your team members.

The Organizational Driving Force

The philosophy is the organizational driving force because it represents the foundation of the organization. It goes without saying that without a strong foundation, you can't build a strong organization. When the organization is small, such as a retail store run by an owner, several other partners, and a few highly committed team members, this is less of an issue. This is because in a small organization it is much more likely that everyone knows why they are in business and where they want to be in the future. With increasing size, however, these attributes become less clear.

Regardless of size, however, an organizational philosophy is absolutely critical to long-term survival and success. Once *all* team members share a clear understanding of the organization's purpose, values, direction, and desired future, many things become self-evident. Team members become empowered and inspired because they know what it is that they are there to do, how they fit into the grand scheme of things, and what's important in the organization. In other words the philosophy defines the "playing field" for every team member. This in turn provides them with a standard by which to make decisions, defines their role, tells them how to act in certain situations, and, above all, confers status and satisfaction because they have a clear understanding that they are part of an organization that accomplishes a valuable and meaningful purpose.

Giving people meaning has always been important. To make this point, I'm fond of quoting Thomas Watson Jr., the son of the founder of that "small" company by the name of International Business Machines. He stated that "the basic philosophy, spirit and drive of an organization have far more to do with its relative achievements than do technological or economic resources, organizational structure, innovation and timing."[11] The reason I like to use this as an example is that very few of us, regardless of how financially sound our organizations are, will ever have anywhere near the resources of this "small" company, better known as IBM. (Now you know why I had *small* in quotation marks.)

Giving people a purpose has taken on an increasing significance in our uncertain world. This was best expressed by Bartlett and Ghoshal:

Institutions like churches, communities, even families, which once provided individuals with identity, affiliation, meaning and support, are eroding. The workplace is becoming a primary means for personal fulfillment. Managers need to recognize and respond to the reality that their employees don't just want to work for a company; they want to belong to an organization. More than just work, companies can help give meaning to people's lives.[12]

The reason why a mission, vision, and values provide people with meaning in their lives is because an effective philosophy provides people with:

- A sense of direction
- A sense of purpose
- A gold standard

In short, one of the most important responsibilities of a *winning manager* is to identify, promote, and nurture the philosophy of the organization. "Okay, coach, you convinced me, now tell me how I can do this good stuff."

Reality Check

The time for action is now. It's never too late to do something.

—Carl Sandburg

CREATING AND INSTALLING AN ORGANIZATIONAL SHARED PHILOSOPHY

What follows next is a six-step process that, if adhered to in the order presented, will help you create and install an empowering and widely shared philosophy in your organization.

Step 1: Determine the Purpose of Your Organization

Figuring out what business you are *really* in may be the single most important exercise that you and your management team will ever wrestle with. Hence, it is important that this question be answered at the highest level of the organization's hierarchy. So, if you are the

CEO, president, or administrator, you are the right person. But please, do not do it alone. (If you are not in charge, find a way to convince the person in charge and get him involved in this process.) Even though this sounds like an easy question, it is a rather complex process that consists of several days of extremely gut-wrenching introspection. If you don't believe the importance of this step, take a look at what happened to Wang Laboratories. They thought they were in the word-processing business, and therefore got stuck when desktop computers came along, which could do much more than *word*-processing. Think of where Wang might be today if they had defined themselves to be in the *information*-processing business.

The best way to accomplish this is to take your management team and several key team members on a retreat. That is, take them someplace where they are not interrupted with operational problems and telephone calls. If you are unable to leave the organization, do it at a time and a place where you will be relatively undisturbed, like on a weekend. You should also consider engaging the services of an effective outside facilitator to help you stay focused and make sure that everyone's time is well spent. Winning organizations have long since learned that the benefits of engaging such a consultant far outweigh the costs.

Now, get this team to answer a number of very basic questions. The first: What business are we really in?

A group of long-term care executives who were stuck in the "comfort zone" answered the question this way: "We are in the long-term care business." Bob Allen of AT&T asked that same question of himself and his management team when they were in the process of converting from being a regulated utility to competing in a worldwide marketplace. His strategic plan called for "developing products to meet the needs of an emerging infocom business." He got rid of that strategic plan and substituted: "AT&T is dedicated to becoming the world's best at bringing people together—giving them easy access to each other and the information and services they want and need—anytime, anywhere."[13] In other words, this question may have a more complicated answer than the one that initially comes to mind. For example, the long-term care executives may really be in the business of providing peace of mind, or continuing care, or convenience, or comfort, or security and safety, and so on. The answer to this basic question will help you define or revise your mission and also provide you with ammunition for the steps that follow.

Having reflected, discussed, and summarized the information above, you and your management team are now ready to craft your mission statement. Although yours will be unique to your organization, let me share three effective mission statements from some of my clients:

A Long-Term Care Facility:
"To enhance the quality of life of our clients/residents by providing superior services in a diverse and dynamic community, guided by the values of dignity, compassion, charity and stewardship."

A Foodservice Company:
"To serve great food, create innovative concepts and provide value for our customers."

An Information Technology Company:
"To provide integrated technologies that enhance our clients' ability to capture, store, retrieve, distribute and use information."

Winning Action Step

Look for team members relying on the organization's philosophy statement to make decisions. Then let them know how impressed you are.

Step 2: Establish the Organization's Vision

The next big question you and your management team need to struggle with is: What do we want to be when we grow up? In other words, what is our vision? To determine your organizational vision, the management team must begin by developing a mental image of what the desired future state of the organization should look like.

According to Bennis and Nanus, this is a critical step because

...when the organization has a clear sense of its purpose, direction, and desired future state and when this image is widely shared, individuals are able to find their own roles... in the organization. This empowers individuals and confers status upon them, because they can see themselves as part of a worthwhile enterprise.... Under these conditions, the human energies of the organization are aligned toward a common end, and a major precondition for success has been satisfied.[14]

Even though the identification of a vision must be a top-down process, these statements alert you to how important it is that the vision be widely shared. Otherwise, it is an exercise in futility. (We'll discuss how to get buy-in from team members later.)

To identify a meaningful vision, I suggest that you have everyone do some dreaming. In other words, get your team to focus on what trends to expect in the future and how those trends might impact your business. To be good at this, it helps to have a crystal ball. Since accurate ones are hard to come by, invite someone who is knowledgeable about future trends to speak to your group. Or, if you can't afford that, your team needs to be coached by someone who is really up on the works of John Naisbett, Faith Popcorn, and other futurists. Also, take a look at the population trends and the projected growth trends for your area, your organization, and your parent company, and any other type of data that allows you to peek into the future.

To maximize your effectiveness, it would help to appoint a leader who is skilled in techniques that promote freewheeling and creative thinking. She, by the way, may not necessarily be the formal leader, i.e., the boss. If this is the case, you can only hope that the boss has mastered the art of "knowing thyself" so that she appoints or hires someone else to facilitate this process.

Now take the information that you and your team have generated and craft your vision. After all, *the best way to predict the future is to invent it.* However, to have meaning to all of your team members and customers, a vision statement must be memorable and readily internalized. This can be accomplished by creating a vision statement that is short and passionate. Here are more examples from some of my clients:

A Smorgasbord Restaurant:

"An intense commitment to satisfy every customer who dines with us."

A Long-Term Care Facility:

"We will be the standard by which quality of living for mature adults is measured."

A Health Care Association:

"To be the leading organization dedicated to creating a world without diabetes."

If you evaluate these, you will see that they are all very different, yet all of them describe a journey instead of a destination. This is important because people at work derive their energy from traveling the journey, not from reaching the destination. In addition, all of these also measure up to the criteria of an effective vision statement I presented earlier (see Exhibit 2-3).

Winning Action Step

Take every opportunity to communicate the philosophy. If you are not sharing it with someone *at least six times* each working day, you are not doing your job! Don't worry about too much repetition. You can't overdo it!

Step 3: Define the Organization's Values

Come on, stay with me now; this stuff is important! With all the ethical issues confronting companies today, it is extremely critical that we identify the organizational values. Values are becoming increasingly more important to people at work, because we live in a rapidly changing and highly complex world—a world where we are constantly being asked to make decisions between confusing and often conflicting options, choices that are frequently in what I call the "gray zone." (Incidentally, when I'm confronted with one of these, I ask myself this question: How would it make me feel if my actions were being reported on the front page of my local newspaper?) To help your team members make these kind of difficult choices, they too need a road map.

The way your management team identifies these values is to answer these questions: What's important to me? What's important to our organization? What's important to our customers? What's important to our team members? Answers will likely include the following:

- A belief in being the best
- A commitment to doing things right the first time
- A belief in the importance of taking care of our people
- A commitment to quality
- A commitment to taking care of our customers
- A commitment to innovation and calculated risk taking
- A belief in extensive informal communication
- A belief in and recognition of the importance of growth and profits (except for nonprofits, of course).

The problem that the management team will be confronted with is that they will have far more information than they can use. So your next step will be to get the management team to narrow all of this down to the five *most important values*. (Why five? Because from experience I have found that people won't remember more that five values. In fact, it will take a lot of energy to get them to remember five. More about that later.)

At this point it will be helpful to share specific examples of organizational values from a variety of companies.

A Hospital:
- A profound respect for all people
- A total commitment to excellence in everything we do
- A passion for service
- A persistent commitment to help our employees grow
- A commitment to finding a better way to do everything

A Jewelry Chain:
We believe in:
- Honesty and integrity.

- Providing quality merchandise and value.
- Building lasting, positive relationships with our customers, team members, and vendors.
- Helping our team members be the best they can be.
- Constant innovation.

Did you read these carefully? Any reaction? A question I like to ask my seminar participants is: "If you knew absolutely nothing about these companies, would you consider working for them?" The answer I usually get is a resounding *yes!* Why? Because these values give you the feeling of passion and compassion, and give you a very clear sense that these organizations care deeply for their team members and customers. In fact, it is a little bit like a religion—which, by the way, is a powerful analogy because, just like a religion, it is something that you (the *winning manager*) and your management team have to believe in. Pretending just won't work.

At this point you and your management team have completed your philosophy statement (the mission, the vision, and the core values) and you're now ready to return to your organization. Once back, there is another critical activity that must be accomplished: You must get buy-in from all of your team members.

Winning Action Step

Consistently practice what you teach. Remember that actions speak louder than words, and that what is important to you tends to be important to your valuable team members.

Step 4: Translate the Philosophy into a Slogan

At this point, the management team has returned from the mountain top with a wonderful philosophy statement that they distribute to all team members. As a result, all team members will be 111 percent committed to the philosophy and deliver consistent excellent service and quality, right? *Wrong!* What you will get instead is the *BOHICA* effect: *Bend Over, Here It Comes Again!* You'll also get the behaviors that go along with this, such as disillusionment, discouragement, disgust, rebellion, and maybe even sabotage. What we need to do before we disseminate the philosophy statement is to get buy-in and ownership. The way I've been able to accomplish that with my clients is to distribute the philosophy statements to all (yes, you read right, *all*) team members as a *draft,* together with a feedback sheet. (If you have e-mail, this is a no-brainer. If you don't, why not?) Ask your team members to review and discuss the document with each other and their team leader and provide you with feedback, questions, and concerns. At the same time, conduct a slogan contest, which will generate lots of excitement and participation. Make sure that you have multiple award categories. For example, you may want to have prizes for the funniest, the most innovative, the rudest, the most outrageous, third runner-up, second runner-up, first runner-up, and the winner, of course. Make sure that every award category has something worth going for and that the grand prize is really *grand.* Also, be sure to give team members guidelines and samples of what you consider to be effective slogans (see below), and, most important, involve the team members in the judging of the submissions. Then get out of their way!

Here are several slogans that team members have come up with:

A Long-Term Care Facility:
   "Caring... we do it best"

A Waterproofing Company:
   "Dedicated to excellence in everything we do"

A Hospital Research Facility:
   "DCI [Department of Clinical Investigation] Is SHARPP: Striving to Help All Researchers from Planning to Publication"

Remember that the main purpose of the slogan contest is to get *every* team member involved so that the team makes the philosophy statement their own. The second purpose is to have the team members translate the philosophy statement into a memorable, concise slogan that provides meaning to every employee and customer.

Winning Action Step

During your next team meeting when people get sidetracked with interpersonal petty issues, ask them: How will the resolution of this issue help us get closer to the attainment of our mission or vision? If they are unable to tell you how, ask: "Do you believe this issue deserves our valuable time and attention?"

An effective philosophy statement and slogan is shown in Exhibit 2-4. (By the way, the team member who came up with the winning slogan won $500.)

Exhibit 2-4: Sample Comprehensive Philosophy Statement and Slogan

A FOODSERVICE COMPANY
"Expect the Best... We'll Do the Rest"

Mission

To serve great food, create innovative concepts, and provide value for our customers

Vision

To consistently exceed our customers expectations

Core Values

- Respect Diversity
- Maximize Team Members' Potential
- Generate Continuous Improvement
- Trust and Empower People
- Commitment to Open and Honest Communications
- Create Fun and Embrace an Entrepreneurial Spirit

I've also provided you with a philosophy check sheet in Exhibit 2-5 so that you and your team members can check the quality of your philosophy statement.

Exhibit 2-5: Philosophy Check Sheet
_____

Our mission describes:
- ❏ What we are in business for
- ❏ What products/services we provide
- ❏ What our products/services will do for our customers
- ❏ What sets us apart from the competition

Our vision describes:
- ❏ Our dream for the future (what we want to be when we grow up)
- ❏ A journey, not a destination
- ❏ What is unique about us
- ❏ What our real priorities are for the next era
- ❏ What we want to accomplish that will cause *all* team members to be committed, aligned, and proud to be part of this organization/ company

Our values describe:
- ❏ What is important to us (what we will *never* compromise)
- ❏ Our commitment to our:
    - ❏ Customers
    - ❏ Quality
    - ❏ Innovation
    - ❏ Employees
    - ❏ Anything else that makes this a better organization/company

---

Reality Check
It is a luxury to be understood.

—Ralph Waldo Emerson

Step 5: Communicate the Philosophy

Now you're ready to begin the process of making your organizational philosophy a reality. Implementation starts with dissemination and "walking the talk." Although a philosophy provides a good start to get your organization to head out in the right direction, it is clear that it will accomplish very little unless it is widely disseminated.

Dissemination should consist of having all team members see the philosophy statement, or at least part of it, every day, over and over again. It begins with a poster prominently displayed on the way to their office or workplace and another one hanging next to their locker or the water cooler. It continues every time they turn their computer on or off. Perhaps you could use it as a screen saver. You might want to have it printed on their paychecks and on the back of *their* business cards. (Yes, I suggest business cards even for your team members. It is, after all, the cheapest way to generate word-of-mouth advertising.) Part of the philosophy can be worn on their uniforms, perhaps on a name tag, posted on laminated sheets on every bulletin board, and placed next to or on every desk or workstation. In other words, wherever team members turn, they should see the philosophy or at least part of it.

Winning Action Step

The next time you have an occasion to coach one of your team members, utilize your philosophy statement to guide your counseling.

But that is not enough. Additional, and perhaps the most effective, dissemination comes from constant reinforcement from you and every other member of the management team. This can be done during counseling sessions, new employee orientations, annual reviews, at daily and weekly meetings, and on and on, ad infinitum. These uses will make your philosophy statement a living document, instead of just an expensive piece of paper. I have found that one of the best ways to make the philosophy come alive is through storytelling, metaphors, myths, and legends. The rule of thumb is for you to talk to someone—team members, customers, co-workers, and anyone else who is willing to hold still long enough—about your philosophy statement a *minimum of six times per day, every* working day! My experience has shown that the day you're getting sick and tired of talking about the philosophy is the day you're getting close to having the majority of your team members internalize and buy into the organizational philosophy.

A beautiful example of disseminating the philosophy to all team members occurred just a little while ago when I received a Federal Express overnight letter. The carrier was extremely courteous, but at the same time very quick and effective. After having me sign for the letter, he passed a wand over the letter. When I asked him about that, he informed me that he places the wand in a computer in the truck, which then "provides us with a precise tracking system for every letter and package which we handle every day." When I complimented him on the efficiency, he answered: "Well, you know we have to be the best; otherwise we will lose market share." Keep in mind that I was talking to one of the drivers, not the president of Federal Express.

To accomplish this kind of commitment to the philosophy, you, as the *winning manager*, must be prepared to "walk your talk," and practice MBWA (more about that in chapter 5).

Winning Action Step

Catch your management team members disseminating the organization's philosophy. When you do, let them know how much you appreciate it.

Step 6: Develop Action Plans

Time to translate theory into action by engaging the power of all your team members to move the organization closer to the attainment of the philosophy. The best way to do this is to conduct another retreat with your management team, but this time also take along as many team members as you possibly can. (The more people involved, the more buy-in you get.) During this retreat, everyone will need to roll up their sleeves and work incredibly hard. But you'll find that this is one of the most important and exhilarating activities your team members have ever undertaken, especially if it is facilitated by someone with expertise in strategic planning. After all, you are inviting your employees to help you and your management team create the future for your organization.

The first step during this retreat is to review your philosophy statement and identify your critical success factors (CSFs) from that statement. These are the factors that every team member must relentlessly focus on to assure that you continue to be in business tomorrow; hence the term "critical." They are also the measurable components of your philosophy, better known as the *metrics*. For most organizations, they include the following:

- Constantly improve customer satisfaction.
- Continually improve team member satisfaction.
- Improve profitability.

Although some organizations include their CSFs in their philosophy, I do not recommend it because they will make your philosophy statement too long and result in information overload. In other words, in this case *less is more*.

Winning Action Step

Check to see if you're measuring, tracking, and rewarding attainment of critical success factors. If not, start today. Remember, *what gets measured, gets done!*

At this point you're probably thinking: "These are obvious. Why bother?" The reason I recommend that your philosophy statement be supplemented with CSFs is that it is important that all team members keep their eye on the ball at all times. I recommend that you develop strategic action plans, goals, and objectives for each CSF. To do that, arrange team members in groups of five to seven for each CSF and have them complete the form shown in Exhibit 2-6.

Successful completion of this process and subsequent implementation of this strategic plan will ensure that every one of your team members is totally focused on the attainment of the mission, vision, and core values, while keeping their eyes on the attainment of the

Exhibit 2-6: Goal Action Sheet

CSF: _____

GOAL: _____

Short (w/in 1 yr.) ____   Intermediate (1-3 yrs.) ____   Long (> 3 yrs.) ____

Start by: _____ Complete by: _____ Supports Core Values 1 2 3 4 5

In accord w/Mission   yes ____   no ____

Moves us closer to Vision   yes ____   no ____

Team Leader (name/dept.) _____

Team Members: _____

Objective	Action Steps	Primary Mover	Start Date	Compl Date
1. _____	_____	_____	_____	_____
_____	_____	_____	_____	_____
_____	_____	_____	_____	_____
_____	_____	_____	_____	_____
2. _____	_____	_____	_____	_____
_____	_____	_____	_____	_____
_____	_____	_____	_____	_____
_____	_____	_____	_____	_____
3. _____	_____	_____	_____	_____
_____	_____	_____	_____	_____
_____	_____	_____	_____	_____
_____	_____	_____	_____	_____
4. _____	_____	_____	_____	_____
_____	_____	_____	_____	_____
_____	_____	_____	_____	_____
_____	_____	_____	_____	_____
5. _____	_____	_____	_____	_____
_____	_____	_____	_____	_____
_____	_____	_____	_____	_____
_____	_____	_____	_____	_____

critical success factors. As a result, your organization will not only be traveling the journey in the *right* direction, it will also experience quantum leaps in performance, productivity, and profitability.

Winning Action Step

The next time one of your team members asks you what to do about *our* problem, answer: What do you think? If they are not sure how to answer the question, ask them what document they could use to help guide their decision. (If you don't know, re-read this chapter, quick!)

PHILOSOPHY POWER AT WORK

When I speak to managers about mission, vision, and core values, I often see their eyes glaze over. That's why I'd like to share with you how a relatively small, but rapidly growing, waterproofing company, AquaGuard, has used their philosophy to set themselves apart from the competition. (See Exhibit 2-7.) But first, in case you have never needed the services of a waterproofing company, I need to make you aware that the reputation of waterproofing is right in the vicinity of used car sales. So what is a quality-driven, customer focused, totally ethical waterproofing company to do? AquaGuard has found the answer. They use their philosophy as their unique selling proposition (USP), by mailing it, along with letters of recommendation, to their pre-qualified prospective customers. In fact, they don't even schedule a sales call until the customer has had a chance to review their philosophy and check out their track record by calling previous customers. Does it work? Absolutely! They have not only been able to achieve 374 percent growth over the past six years, they also have their customers raving about them. More important, they have been able to set themselves apart in the marketplace from all the fly-by-night outfits that usually dominate this industry.

Vivid proof of just how important their philosophy statement is was brought home to me when I received a call from a manager at Time-Life Libraries. He wanted to know if we could help them establish their mission, vision, and core values. When I queried him as to how he found out about us, he told me that he had his basement waterproofed by AquaGuard. Of course, as part of the advance packet, he had received their philosophy statement. That statement, according to this customer, "cinched the deal" for AquaGuard because it conveyed integrity, quality, and pride—exactly the attributes this customer was looking for when he needed to entrust his most valuable asset to a group of strangers.

Exhibit 2-7: AquaGuard's Philosophy Statement

AquaGuard
"Dedicated to excellence in everything we do"

Mission:
To achieve unrivaled customer satisfaction and "peace of mind" by providing the highest quality, most innovative waterproofing services

Vision:
To consistently exceed our customers' expectations and become the standard by which all waterproofing companies are measured

Core Values:
◆ an uncompromising integrity and pride in everything we do

◆ a commitment to helping all team members strive to be the best they can be

◆ an obsession to provide high quality workmanship and value

◆ an intense desire for continuous improvement and growth

◆ a resolution to create a friendly and fun atmosphere where participation and creativity are valued

Critical Success Factors
◆ Anticipate and constantly improve customer satisfaction
◆ Continually improve employee satisfaction
◆ Increase sales and profits

SUMMARY

- Your personal values determine how you deal with and manage people.
- The mission identifies the purpose of the organization.
- The vision describes the desired future for the organization.
- Organizational values help people determine what's right and what's wrong.
- The organizational philosophy consists of the mission, vision, and core values.
- An effective philosophy provides people with a sense of direction, a sense of purpose, and a gold standard.
- An organizational shared philosophy can be created and installed by:
  — Determining the basic purpose of the organization
  — Establishing the organization's vision
  — Defining the organization's values
  — Translating the philosophy into a meaningful and memorable slogan
  — Communicating the philosophy by walking the talk
  — Establishing strategic plans that will transform the philosophy into reality

Winning Action Step

Starting tomorrow, let your team members call you by your first name, except those you call by their last name.

NOTES

1. Adapted from W. J. Rinke, *The Winning Foodservice Manager: Strategies for Doing More with Less,* 2nd ed. (Clarksville, MD: Achievement Publishers, division of Wolf Rinke Associates, Inc., 1990), pp. 174–175.
2. L. Larwood et al., "Structure and Meaning of Organizational Vision," *Academy of Management Journal* 38, no. 3 (1995): 740–769.
3. Ibid., 765.
4. T. A. Stewart. "Company Values That Add Value," *Fortune.* 134, no. 1 (1996): 145.

5. "Inc. Reader Survey," *Inc.* 15, no. 5 (January 1993).
6. The story is similar to one told by Thomas J. Winninger, CEO, Winninger Institute for Market Strategy, Edina, MN.
7. P. F. Drucker, *Management: Task, Responsibilities, Practices* (New York: Harper and Row, Publishers, 1974).
8. M. deVries, "The Leadership Mystique," *Academy of Management Executive* 8, no. 3 (1994): 4.
9. C. S. McCoy, *Management of Values: The Ethical Difference in Corporate Policy and Performance* (Marshfield, MA: Pitman, 1985).
10. C. A. Bartlett and S. Ghoshal, "Changing the Role of Top Management: Beyond Strategy to Purpose," *Harvard Business Review* 72, no. 6 (November–December 1994): 80.
11. T. J. Watson Jr., *A Business and Its Beliefs* (New York: McGraw-Hill Book Company, Inc., 1963), p. 5.
12. Bartlett and Ghoshal, "Changing the Role of Top Management," 86.
13. Ibid., 82.
14. W. Bennis and B. Nanus, Leaders. *The Strategies for Taking Charge* (New York: Harper and Row, Publishers, 1985), pp. 90–91.

Winning Action Step

Hold brief NETMA (nobody ever tells me anything) killer meetings on a regularly scheduled basis.

Climate-Building

3

You develop people just like you mine gold. When you mine gold, you don't go into the mountain looking for dirt. You look for gold, no matter how small, or how much dirt you have to push aside.

—Andrew Carnegie

Every organization, just like your family and your country, has a climate, also referred to as a *culture*. That climate can be one that is positive, warm, and supportive, where people are appreciative of each other and enjoy working together toward mutually shared personal and organizational goals. Believe it or not, it can even be a place where people have fun and *want* to come to work. Conversely, there are many companies where people basically dread coming to work and, in fact, they would just as soon not, except that they need the money.

I'm sure that at this point you are saying to yourself: "Okay, coach, what's new about this climate business?" Well, nothing really, except that you as the *winning manager* in your organization can create any climate you want! This may be difficult for you to accept, but if you will stick with me and tune into this chapter, I will not only convince you but provide you with the information that will enable you to create the climate you desire in your organization. (I know that some of this may not sound logical. Just remember, if everything were logical, *men* would ride sidesaddle. Hold on, that deserves at least a smile. If you did not catch it, I would like you to get another cup of coffee because we are getting into some important stuff that requires you to be alert!)

PREVIEW OF COMING ATTRACTIONS

Now that you have installed an empowering mission, vision, and core values, and have supplemented this philosophy with specifics, such as organizational goals and objectives, it is time to figure out how you can create and then maintain a positive organizational climate in your company, unit, or organization. This is precisely what you will have a chance to learn in this chapter. First, you will find out what most team members want from their job and what causes employees to quit or to stay; then you will learn specific strategies to help you consistently treat all of your employees as adults, winners, and team members. Next, you will find out what specific techniques will facilitate and maintain a positive organizational climate, and how to use reward and recognition strategies to achieve improved performance and increased job satisfaction. You'll also learn how to avoid common reward follies, apply punishment strategies more effectively, and take advantage of the employee–customer satisfaction connection to build high-performance organizations that achieve dramatic improvements in performance, productivity, and profitability.

Reality Check

The foundation of management effectiveness is to accept people the way they are, not the way they ought to be.

—Wolf J. Rinke

CLIMATE-BUILDING SKILLS: A SELF-ANALYSIS

Let's get started by having you do a quick self-analysis of your climate-building skills by completing Exhibit 3-1. Please take the time to do that now.

Exhibit 3-1: Climate-Building Skills: A Self-Analysis[1]

Instructions: Using the following scale, circle the number that corresponds to your level of disagreement or agreement with each statement. (People have different preferences and opinions; therefore, there are no right or wrong answers.)

SCALE: Strongly Disagree   Disagree Neutral Agree Strongly Agree
              SD   D   N   A   SA

	SD	D	N	A	SA
1. Most employees must be closely supervised to ensure that they are really productive.	1	2	3	4	5
2. Employees want to do their best at work.	1	2	3	4	5
3. Employees should be trusted.	1	2	3	4	5
4. Employees tend to goof off unless someone supervises them.	1	2	3	4	5
5. I make it a practice to manage the exceptions.	1	2	3	4	5
6. Most of my employees are working at their full potential.	1	2	3	4	5
7. Before I ask an employee to do something, I ask myself how I would feel if I were asked to take this action.	1	2	3	4	5
8. If in doubt, I assume that the employee had a valid reason for being late.	1	2	3	4	5
9. I tend to counsel my employees while I'm still upset so that I do not omit important details.	1	2	3	4	5
10. While counseling, I generally focus on the act, instead of the actor.	1	2	3	4	5
11. At least half of my counseling sessions are dedicated to disciplining employees.	1	2	3	4	5
12. I look for people doing things right.	1	2	3	4	5
13. My best employees do their work exactly the way I tell them.	1	2	3	4	5
14. Work is a place where employees should have fun.	1	2	3	4	5
15. Generally speaking, satisfied employees are more loyal than unsatisfied employees.	1	2	3	4	5
16. I usually find something to compliment my employees about every day.	1	2	3	4	5
17. I make it a practice to tie rewards to performance.	1	2	3	4	5
18. Recognition programs should recognize about 15 percent of the top achievers.	1	2	3	4	5
19. I make it a practice to punish in private.	1	2	3	4	5
20. I make it a practice to reward in private.	1	2	3	4	5

TOTAL: _____

Scoring Instructions:

Score each item in accordance with the number you have circled, *except items 1, 4, 5, 6, 9, 11, 13, 18, and 20,* which have to be scored by reversing the scale, so that 1 = 5, 2 = 4, 3 = 3, 4 = 2, 5 = 1. Then total the scores in the space provided.

Examples:

1. Most employees... 1 ②3   4   5 = 4
2. Employees want to .... ①2   3   4   5 = 1
3. Employees should... 1   2   3 ④5 = 4

Climate-Building Skills: What Your Score Means:

95–100   *You sure know your stuff*—please call me, I could use an associate like you.

85–94   *Excellent*—you are well on the way to becoming a *winning manager.*

75–84   *Very good*—you are primed to learn some powerful new techniques, which will help you to catch people doing things *almost right.*

65–74   *Good*—but you need help. Better start paying attention.

55–64   *Okay*—but you can do much better. So read carefully and you too will learn powerful new strategies to help you build a winning team.

<55   I'm really pleased for you, because you will get your money's worth from this book. In fact, if you apply the strategies in this chapter, the book will pay for itself many times over.

Winning Action Step

Teach yourself and your team members to learn from mistakes. Then forget about all those that have been made in the past! *Really* forget about them!

ARE YOUR TEAM MEMBERS HAVING FUN YET?

Now that you know how skilled you are at building a positive climate, I would like you to take a minute and think about how your organization's climate compares to what I find in many organizations. As a consultant I occasionally have the opportunity to observe companies that are built on an assumption of mistrust. Frequently, employees are assumed to have interests different from management's. Signs that tell people what *not* to do are all over the place. In fact, very rarely do I find signs that tell team members what *is* expected of them. Most often employees are watched because as one supervisor said, "You can't trust 'em. All they want to do is goof off whenever they can." When they make a mistake, employees are scolded much like children. When they come in late, they must report to the boss so that they can get chewed out, and the list goes on ad infinitum.

The element totally overlooked in these organizations is that virtually all people basically live up to other people's expectations, especially those people who are important to them. So, if you expect your employees to goof off, they will not disappoint you. Similarly, if people are treated like children, they will behave like children. A basic and very important concept I would like you to recognize is this: *You, the manager, play a key role in determining how people behave and perform in your organization!*

"But," you say, "my employees seem to like it that way. In fact, they seldom, if ever, complain to me." That may be the case. One reason is that you, as the manager, have a difficult time finding out just how your team members truly feel. Few employees will bring you any kind of bad news, especially in this era of downsizing and "squashing of the pyramid." That handicap is magnified if you are an autocratic manager who does not encourage or even reward team members for bringing you negative information. (No, that is not a typo. I do mean *reward* people for *information you do not want to hear.*)

Even though employees tend to not complain, research tells us that only 19 percent of employees "truly enjoy" their job. On the other hand, "one worker in four equates the workplace with a 'prison.'"[2] Under such circumstances, it is virtually impossible to get employees to have fun and perform at their maximum potential.

Reality Check

The deepest principle of Human Nature is the craving to be appreciated.

—William James

WHAT DO YOUR TEAM MEMBERS REALLY WANT?

Let's step back for a moment and take a look at what research tells us employees want from work.

If Fred Herzberg, famous for his two-factor theory, is correct, then employees are motivated by the work itself, recognition, responsibility, advancement, and growth.[3] Similarly, research conducted by Heskett et al. has demonstrated that the one thing employees value more than anything else is the ability and authority to achieve desired results for their customers.[4] (More about the employee–customer satisfaction connection at the end of this chapter.)

MCI, in a study of its seven telephone customer service centers, found that the factors that impacted most on employee job satisfaction were, in order of importance:

- Satisfaction with the job itself
- Training
- Fair pay
- Fair opportunities for advancement
- Being treated with respect and dignity
- Teamwork
- The company's interest in their well being[5]

I don't know about you or your organization, but these findings simply do not mesh with the stereotypical explanation that most managers use when they tell me what's important to their employees.

But let's look at the other side of the coin. What makes people quit? According to a study of 150 Fortune 1,000 companies conducted by Robert Half, a full 34 percent left because they received limited recognition and praise at work. (See Exhibit 3–2.)

Exhibit 3-2: The Most Common Reasons Employees Leave a Company[6]

Limited recognition and praise	34%
Compensation	29%
Limited authority	13%
Personality conflicts	8%
Other	16%

The employment firm of Challenger, Gray and Christmas conducted another study that looked at what caused *employed* people to look for another job. They found that dislike for the boss was the number one reason people looked for something better. The second most common reason job hunters cited was that they felt under-used in their current job, and money was the third reason.[7]

These findings blow my mind, because it tells me that if we are able to master the principles in this book and become *winning managers,* challenge our team members, and then recognize and praise them more often, we will be able keep more of our excellent team members. Something so easy and inexpensive, and managers still do not do enough of it. In other words: "Ninety-five percent of American managers today say the right thing. Five percent actually do it."[8]

Of course, you are different! After all, that's why you are reading this book. So let's roll up our sleeves and establish a positive climate that will result in your team members wanting to come to work, give you all they've got, stay with you over the long term, and help you build a high-performance organization. An organization that consistently achieves high levels of productivity and profitability.

FOLLOW THE GOLDEN RULE

A positive climate is established by going back to basics, that is, by treating every human being the way you yourself wish to be treated or, better yet, the way they want to be treated. (That is called the *golden rule* and it has been around for a while.) A good way to start on this journey is to ask yourself what you want from a job. Until you find out otherwise, it is a safe assumption that you and your team members want similar things from a job. So give it to them because it won't take anything away from you.

Reality Check

You can get anything in life you want, if you just help enough other people get what they want.

—Zig Ziglar

Treat People Like Adults

Earlier in the chapter you found out that most people want knowledge, accountability, respect, and responsibility from their job. Now let's just assume that for the next twenty-one days you consistently approach every one of your team members with the assumption that they want these positive things from their job, instead of the assumption that they want to goof off or take advantage of you or the organization. What I'm saying is this: Treat all of your people as adults, which you can accomplish by *trusting all of your people all of the time!* Now, I can hear you groaning all the way over here, saying something like: "That is the trouble with these Ph.Ds (consultants, authors, or what ever description you are using), they hang out on cloud nine. You just don't not know my people; there is no way that I can possibly trust them, or can I?" I recognize that it is difficult to fly like an eagle when you work with a bunch of turkeys, but I'm glad that you left the door open just a little bit because the answer to that question is actually very simple. You can trust your people or mistrust them; it is *your choice.* The bigger question is: What do you want? Do you want them to trust you and behave as independent, empowered, and mature adults, or like little kids who have to be led by the hand to do everything? The choice is yours! But let's get a little more specific.

Trust, a Vanishing Act

The one attribute I find missing more often than any other in corporate America is that five letter *T* word, *trust!* No wonder: With all the reengineering, layoffs, downsizing, and rightsizing employees find it increasingly difficult to trust management. And yet, it is in my opinion the single most important variable that will determine whether or not you'll be able to practice *winning management!* If it is that important, perhaps we should take just a moment and define it. Hosmer, who conducted a comprehensive review of the philosophical ethics and organizational theory literature, defined *trust* as:

> The expectation by one person, group, or firm of ethically justified behavior—that is, morally correct decisions and actions based upon ethical principles of analysis—on the part of the other person, group, or firm in a joint endeavor or economic exchange.[9]

I don't know about you, but to me that is just a bit vague. So what does trust mean to me? To me it means that your word is as good as gold, that I never have to second-guess anything you tell me, and that I can count on you to do right by me, our customers, and our company. In short, it is the foundation upon which our relationship and interactions are built! And once that foundation is destroyed, our relationship and interactions will no longer function smoothly, effectively, or productively. Hence all organizational interventions, especially empowerment, are dependent on trust, and without it they will surely fail!

Reality Check
Trust is the glue that holds every relationship together.
—Wolf J. Rinke

Trust, How to Make It Work

You, as a *winning manager,* can make trust work by keeping the following eight cardinal principles in mind:[10]

1. Trust is an either/or proposition. It's not possible to partially trust people—you either do or don't. (I guess that's why trust is like being pregnant.)
2. Trust requires accountability. Since it is difficult to establish accountability among more than about fifty people, make sure that you subgroup your organization into small business units of (ideally) no more than fifty per group.
3. Trust must have boundaries. Trust works when people know that they can count on each other to do a certain thing a certain way. How things are done is defined by the organization's mission, vision, and core values. (I told you crafting an organizational philosophy is important!) Once the boundaries are in place you can then assume that your team members are going to operate within those boundaries. Control in such an environment comes after the action, when results are assessed, instead of telling people what to do or having them ask permission before taking action.

4. Trust requires lifelong learning. Trust can only come about if people can count on each other to perform at peak performance. Such performance is not possible unless everyone is fully committed to lifelong learning, constant renewal, and change. (More about this in chapter 7.)

5. Trust has to be ruthless. People who have *intentionally* abused trust must be removed from the organization because you must be able to trust all of your people all of the time. Otherwise you will revert back to being an autocratic manager—a manager who does the checking and controlling *in advance,* as opposed to operating like a *winning manager* who lets the organizational philosophy do the checking and controlling and only deals with those team members who *intentionally* violate that gold standard. In other words: Trust "is incompatible with any promise of a job for life."[11]

6. Trust requires you to "walk your talk." Trust comes alive as a result of reinforcing your words with actions. People are much more influenced by what you do than by what you say. I have my seminar participants prove this to themselves by having everyone stand and look at me, and follow my directions. I tell them to extend their right arm, just as I am doing. Next I tell them to form a circle with their index finger and thumb, and place that circle on their cheek. As I say "cheek," I put my thumb and index finger circle on my *chin.* What happens next is quite comical. Most people look like they have early onset of Alzheimer's disease because their arm will tremble as they waver between cheek and chin. Others place the circle on the chin and can't quite understand what the fuss is all about. Typically a minority actually follow my *verbal* instructions and place the circle on their cheek. Next I have them look at each other, which results in another salvo of snickers and laughter, and have them tell me what happened. Of course, they tell me that they were influenced much more by my *actions* than my words. That's why you must be the standard bearer and walk your talk.

7. Trust requires "high touch." High-tech will increasingly be the norm as we move toward virtual organizations. Without high touch, however, in the form of organizational retreats, confer-

ences, and meetings, trust will wither on the vine. There simply is no shortcut to developing trust with another human being. It can't be done via the Internet, voice mail, faxes, or other electronic media. It requires you to be belly to belly, nose to nose, eye to eye, so that you can make sure that a person's body language reinforces and supports his words.

8. Trust requires *winning management* and all the attributes, strategies, and skills that I'm describing in this book!

Winning Action Step

Starting tomorrow, trust all of your customers and team members all of the time, until they prove you wrong. Give yourself a pat on the back every time you trust someone you tended to mistrust before. If you have a team member who can't be trusted by anyone on the team, despite receiving a fair share of assistance, begin to remove her—now.

Take Advantage of the Odds

But perhaps you still don't believe that trust is a big deal. Let me use a different analogy. Do you believe in odds? Most people do. Some play the odds even if they are way out, such as one in one million to win big in the lottery. I'm going to be more conservative and ask you whether you prefer to be right 3 percent of the time, or 97 percent of the time? I'm sure that that was a very simple decision for you. You picked 97 percent, right? After all, you know how to play the odds. So why don't you operate that way when you make assumptions about your employees? You see, if you trust all of your employees and customers all of the time—I mean totally trust them beyond a shadow of the doubt—they will prove you *right* about 97 percent of the time. The irony is that most managers prefer to play a losing hand when it comes to people management, because they manage people as if all belonged to the exception (3 percent), instead of the rule (97 percent). That's like being distraught every night when you go to bed because you know that someday you won't wake up again. Now, I don't know about you, but I just don't worry about that when I go to bed. Yet, at one time I used to manage my people as if they belonged to the exception. My recommendation? Play the odds *and trust every one of your team members until they prove you wrong.* At that point, talk to him to find out why he did not live up to your expectation.

When people do disappoint you, which they will about 3 percent of the time, always be sure to depersonalize the situation by separating the act from the actor. For example, if you assumed that Mary would show up for work because she knew that you were "short," and she does not make it, find out why before you take any action. Yes, that means before you get upset and scream at her. Remember that even if she did not have a valid reason, she is not a bad or lazy person; *she acted or behaved inappropriately.* Attacking Mary as a total person will diminish her self-esteem, which is what you have been attempting to build by trusting her. Treating the action treats the problem and helps to make the person get better, instead of making everything worse. It also retains Mary's self-esteem, which she needs so that she can provide consistent quality to you, her team members, and the customers. Self-esteem is also needed if you want her to trust you.

Reality Check
You can't give away something you do not have.
—Wolf J. Rinke

Treat People Like Winners
It was Ken Blanchard of *The One Minute Manager* fame who stated that "Everyone is a potential winner, some people are disguised as losers, don't let their appearances fool you."[12] This axiom is a poignant reminder to all of us that all people like to think of themselves as winners. (Doubt it? Next time you meet with all of your team members, ask for a show of hands of how many perceive themselves as a winner.) Some people have problems with that because their self-esteem is not at an optimum. Now what business is that of yours as their *winning manager?* Well, quite a bit actually. First of all,

research has demonstrated over and over again that our perceptions are our reality and that our self-image controls our life. This effect exists because of the self-fulfilling prophecy. In addition, there is a second force at work, which is equally powerful; it is called the *looking-glass theory.*

Mirror, Mirror on the Wall...

The looking-glass theory maintains that we see ourselves as others see us. If the people who are important to me, like my boss or spouse, see me as a loser, I will begin to doubt my own abilities and, in the long run, begin to see myself as a loser. In other words, my doubts will begin to diminish my self-esteem. Of course, it works just as effectively in a positive direction. This phenomenon gives you, the *winning manager,* spouse, or parent, far more power over others than you ever imagined in your wildest dreams. It literally allows you to create winners or losers by following the strategies I'm outlining in this and the following chapters. Isn't this awesome?

Make It Easy for People to Succeed

A powerful way to reinforce your expectation that your team members are winners is to help them succeed. It is odd, but for some reason we utilize this concept with little people (my preferred terminology for children) but either forget or think it is inappropriate with adults. If you are a parent (if not, use your imagination), think back to the time when you were teaching your daughter to ride a bicycle. Did you jump on your bicycle, parade in front of her to show her how to do it, then put her on it, give her a big push, and let go? When she didn't make it the first time and fell, did you call her a dummy? I know the answer is not just no, it's *hell no!* Instead, I'm sure you put her on a small bicycle with training wheels. Then, once she barely propelled the bicycle forward, your spouse had to come out and goo-gaa over her accomplishment. Continued repetition, positive reinforcement, and near-tries finally led to your daughter getting enough confidence to take off the training wheels. At that point you called Grandma, who had to congratulate your Olympic champion. Then you started the whole process over again and, after much more practice, complimenting, and encouragement, your daughter finally rode that bicycle all on her own.

If you use this simply elegant and extremely basic approach to treat your team members when they are learning the things they need to know in your organization, you will not only have people who know what they are doing, but will, at the same time, also have team members with high self-esteem. Of course, the skeptics in my *fun*-shops object, saying that employees will find such treatment degrading. I disagree vehemently. As long as you start with what they currently know, build on that in small increments, reward near-tries as if they were giant accomplishments and substitute a pat on the back for oohing and aahing, your adult team members will not consider it demeaning or degrading. Every human being, regardless of age, is a much more effective learner if she can learn with training wheels on and receive consistent positive reinforcement.

Winning Action Step

When assigning projects to your team members, break down the projects into manageable steps, remind them of when they succeeded before, and express your confidence in their ability. Then take your hands off until they ask you for help.

CREATE AND MAINTAIN A POSITIVE ORGANIZATIONAL CLIMATE

Quality or excellent service are much more effectively delivered if people are working in a positive climate. To create such an environment, *you* have to begin by developing and maintaining a positive attitude.[13] (I know you are getting tired of hearing that you have to manage by example.) You simply cannot expect that your team members will treat you, your customers, or each other with courtesy, cheerfulness, and a positive attitude if you treat them with rudeness and contempt and, in general, behave like a grouch. You, by virtue of your position, have to be the role model for just about everything you want to have happen in your organization.

"Okay, coach, I'm with you, but my problem is that I'm just not a positive kind of a person. So tell me, how do I become positive?" I hear you, so let me ask you a question: How did you become negative? After you give that some thought, I think that you will be able to answer that question without too much difficulty. You become positive the same way you become negative! You make a decision to *be* positive, because *you,* and only you, are in charge of your *psyche* (the mind), which in turn controls *soma* (the body). In turn, both communicate with each other to decide how you feel! Not the weather, not your employees, not your spouse, not the government, just *you* and no one else makes that decision! It is just like Abraham Lincoln said: "Most people are about as happy as they make up their minds to be." (If this feels uncomfortable, I'd recommend that you devour one of my other books.[14] It describes how I transformed myself from a pessimist into an eternal optimist. And if I can do it, I know you can, too!)

Get Your MBA

In addition to displaying a positive attitude, you must also unlearn just about everything you were ever taught about managing people. The reason is that most of us were taught to manage people by catching them messing up. Someone even gave it a name: *management by exception.* You already know from our earlier discussion that people will live up, or in this case down, to your expectation. To reverse this, you will need to learn to catch people doing things *right* or, or better yet, *almost right.*[15] Let's face it, some people find it very difficult to get it right, at least the way you define *right.* When you catch someone getting it *almost right,* it's your job to compliment or recognize that positive performance in some way. Once you have mastered this, you'll be practicing what I refer to as *management by appreciation* (MBA). Although somewhat difficult to master, it is a more powerful strategy than you will ever learn in any university MBA program.

"Okay, coach, if it is difficult to learn, how do I do it?" To start with, you must become less of a perfectionist because I'm going to ask you to learn to *look the other way.* Now I can see you getting really upset, so let me give you a safety hatch. Look the other way only in cases that are not critical or will not endanger or compromise your customers' expectations or your organizational philosophy. (By the way, *perfectionitis* is a terrible disease that will give you hardening of the "categories.") Your philosophy will help you decide when you should, or should not, look the other way. If one of your team members goofs and it compromises your philosophy, you must address it. If it does not, you should do everything you can to look the other way. Furthermore, if you have implemented the strategies described in the previous chapter, your team member will already know that he goofed because he knows the philosophy just about as well as you do. What about correcting your team member? Are you going to tell him in no uncertain terms that he is a dummy because he should know better? Well, no, you are going to master the art of correcting without destroying.

Reality Check

People who feel bad about themselves, bad about the boss, and bad about the company they work for will not produce excellence or deliver excellent customer service.

—Wolf J. Rinke

Correct without Destroying

Most of us spend too much of our mental energy on the past. Let me explain with a proverbial "spilled milk" example. I like to ask members of my audience what happens when their son spills his milk after you, his mom or dad, have told him about a thousand times to be careful not to spill it. Well, most parents say that they get mighty upset, many rant and rave, calling their son a stupid, clumsy bumbling fool. (I know, I've done it.) I then ask the participants whether it works; in other words, does it have a positive impact on the bottom line? If you rant and rave long enough, will the milk pick itself up and jump back into the glass? I have yet to come across anyone who has been able to accomplish that. What you will accomplish, however, is far more destructive. By punishing the actor instead of the act, that is, by not separating the inappropriate behavior from the person, you will significantly diminish that person's self-esteem.

The same is true when you find out that one of your team members, let's call her Susan, has screwed up a major proposal. Now, you have a choice. You can jump all over her, telling her what an idiot she is, that she will never learn, _____ . (You fill in the rest of the blanks.) Or you can take a deep breath (to help you deal with your frustration) and ask Susan to see you at a later time before she goes home.

When Susan comes to see you, you will have gotten over your anger, which is the first benefit of using this strategy because most angry people are unable to communicate effectively. At this point you might ask her what happened. Her explanation might provide you with information of which you were totally unaware, like: "John, I had a very tough time finding out what the client's real needs were because I was only able to talk to the head of the accounting department, who was collecting proposals on behalf of the client." Or, at worst, you might find out that it was the result of making a critical error. (Haven't you ever made those?) Regardless, you should ask her what she learned from this. If she is clear about answering that question, and it makes sense, then you end the conversation by defining your expectations. For example, you might say: "Susan, I know you are aware how tough it is to get these contracts. And I can tell that you've learned many valuable lessons for future proposals. As a result, I'm confident that you will be even more persistent in the future. After all, you are one of my most experienced and valuable team members and many of the younger team members look up to you as a role model." In other words, you want to maintain a future orientation. When the proposal came back, Susan was fully aware of the fact that she messed up. Telling her that or, even worse rubbing it in, adds no new information, will only frustrate her even further and certainly will not fix the problem. By being future oriented, you expressed what you want to have happen in the future, giving Susan desirable objectives to work toward. You also took the opportunity to repair her slightly damaged self-image by telling her how important she is to the overall effectiveness of your organization.

Just about now you are probably saying to yourself, "That sounds great, but who does this guy think I am, Superman?" No, not really, but you are becoming a *winning manager.* However, using this approach leaves two unanswered questions. One is, "How do you handle your own anger and frustration?" The answer to that is any way you like, as long as you do not take it out on someone else and diminish his self-esteem. For example, you might find it therapeutic to go outside and let out a long scream. Better yet, engage in a daily physical exercise program such as swimming or jogging to help you deal with the frustrations of your job and keep your cardiovascular system in good shape at the same time. Is containing your anger easy? Well, it is once you have learned how to do it. Until then it will take a lot of practice and hard work. Who said being a *winning manager* is easy anyway? If it were, everyone would do it!

The second question that I'm asked most frequently is: Isn't it phony to compliment people when it is not deserved? The answer to that question is an emphatic yes! In fact, I do not recommend you do that! Catching people doing things *almost right,* means that you use your abundant mental energy to look for something that people are doing that deserves a positive comment instead of using the same amount of energy to catch them messing up. If you look hard enough, you will find that most people do something each day that they feel good about. Find it, and then be sure to make a big deal about it. If you have difficulty with this, I would encourage you to master the PIN technique.

Winning Action Step

Tomorrow, analyze your calendar to figure out how much time you are spending with your team members and your customers. If it is less than 70 percent, you need to take action! Set up an action plan to increase the time you spend with your team members and customers by 5 percent each month until it is up to an average of 70 percent.

PIN It, Don't NIP It

The PIN technique will help you become positively focused, faster. I know because internalizing and consistently applying the PIN technique has helped me in my transformation from a pessimist to an eternal optimist. It will do the same for you!

Mastering the PIN technique requires you to use a sequential three-step mental process that *first* focuses on what is positive (P), *next* on what is interesting or innovative (I), and *last* on what is negative (N). I have found that PINing it, instead of NIPing it, provides me with the ability to focus my inordinate mental energies on positive thoughts instead of squandering them on negative and nonproductive stimuli. NIPing it closes the proverbial mental shade, while PINing it allows people to go beyond their customary response pattern and provides them the opportunity to discover the positive, even when initially it did not appear to be there.

Here is an example of how the PIN technique might come in handy for you. Let's say that one of your team members comes into your office and says, "Boss, I have a super idea that will enable us to save an incredible amount of money. Let's fire all of our salespeople and do only direct mail." Given that you have relied on a highly effective sales team since you started your business, your initial internal response goes something like this: "I wonder what she is smoking today." Instead of falling into your prevailing habit pattern and NIPing that idea in the bud, I suggest that you PIN it, by first thinking about the positives, which might include:

- It would save an incredible amount of money.
- I would have fewer personnel problems.
- It would allow me to get rid of Harry, who is no longer pulling his weight.
- It would enable us to move to a smaller office space closer to home.

Next think of what is interesting or innovative about this idea:

- It's interesting how much she has grown and become her own person.
- It's great that she is using her head to help us do better.
- It is an incredibly innovative idea that certainly deserves exploration.

After you have explored all of the potential positive and interesting possibilities, it's time to identify the negatives. After all, I don't want you to be on cloud nine and get yourself into serious trouble. However, I'm not going to give any examples here because I've learned that most people don't need any extra help with this step.

Consistent application of the PIN technique will enable you to enhance your self-esteem, as well as that of others. As a bonus, it also facilitates creativity and provides a powerful basis for establishing an organizational climate where people are willing to take risks and feel free to experiment, thereby empowering them and letting them maximize their own, and the organization's, effectiveness. (The PIN technique alone is worth the price of this book. Be sure to apply it today, so that you can get your money's worth!)

Reality Check
Our cup of appreciation never, ever runneth over.
—Wolf J. Rinke

Master Three Magic Words

In real estate, the three magic words are *location, location, location.* In management, they are reward, reward, reward! In fact, I'm convinced that *our cup of appreciation never runneth over.* If you have any doubts about that, when was the last time you said to your boss, "Please don't compliment me anymore"? (I'll bet you have never done that!) Before we get into the specifics of how and when to reward people, I would like to dispel a few myths. The first is that, in order to be meaningful, a reward has to be valuable to the individual receiving it. That may be true of rewards per se (e.g., getting a ham for Christmas does not mean much if you are Jewish), but is not true of positive recognition because recognition is an end in itself, instead of a means to an end. Any type of recognition works, be it a pat on the back, buttons, badges, an hour off, medals, ribbons, or anything else, especially if it is done in front of the employee's peers. In fact, if you believe in Herzberg's research[16] (and a lot of people do), money is not even a motivator; it is a satisfier, which if absent results in dissatisfaction, while if present results in very little motivation.

Research concerned with the consequences of gain sharing found that a *fair* bonus program tied to the documented productivity improvements of a team led to improved and increased communication and learning among team members, which in turn led to positive changes in the behavior of team members and improved long-term job performance and positive employee attitudes. What is most startling about this research is that these positive outcomes continued even after the bonus was eliminated. In other words, the potential of making more money encouraged team members to more effectively communicate with and learn from each other. As a result, they were more productive and more satisfied, which in turn changed the long-term behavior of the team members. This change in behavior sustained itself even after there were no longer any bonuses.[17]

For managers, however, the findings were different. Werner and Tosi studied the compensation practices of eight hundred organizations and two hundred thousand managers, and found that higher salaries, greater bonuses, and more long-term incentives did not result in increases in performance of managers, nor did higher-paying organizations perform more effectively than other types of organizations.[18]

Regardless of how you feel about this research, I take exception to the findings that money is not a motivator. It's been my experience that money is very important to most team members, especially if it is tied to performance, like in sales. It's also critically important to the lower-paid front-line employees, especially those in the service industries. In general, service employees receive too little compensation for the type of work they do. Even for those who receive sufficient compensation to satisfy their basic needs, money becomes the scorecard by which perceived success is measured. In any event, generally speaking, I agree that money by itself will not, over the long term, assure that people will go the extra mile. Positive reinforcement and hoopla will accomplish that, especially if it is done correctly. "Okay, coach, you've got me convinced. So tell me how to do it right."

Winning Action Step

Check your compensation practices to see if there is a clear connection between how well a job is done and the reward received. If your top performers get the same compensation and recognition as the slackers, do something about it now!

The Most Powerful Management Principle of All Time

After having instructed a recent client on the importance of rewards and hoopla, I received a call about a week later. He said: "Wolf, I have been telling my employees what a great job they are doing, and it seems that people are happier, but they surely are not more productive." He probably was right, because he had violated the most important management principle of all time: He had not *tied rewards to performance*. A number of years ago, Professor Adams developed an interesting theory that he called the *equity theory*. Without boring you with all the details, it says that people in organizations are acutely aware of what other people receive for their efforts. He demonstrated that if you and I work for the same company, have similar backgrounds, hold similar jobs, and get similar pay, equity exists. If, on the other hand, you perceive yourself as working much harder, inequity exists, which you will attempt to restore by either getting more for what you do or working less. Adams also found that the reverse holds true; that is, if you are working less than I am and getting paid the same, you will increase your output to restore equity. As you can imagine, in this case people are much more tolerant of the inequity than in the former case.[19] Although the theory is a bit more complex, it is very instructive for the topic at hand because it alerts us that if you want rewards to be effective you have to be sure that they are given to the people or teams who have earned them. Fortunately, American companies are finally catching on, as more and more companies are linking pay to performance, productivity, profit gains,[20] or incentives.[21]

Now let me shift gears and share with you how *not* to do it. A top executive of a hospital was fond of meetings that were designed to motivate the troops. Invariably, these involved a pep talk, which was always very eloquent and inspiring. Somewhere along the line, however, he always complimented the *entire* group for doing a superb job. The group, by the way, tended to be very large because of the size of the medical center. Initially, these compliments were well received. After having listened to this type of positive reinforcement several times, I noticed that people began to discount it as empty platitudes. I was curious about the effect and asked some of the attendees how they felt about the complimentary comments during the meetings.

The bottom line was that most people did not care for it. Here is what one person said: "I'm busting my butt, and next to me sits Larry, who has been goofing off, and he tells both of us that we are doing a great job. That's a bunch of B.S. I guess the boss just doesn't care if people are doing a great job, and if he doesn't, why should I?" You see? That was an example of the equity theory at work. The lesson: Never tell a large group of people that they have done a great job unless it is for a specific action that *everyone* did in fact contribute to, such as one team having out-performed another, or unless you are sure that everyone did in fact do a great job.

It is far more powerful to recognize individuals, or groups of individuals who recognize themselves as a team, for specific actions or accomplishments.

Winning Action Step

Analyze your time usage to see how much time you're spending with troublemakers and top achievers. If you are spending more than 50 percent of your employee coaching time with troublemakers, begin to decrease that time by 5 percent right now! Then decrease it by another 5 percent for the next several months until virtually all of your time is spent with the team members who are responsible for your success.

Recognize About Three-Quarters of Your Performers

Most organizations tend to recognize only the truly outstanding performers, perhaps the top 10–20 percent. That is not enough for two reasons. If you do it that way, you will tend to recognize the same people most of the time. These are the people I call "water walkers." They will tend to outperform everyone else because of their mental make-up. They would probably do better than everyone else even if they were never rewarded. The second reason is that the average employees—most of the folks who work for you (that's what average means)—will be frustrated by this strategy because they can't visualize themselves getting rewarded. Instead of being motivated, they will become de-motivated because recognition appears to be out of their reach. (By the way, I've learned that there is no such thing as an average performer. I've come to this conclusion as a result of asking countless audiences to raise their hand if they are an above-average performer. Virtually all of the hands go up. Ask how many are average performers and virtually no hands go up. This also reinforces my belief that there is no reality, only perception.)

A more effective strategy is to set up your recognition program so that all average performers, or roughly about the top three-quarters, perceive that they have a chance to be recognized. (For lots of innovative and inexpensive ideas on how to reward your team members, see Nelson.[22])

Do It in Public

To get the maximum benefit from your recognition program, it should be public. If you have any doubts about the effectiveness of this approach, just watch the changes in physical appearance of someone who is being recognized in front of his peers. The shoulders go back, the chin goes up, and the chest comes out. At the same time, his self-esteem grows by leaps and bounds. (By the way, I believe that the building of self-esteem of your team members is one of your critical responsibilities.[23]) Is this the only way to do it? No, absolutely not. It is far better to recognize people in private than not to recognize them at all. In fact, just spending time with your team members in their work area, recognizing team members by name, and wishing them a great day is recognition. (More about this when we talk about managing by walking around.)

Winning Action Step

Take a look at how people are told that they have done a good job in your organization. If fewer than two-thirds of your team members have been publicly recognized during the past year, change your recognition program so that ultimately 75 percent of all team members receive public recognition every year.

If It's Fun, It Gets Done

People love to have fun! Yes, even grownups! Why do you think TV game shows are so successful? Some companies are finally catching on to this truism and, in some cases, use it as both a management and a marketing strategy. So when you have your daily meeting, or your weekly team member get-together, make it fun. Find out from team leaders, from team members, from the suggestion box, and from your own observations who has done something *almost right*. Invite the honorees to "come on down," say a few words about them and publicly recognize them for their accomplishments. Have everyone else whoop it up and congratulate the awardees. Use this, as well as other innovative approaches that your team comes up with as often as you have a chance. This will be often because you are now in the habit of catching people doing things *almost right*. (By the way, contrary to what you may have heard, suggestion boxes can be extremely effective, especially if you react to the suggestions in a speedy manner and if there is something in it for the suggestor. A suggestion box helped Marty Edelston build a highly successful multi-million dollar publishing company.[24])

In addition to "tying rewards to performance," I recommend you also have a mechanism that recognizes people at random. One way to do this is to have birthday parties or use other occasions to recognize specific individuals at random, such as the "spotlight is on (employee name)" approach. This can be done by having all team members place their names into a hat and then have one of them publicly draw one or more names. Whoever is drawn is then spotlighted on the bulletin board, the company newspaper, e-mail, or some other public medium. This random approach communicates to all team members that *every* individual is an important and valued member of the team. I can't overemphasize the importance of creating this sense of belonging. All human beings have a need for affiliation. However, in today's society our typical sources for fulfilling that need—the family, church, and communities—are crumbling. And as they erode at an ever-escalating rate, people look to their place of work to gain a sense of affiliation, identity, and support. One example of the organizational impact was best expressed by a participant of a *fun*shop who said: "I've had many opportunities to leave my company. In most cases, it would have meant more money. Still, I didn't do it because my team members need me."

Reality Check

Employees don't just want to work for a company. They want to belong to an organization.

—Christopher A. Bartlett and Sumantra Ghoshal

Check Your Reward System

In spite of the powerful outcomes associated with *effective* reward *systems,* the stark reality is that most reward systems are simply screwed up in most organizations. And according to an *Academy of Management Executive* update, things have improved very little over the past twenty years. The causes are common system follies that, according Steven Kerr, reward A while hoping for B.[25] Exhibit 3-3 provides you with a summary of the common follies that managers perpetrate. I hope they will cause you to pause and evaluate your reward system to make sure that you are not perpetuating these follies in your organization.

The way most of us conduct meetings provides a specific example of how we want one thing and reward just the opposite. Let's say that you've called an important meeting for 10:00 a.m. and expect twelve people to attend. You arrive shortly before 10:00 a.m., and only Susie is already there. By 10 o'clock, only five people have arrived. Everyone chats and waits. At 10:11 a.m., the eleventh person finally arrives. At this point you're feeling a bit impatient, but you tell the group that you'll wait just a few more minutes because you have an important announcement which has ramifications for everyone. At 10:13 a.m., John finally rushes in, providing you and everyone else with an excuse, and the excuse is not even very original. You start your 10:00 a.m. meeting at 10:14 a.m.

Ask yourself what you have just done. You rewarded the wrong behavior, and worse, punished the right behavior. Here is what I mean. You punished Susie and the other four teammates who made the effort to make it to the meeting on time. In effect, you've said to them: "Hey, you're pretty stupid for trying so hard to do what I want." You also wasted their most precious resource—their time—and communicated to them that they are not as important or valuable as the people who arrive late. To make matters worse, you have rewarded John and all the others who were late by saying, in effect, "Coming to meetings on time is not important. Feel free to waste other peoples' time, devalue me and your team members because, after all, you are the most important person in this organization."

Exhibit 3-3: Common Reward Follies[26]

We want...	**But reward...**
— teamwork	— individual performance
— collaboration	— competition
— productivity	— number of hours of "warming the chair"
— risk taking	— not making waves
— trust	— people "telling" on each other
— candor	— "yes" men and women
— innovative thinking	— conformance
— people skills	— technical achievements
— long-term growth	— quarterly earnings
— total quality	— getting orders out on time at any cost
— environmental responsibility	— making budgets
— stretch goals	— "making the numbers"
— to exceed customer expectations	— adhering to policies and procedures
— "rightsized" organizational structures	— adding staff
— employee involvement	— speed
— empowerment	— tight control
— learning organizations	— lean training budgets

Since human behavior is fairly consistent, this has significant implications on how people feel about you, themselves, and the organization and how they treat each other and their customers. Over the long term, this kind of behavior will have a negative impact on the organization's discipline, productivity, performance, and profitability.

The moral of this story is to always start and stop your meetings on time. To encourage people to show up on time, cover the most important information at the beginning, and be sure not to review when the last person arrives. (Latecomers should get the information they missed from someone else *after* the meeting.) Also, to combat excuses, just ask the person if they would have made it on time if their job depended on it. They'll catch on, sooner or later.

Winning Action Step

Review your current reward and recognition system. Compare it to the common reward follies described in Exhibit 3-3. If you are currently rewarding undesired outcomes, publicly admit you've screwed up and begin to fix it right *now!* Solicit input; better yet, seek volunteers for the "recognition project" and put the people who are directly affected in the driver's seat of the project. Ask them to come up with a reward and recognition program that accomplishes the outcomes they and you desire.

How to Make "Carrots" Work

Here are the five steps to take to make sure your reward system produces the tangible results you and your organization want:

Step 1: Establish Reasonable and Fair Objectives

Make sure that they are easy to understand, measurable, and tied to specific goals you and your company want to accomplish. Have people compete against themselves or against standards. Avoid having people compete against each other within the same company. Also make sure that the objectives are perceived as attainable by the majority of your team members. If they don't think they can make them, they won't even try.

Step 2: Measure the Right Objectives

Make sure you are measuring what you want to accomplish and what team members can have an impact on. Typically managers measure global indicators, such as sales, over which many team members have absolutely no control. Your team members have no reason to stretch if they can't influence the outcome.

Step 3: Communicate, Communicate, Communicate

Let your team members know how they are doing more often than you think is necessary. Distribute status reports using a variety of media. Make liberal use of charts and graphs. Remember, a picture is worth a thousand words. When the enthusiasm wanes, it's time for more communication. In other words, tell people more, and more often than they want to know (more about that in chapter 5).

Step 4: Offer the Right Stuff

Make sure that awards and incentives are important to your team members. How do you figure that out? You ask them! Or better yet, involve them by inviting employees to become members of the awards team.

Step 5: Celebrate More, and More Often Than You Think Is Wise

Whenever you have a chance, celebrate achievements and performance. Having fun is what this is all about, so do it up right and do it as often as possible! Do it in front of team members, and be sure the rewards are proportionate to the achievements. Follow this five-step model and you won't have a need for the information in the next paragraph.

Reality Check

Punishment does not work. The primary reason it's used is that it does something positive for the person who is doing the punishing.
—Wolf J. Rinke

When All Else Fails...

At this point, I'd better bite the bullet and address the issue of punishment. Earlier in the chapter, I stated that you should learn to look the other way when your people mess up unless they violate the basic philosophy of your organization. But what do you do if they repeat the same mistake over and over again? For example, let's say you run a service company, and your customer satisfaction surveys repeatedly identify one of your employees as providing discourteous and rude service. Since providing consistently outstanding service is one of the key elements in your philosophy, you certainly should not look the other way. (That is one of your values, isn't it?) Worse, you have talked to this employee a number of times and have used every positive approach in this book. Nothing seems to work. At this point, you obviously need to shift gears and find stronger medicine. This medicine, which should be used extremely sparingly, is punishment.

Here are seven rules that will help you use punishment more effectively when you believe you *must* use it:[27]

- *"Hot-stove" rule.* Punish as soon as possible after the noted infraction occurs. This is called the *hot-stove rule* because when you were little your mother told you not to touch the stove because it was hot. Like any red-blooded youngster, you, of course, did not believe your mother and touched it anyway. Given that you are a fast learner, you only did that once because you found out immediately that Mother does not lie.

- *Clarity rule.* Be very clear about what is being punished. In our example, you would be able to show the team member copies of the surveys, which specifically and repeatedly identified him as being rude and discourteous to customers.

- *Depersonalization rule.* Punish the act, not the actor. Just because Mr. Brown gave poor service does not mean he is a loser or a bad person.

- *Future orientation rule.* Identify clearly what can be learned from the past, what Mr. Brown can do to improve himself, and what the consequences will be if he does not comply with your expectations.

- *Equitableness rule.* Let the punishment fit the crime. In other words, you need to follow some sort of schedule to assure that the punishment is equitable. For example, being discourteous to a customer should not result in the same punishment as physically attacking a customer. (Don't laugh; I've experienced it, and it is not funny.)

- *Positiveness rule.* Conduct the session in a positive and supportive climate. Avoid counseling your team member while you are angry, upset, or hostile. I know this sounds like an oxymoron, but remember that being firm is not the same as being angry or upset.
- *Consistency rule.* This rule is the Achilles' heel of punishment. Punishment can have positive short-term outcomes; that is, the employee won't do what he was punished for anymore, at least not while you are around. Unfortunately, it won't be effective in the long run because it is virtually impossible to punish employees in a consistent manner. To do so would require *constant* supervision and, worse than that, would result in far more undesired behavior because, as stated earlier, if you treat people like children, they will behave like children.

Remember to use *punishment only as a last resort* because it does *not* work in the long run. The reason is that punishment is extremely difficult to control, is often used by employees as a means of getting attention, results in deceitful behavior (compliance may occur only while the punisher is present), and has numerous other negative consequences.

Reality Check

The busy worker is the happy worker—until he finds out that the lazy worker is being paid the same or more.

—Bob Talbert

Firings Will Continue Until Morale Improves

Did this headline cause you to chuckle? If not, maybe you need to take a stretch and exercise your funny bone because we're ready to consider a very serious question: What do you do with a truly ineffective employee or troublemaker? Especially one who has been provided every opportunity to improve, has been offered work in another area of the organization, has received some type of peer review, and has been coached and counseled repeatedly, all without lasting success. This individual should be removed (yes, fired) as soon as possible to minimize the negative influence that such an employee can have on the climate of your organization. Although unpleasant (if you are like me you absolutely hate it), this is one of the responsibilities you get paid for as a manager. Besides that, I believe that removing an employee who does not fit, and doing it in an expeditious and positive manner, will often *help* the employee in the long run. (You can help your company, too, by sending him to the competition.) This is because you are giving the employee the opportunity to find another job, one that may enable him to build on his strengths, which means that, in the long run, you may be helping the employee to maximize his potential. (I know he won't put his arms around you to thank you for firing him now, but he may do just that several years from now.)

One last rule of thumb before we leave this subject. If you punish more than once in ten counseling sessions, you are punishing too much. So keep track of it in your calendar, or use the ten-penny system. Put ten pennies in your left pocket. Every time you catch someone doing something *almost right* and let them know about it, transfer one penny from your left pocket to your right pocket. When you punish someone or provide negative reinforcement, reverse the process; this time move three pennies back to the left pocket. At the end of the day you ought to have all pennies in your right pocket. Otherwise you have messed up and you need to continue the process tomorrow until all the pennies are in the right pocket. At that point it's time to start all over again until you've internalized this new habit. If that seems too complicated, use the rubber band system instead. Put a rubber band on your wrist and snap it every time you punish a team member. You'll catch on quickly!

Winning Action Step

During the next five days, keep a written record of how many times you say something positive or negative to your team members. If the positives do not outweigh the negatives ten to one, set up an action plan, which will force you to practice management by appreciation (MBA). Track your progress on a "Catch People Doing Things Almost Right" chart or start using the ten-penny technique today.

TAKE ADVANTAGE OF THE EMPLOYEE–CUSTOMER SATISFACTION CONNECTION

Research regarding the impact of satisfaction and job performance has provided us with powerful data that you as a *winning manager* need to take advantage of. Heskett et al.[28] have been able to demonstrate that there is a very clear connection between creating what they refer to as an *internal service quality* and employee satisfaction. (I call it the *exceptional quality service* [EQS] *culture*).[29] They found that "a primary source of job satisfaction was the service workers' perception of their ability to meet customer needs."[30] That is to say, employees are significantly more satisfied in:

- Organizations that provide them with a powerful service strategy
- A well-organized service system that enables them to take independent care of the customer
- A powerful selection system that focuses on selecting only those employees with a service personality.

Employees also want access to continuing education and training, and the right tools at the right time. Last, but not least, service providers want organizations to tie rewards and benefits directly to their efforts.

Heskett et al. were further able to demonstrate that satisfied service employees were much more loyal than unsatisfied employees, resulting in significantly higher employee retention and productivity. In turn, service systems that consistently exceed customers' expectations and deliver value—organizations such as Taco Bell, Southwest Airlines, MCI, and Service Master—enjoy relatively high customer satisfaction levels, which leads to customer loyalty, incredible revenue growth, and profitability. (See Exhibit 3-4.)

An example of this service–profit connection is Taco Bell, a subsidiary of PepsiCo. Taco Bell is an aggressive leader in the fast-food industry that has bought heavily into customer service, empowerment, and team building. They are truly service-driven. For example, to make sure that they are meeting their customers' needs, they collect feedback from some eight-hundred thousand customers yearly. Then they tie those results to employee compensation. Taco Bell has also discovered that the quality of their service providers and the service providers' level of satisfaction impacts not only on customer satisfaction but also on Taco Bell's profitability. By carefully monitoring turnover data, "Taco Bell has discovered that the 20% of the stores with the lowest turnover enjoy double the sales and 55% higher profits than the 20% of the stores with highest employee turnover rates."[31] These findings have convinced Taco Bell of the importance of reversing the "cycle of failure that is associated with poor employee selection, subpar training, low pay, and high turnover."[32]

Exhibit 3-4: The Employee–Customer Satisfaction Connection[33]

As a *winning manager,* I know that you will make sure that you do everything in your power to take advantage of the employee–customer satisfaction connection and have not only happy people, but happy *and* productive team members and customers who will keep coming back for more!

Winning Action Step

If you have not conducted a comprehensive employee satisfaction survey during the past twelve months, conduct one during the next month. Address any unsatisfactory ratings immediately. Then let employees know what you have done to address their concerns. Get aggressive about consistently exceeding your team members' expectations by repeating this process every six months thereafter.

SUMMARY

- Most employees want work that provides them with satisfaction, recognition, responsibility, training, fair pay, respect, dignity, advancement, and growth.
- Research findings indicate that about a third of all employees believe that they do not receive enough praise and recognition.
- Employees tend to leave their job when they dislike their boss and do not feel fully utilized.
- Establishing and maintaining a positive organizational climate is facilitated by:
  — Treating employees as adults
  — Trusting all employees until they prove you wrong
  — Treating employees like winners
  — Helping people build their positive self-esteem
  — Providing employees with the opportunity to succeed
  — Catching people do things *almost right*
  — Helping team members learn from the past and focus on the future
- To focus on the good stuff master the PIN technique by focusing

first on what is positive (P), then on what is interesting or innovative (I), and only *last* on what is negative (N).

- An effective reward and recognition program is one that:
  — Ties rewards to performance
  — Recognizes about three-quarters of all employees
  — Is conducted in front of peers
  — Uses lots of hoopla
  — Is fun
  — Instills a team feeling
  — Avoids common reward follies
- As a general rule, punishment is ineffective and should only be
  used as a last resort.
- To increase the effectiveness of punishment, the *winning manager*
  will:
  — Punish as soon as possible after the infraction occurs.
  — Depersonalize the discussion.
  — Be equitable.
  — Be positive.
  — Be consistent.
- To achieve low employee turnover, increased sales, and greater
  profits, take advantage of the employee–customer satisfaction
  connection by:
  — Implementing a powerful service strategy
  — Empowering all employees to take care of the customer
  — Hiring only those employees who have a well-defined
    service personality

Winning Action Step

Collect employee turnover data. Benchmark your data against the
leader in the industry. Cut turnover by 10 percent this year and
every year after until your turnover is below the industry leader.

NOTES

1. Adapted from W. J. Rinke, *The Winning Foodservice Manager: Strategies for Doing More with Less,* 2nd ed. (Clarksville, MD: Achievement Publishers, division of Wolf Rinke Associates, Inc., 1990), pp. 199–200.
2. R. McGarvey, "Are We Having Fun Yet?" *Entrepreneur* 21, no. 8 (1993): 102.
3. F. Herzberg, "One More Time: How Do You Motivate Employees," in *People: Managing Your Most Important Asset* (Boston: Harvard Business Review, 1986): 26–35.
4. J. L. Heskett et al., "Putting the Service–Profit Chain to Work," *Harvard Business Review* 72, no. 2 (1994): 164–174.
5. Ibid., 169.
6. "A Pat On The Back," *Personal Selling Power* 14, no. 8 (November/December 1994): 79.
7. "Digest," *Washington Post,* 3 January 1995, p. E-1.
8. J. Huey, "The New Post-Heroic Leadership," *Fortune* 129, no. 4 (1994): 42.
9. L. T. Hosmer, "Trust: The Connecting Link Between Organizational Theory and Philosophical Ethics," *Academy of Management Review* 20, no. 2 (1995): 399.
10. C. Handy, "Trust and the Virtual Organization," *Harvard Business Review 73,* no. 3 (1995): 40–50.
11. Ibid., 46.
12. K. Blanchard and S. Johnson, *The One Minute Manager* (New York: William Morrow and Co., Inc., 1982), p. 71.
13. W. J. Rinke, "How to Develop a Positive Attitude. How to Maintain a Positive Attitude," *Bottom Line Personal* 15, no. 9 (1994): 9.
14. W. J. Rinke, *The 6 Success Strategies for Winning at Life,* Love and Business (Deerfield Beach, FL: Health Communications, Inc., 1996).
15. Blanchard and Johnson, *The One Minute Manager.*
16. Herzberg, "One More Time."
17. S. C. Hanlon, D. C. Meyer, and R. R. Taylor, "Consequences of Gainsharing: A Field Experiment Revisited," *Group and Organizational Management* 19, no. 1 (1994): 87–111.
18. S. Werner and H. L. Tosi, "Other People's Money: The Effects of Ownership on Compensation Strategy and Managerial Pay," *Academy of Management Journal* 38, no. 6 (1995): 1672–1691.
19. J. S. Adams, "Toward an Understanding Of Inequity," *Journal of Abnormal and Social Psychology* 67 (1963): 422–436.
20. B. Wysocki Jr., "Unstable Pay Becomes Ever More Common," *Wall Street Journal* 4 December 1995, p. A-1.
21. T. Burdick and C. Mitchell, "More Companies Abandon Sticks for Carrots," *Washington Times,* 6 April 1995, p. B-8.
22. B. Nelson, *1001 Ways to Reward People* (New York: Workman Publishing, 1994).
23. W. J. Rinke, "Maximizing Management Potential By Building Self-Esteem," *Management Solutions* 33 (March 1988): 11–16.

24. M. Edelston and M. Buhagiar, *I Power* (Fort Lee, NJ: Barricade Books, Inc., 1992).

25. S. Kerr, "On the Folly of Rewarding A, While Hoping for B," *Academy of Management Executive* 9, no. 1 (1995): 7–16.

26. Ibid., 12,15.

27. Adapted from W. J. Rinke, *The Winning Foodservice Manager,* 199–200.

28. Heskett et al., "Putting the Service–Profit Chain to Work."

29. W. J. Rinke, *Exceptional Quality Service (EQS): How to Consistently Exceed Your Customers' Expectations* (Clarksville, MD: Wolf Rinke Associates, Inc., 1995).

30. Heskett, et al., "Putting the Service–Profit Chain to Work," 169.

31. Ibid., 169.

32. Ibid., 170.

33. Ibid., 166 (adaptation).

Winning Action Step

Do whatever you can to make sure that people enjoy coming to work.

Coaching and Empowering

4

The best executive is the one who has sense enough to pick good men to do what he wants done, and self-restraint enough to keep from meddling with them while they do it.
—Theodore Roosevelt

Having established a shared organizational philosophy and a powerful positive climate in your organization, you are now ready to learn how to coach and empower so that you can put your team members in the driver's seat.

PREVIEW OF COMING ATTRACTIONS

In this chapter, you will have an opportunity to assess your current empowerment skills, discover the two basic ways of managing people, gain a better understanding of what power is all about, and learn about the outcomes associated with powerlessness and empowerment. You will find out how to become a coach and what specific steps you must take to coach someone effectively. You will then learn five specific strategies that will enable you to empower others. We'll conclude this important chapter by providing you with a litmus test that will enable you to assess whether you have mastered the critical skills to achieve extraordinary results with ordinary people and whether you have empowered your team members. So, let's get set and put the pedal to the mental metal.

┌─ **Reality Check**

Employees don't just suddenly feel empowered because managers tell them they are.

—David E. Bowen ─┘

COACHING AND EMPOWERING: AN ASSESSMENT OF YOUR CURRENT SKILLS

Let's start by having you assess your current level of coaching and empowerment skills so that you can figure out how important this chapter is to you. Please complete the self-assessment instrument in Exhibit 4-1 before reading further.

Exhibit 4-1: Coaching and Empowerment Skills Inventory[1]

Instructions: Using the following scale, circle the number that corresponds to your level of disagreement or agreement with each statement. (People have different preferences and opinions; therefore, there are no right or wrong answers.)

SCALE:

Strongly Disagree	Disagree	Neutral	Agree	Strongly Agree
SD	D	N	A	SA

	SD	D	N	A	SA
1. My preference is to motivate by instilling desire rather than fear in my team members.	1	2	3	4	5
2. When push comes to shove, I feel that I can order people to get the job done.	1	2	3	4	5
3. Because I am a manager, I believe I'm entitled to such perks as reserved parking, a nice office, etc.	1	2	3	4	5
4. I am comfortable admitting to my employees that I've made a mistake.	1	2	3	4	5
5. Giving power to my team members makes me more powerful.	1	2	3	4	5
6. As a manager, I think that one of my most important responsibilities is to be a coach to my employees.	1	2	3	4	5

7. The best way to coach someone is to show them what to do.   1 2 3 4 5

8. My employees believe the management team has their best interest at heart.   1 2 3 4 5

9. I tend to be more concerned about getting the work done than about the people who are doing the work.   1 2 3 4 5

10. I usually give people more responsibilities than they think they can handle.   1 2 3 4 5

11. I make it a habit to focus on my people's strengths and overlook their weaknesses.   1 2 3 4 5

12. When evaluating people, I tend to compare them to myself.   1 2 3 4 5

13. Generally speaking, my team members know how they are doing at all times.   1 2 3 4 5

14. My employees have fun while they are at work.   1 2 3 4 5

15. I make sure that all my employees have an opportunity to participate in some sort of self-improvement training at least once a year.   1 2 3 4 5

16. I tend to share the "big picture" with all my team members.   1 2 3 4 5

17. I believe I have to monitor performance to make sure my employees are really productive.   1 2 3 4 5

18. I tell my team members that they should make their own decisions.   1 2 3 4 5

19. Being empowered means that employees are free to do what they want to do.   1 2 3 4 5

20. Compared to supervisory pressure, peer pressure is more effective in getting people to do things.   1 2 3 4 5

TOTAL: _____

Scoring Instructions

Score each item in accordance with the number you have circled, *except items 2, 3, 7, 9, 12, 17, and 19, which have to be scored* by reversing the scale so that 1 = 5, 2 = 4, 3 = 3, 4 = 2 and 5 = 1. Then total the scores in the space provided.

Examples:

1. My preference is to motivate .... 1 2 3 4 ⑤= 5
2. When push comes to shove, I .... 1 2 3 ④ 5 = 2
3. Because I am a manager, I believe .... 1 ② 3 4 5 = 4

Coaching and Empowerment Skills: What Your Score Means

95–100   You know how to empower and coach people better than anyone I have ever met. Perhaps you should consider becoming a consultant. This business can use a few more good men and women.

85–94   Excellent—you are a veritable genius at empowering and coaching others. What is your secret formula?

75–84   Very good—you are on your way to learning how to empower and coach others. Build on what you already know and you're sure to be a *winning manager*.

65–74   Good—but you have the potential to do much better. Put your concentration cap on and pay close attention to this chapter.

55–64   Okay—but I would like to help you improve your skills at empowering and coaching your team members. So start paying attention.

<55   Time for making up that self-improvement action plan so that you can enhance your empowerment and coaching skills.

Now that you have a better idea about your strengths and weaknesses as they relate to coaching and empowering, let's take a look at the two basic ways of managing people.

Winning Action Step

Get rid of *all* preferential treatments for you and your managers. Start with your reserved parking space—turn it into the "Team Member of the Month" parking space. Next, do away with the private executive dining room and go on from there until managers receive only those preferential treatments that are absolutely necessary to help them accomplish their jobs.

FEAR VERSUS DESIRE

As a manager, you have a basic choice to make about how you manage people. You can manage by instilling fear or desire. Adhering to the principle of fear, you can closely supervise people and tell them exactly what, when, where, and how to do things. If they don't comply, you can order them to do it, and if that doesn't work, you can take punitive action. Will that get the job done? Well, let's assume that I'm your boss and I order you to "serve that customer right now, or you will be fired!" Will you serve the customer? I guess the answer in most cases will be yes—after all, you have to put bread and butter on your table. But how will you serve the customer? Will you be smiling? Thinking revenge? Angry, hurt, confused, disappointed, tired, and generally defeated? Even if you have a super disposition and nothing bothers you, *how will you behave when I'm not around?*

The weakness of any supervisory action that is based on fear and raw power—what Herzberg[2] called KITA (a *kick in the ass*—I'm sorry but that's what Herzberg called it)—is that it results in only short-term change, which will probably be reversed when the supervisor is gone. In extreme cases, such as occurred in the American automobile industry in the early 1970s, it results in dysfunctional and destructive behavior such as work stoppages, sabotage, and frequent strikes.

Research conducted by Arthur and summarized by Cole[3] evaluated the manufacturing performance and employee turnover rates in thirty U.S. steel minimills that utilized two different strategies for human resource management. One approach emphasized tight *control* by enforcing employee compliance with detailed policies and procedures. The other emphasized *commitment* by involving employees in decision making and problem solving. "Arthur found that the commitment approach resulted in higher labor efficiency and lower scrap rate."[4] On the other hand, turnover was significantly higher in those mills that relied heavily on a rule-oriented control approach.

In other words, instead of using raw power, you can choose to multiply your productivity by instilling desire and commitment by empowering your team members. It's like wanting to move a five-ton elephant. You have two basic choices to get the job done. One, you can get behind the elephant and try to push him. At this point you might want to stop and visualize this. Look up! Is this really a good place to be? (If you are not squirming, you're not doing a good job of visualization.) Instead of brute force, you can invoke desire by reaching in your pocket, getting out a couple of peanuts, putting them in the palm of your hand, and walking in front of the elephant. I think the choice is obvious. But since this chapter is about coaching and giving your power away, let's take a look at some of the basic issues concerning power, where it comes from, and how you can use it to help your team members maximize their potential while building a high-performance organization.

Reality Check

Power does not corrupt men; fools, however, if they get into a position of power, corrupt power.

—George Bernard Shaw

POWER: A DIRTY FIVE-LETTER WORD?

Managers and supervisors have five basic types of power over their employees:[5]

Reward power—the ability to extend rewards—such as money, time off, and titles—that are valued by employees.

Coercive power—the ability to use resources that cause employees to experience unpleasant or adverse outcomes, such as "catching hell" or getting fired.

Legitimate power—having attributes or resources that employees perceive as legitimate and feel compelled to obey. Such power may be derived from the values of a group, culture, or organization; from a position that an individual holds, such as being a supervisor; or from receiving power, such as when it is delegated.

Referent power—having attributes—such as attractiveness, fame, or charisma—that cause employees to be attracted to or identify with the manager. This is the power that you have when your team members perceive you as a role model and coach.

Expert power—having knowledge, expertise, or skills that can be useful to employees. For this type of power to work, your employees must perceive you as credible and trustworthy. This is the power you have when your employees perceive that you know what you are doing.

In addition to the five classic sources of power, there is one more that is taking on increasing importance in this age of information overload. It is *information power*—having access to and control of information valued by others.

You can see that power, contrary to most people's thinking, is not a dirty word. I suspect that power has such a bad reputation because most people assume that all power is coercive power. Instead, most forms of power represent positive behaviors that help people get the job done.

Winning Action Step

At the close of your day today, reflect on how often you have used coercive power to get something done. Commit to reducing that number by one tomorrow and by one each day after until you rarely, if ever, resort to it.

Powerlessness: How to Get People to Do Less with More

Lack of power, although not as destructive as coercive power, can be equally debilitating. One of the best examples of an organizational structure often accompanied by powerlessness is a bureaucracy, especially one that is very large, prescriptive, and controlling. This type of organization has too many rules and regulations that attempt to tell people exactly how to behave in virtually all situations. (Sounds like the federal government, doesn't it?) Because of this heavy top-down approach, this type of organizational structure tends to have employees who:

- Are vulnerable
- Feel dependent
- Avoid taking responsibilities
- Feel overwhelmed
- Are disillusioned
- Feel helpless
- Lack creativity
- Are mistrusting
- Lack motivation
- Are activity focused instead of results focused[6]

Having employees who exhibit these types of behaviors will cause you to quickly lose your competitive advantage in this rapidly changing global economy.

Winning Action Step

Starting today, treat every one of your team members as if they were a *volunteer.* You will know how good you've become at this by counting the number of times you use these powerful words per day: *please; would you be so kind; would you please do me a favor;* and *thank you.*

Empowerment: What It Is and What It Is Not

Before we take a look at what you can expect when you empower your team members, let's first define it. My experience is that everyone has their own idea of what it means to be empowered. Some managers think that to empower means to take their hands off and abdicate their responsibilities. Some employees think that they can do whatever they please. After all, they have been told that they have the power. Of course, both points of view are way off. One of the best definitions that I have come across is courtesy of my friend Joe Batten, who stated that to empower means "to create and foster relationships in which people understand their significance, possibilities and strengths. People who are empowered have a clear understanding of their authority, responsibility, accountability and valued roles in the team, and they have autonomy that is symbiotic with others."[7]

Another view very closely aligned with *winning management* has been advocated by Ford and Fottler, who suggest that "empowerment enables individuals or teams to make responsible decisions about the jobs they do: it involves management sharing relevant information about and control over factors that impinge upon the effective job performance."[8] Even more important, they stress that empowerment is a matter of degree, best visualized in Exhibit 4.2.

This model, I believe, can clear up a lot of confusion in regard to what empowerment really is and is not. It views empowerment to be a matter of degree in relationship to job content, which has to do with the tasks and procedures that are necessary to get the job done (horizontal axis). The vertical axis has to do with job context, which is concerned with the big picture. Why do we need to get this job done, and how does it fit within the parameters of our philosophy and our goals and objectives? (There is that mission, vision, and core values stuff again. I hope by now you have figured out that indeed it is important!)

Exhibit 4-2: Employee Empowerment Grid[9]

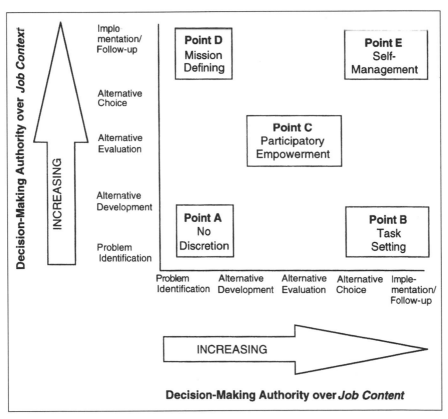

Ford and Fottler identified five specific points in their model to help you better understand the different degrees of empowerment. (Keep in mind that the number of points and the degrees of empowerment are infinite.)[10]

- Point A—no discretion. Really no empowerment at all. It's good old autocratic management, period!

- Point B—task setting. At this point employees are empowered to figure out how to get the job done, but they have little or no input in determining the organization's philosophy, goals, and objectives. This approach is used most frequently in American industries. Research has demonstrated that employees find such "enriched" jobs more satisfying and motivating, often leading to improved work quality. This approach is highly dependent on management's support, reinforcing reward systems, and organizational structure.

- Point C—participatory empowerment. This provides employees with some control over job content and context. This approach is often referred to as *autonomous work teams*. Saturn, the automotive subsidiary of General Motors, has made such teams work well.

- Point D—mission defining. This is a highly unusual approach where labor, perhaps in the form of a union, gets involved with determining the scope of an organization without having control over how the job gets done. An example might be a union being called upon to help decide whether or not a certain component should be outsourced. This approach is seldom found in U.S. organizations.

- Point E—self-management. This represents the ideal form of empowerment. So ideal, in fact, that it is seldom extended to employees and, in the U.S. at least, is more representative of the control accorded to top-level management. (One exception that comes to mind is W. L. Gore and Associates, makers of Goretex, which has practiced self-management to the max with awesome positive financial results for more than thirty years.[11]) Although rare, this is the level of empowerment that a *winning manager* constantly moves toward. (Remember, practicing *winning management* is a journey, not a destination.)

To me, the important thing about empowerment has more to do with what you do *not* do as opposed to what you do for your team members. What you do *not* do is practice what Ken Blanchard calls "seagull management." That's when you fly in, make a lot of noise, cause a lot of confusion, crap on everybody, and fly away. (Are you smiling? If not, time for a break.)

However, there are some things that you must do if you want to empower your team members. For one, you must do everything in your power to get rid of obstacles, like rules and regulations, that prevent team members from doing their job and taking care of the customer. Get rid of obstacles like systems and technologies (you've heard it before: "the computer won't let me do that") that stand in the way of getting the job done. Omit obstacles like unnecessary hierarchies that impede the communication flow among team members. And remove obstacles like managers who believe it is their job to think for or control their team members. Of course, there are things you must provide. You must provide team members with the tools and technologies that make their job easier; you must provide them with the authority to take independent actions; you must provide them with the financial resources to get the job done; you must provide them every opportunity to learn and continuously get better; you must have 111 percent confidence in their ability to get the job done; and, most important, you must get out of their way! In a nutshell, that's what empowerment is all about.

Reality Check
The measure of a man is what he does with power.
—Pittacus (650–569 B.C.)

Want to Increase Your Power? Learn to Give It Away

Since our rapidly changing times demand that we do business differently today, managers must learn to leverage themselves by empowering *all* team members in their organization. However, many managers are unwilling to grant power to their team members because they fear that doing so will reduce their own power. My own experience, and that of my clients, has demonstrated just the opposite. Giving power to others not only multiplies your own power, it also (in the long run) enhances your ability to be an effective coach. In fact, the ability to empower others is a key skill of winning managers. The reason is that empowered team members tend to be:

- Results oriented instead of activity focused
- Less concerned about doing something wrong or making mistakes
- Less dependent on supervisory approval to make decisions about what needs to be accomplished
- Willing to take calculated risks to achieve innovative results
- Able to communicate effectively because they can express their needs and desires
- Able to build effective networks and partnerships that help them get things done
- Able to influence others, including their supervisors, to get the job done
- Opportunity focused, looking beyond their own area of responsibility to make contributions that add value to customers, team members, and the entire organization

---

Winning Action Step

Anytime you are asked to make a decision for someone, ask him: "What do you think?" Then let him go with that decision unless it will inflict harm to customers, is contraindicated by the organizational philosophy, or costs more than you can safely sustain.

STRATEGIES TO COACH AND EMPOWER OTHERS

Given the alternatives, it is clear that empowerment is a critical strategy that demands your attention. Of course, if you are currently an effective delegator, you might say that you are already empowering your employees. Although I partially agree, coaching and empowerment go beyond delegating because they represent an entirely different way of managing people. Instead of playing cop, you will be expected to assume the role of coach, facilitator, and team leader. In this age of teams and project management, mastering these roles represents a survival strategy. You learned how to begin this transformation in the previous chapter, which described how to treat your people as adults, winners, and team members; develop and maintain a positive orientation; and tie rewards to performance. So let's go on from there.

Reality Check

Unconditionally accept others for who they are, instead of who they ought to be.

—Wolf J. Rinke

Coaching: A Definition

To me, coaching is a system that "grows" people by enabling them to learn through *guided discovery* and hands-on experience. The important element in this definition is that learning occurs through guided discovery, not by showing or telling people what to do. Rather, coaching assumes that team members learn by doing. Implicit in that definition is that effective coaches have three major responsibilities:

- Guiding people to discover the tools they need to get the job done
- Building confidence
- Motivating team members to be the best they can be

Building confidence and keeping team members motivated is an important aspect of your job as a *winning manager* because you are in the process of growing people. Some people will take on additional responsibilities with open arms. No problem there. But what about those who are always running away from additional responsibility? Well, you must make very clear what's in it for them and then reward any degree of success. (Remember, all of us listen to our favorite radio station, WIIFM—*what's in it for me.*) Some employees are afraid of taking on anything new because they are not sure of their own capabilities. Here you must engage them in incremental learning, as we discussed earlier. In addition, you should point out where and when they have succeeded in the past. Then you must express confidence in their capabilities by saying, for example, "I know you can provide leadership to this team. Remember how well you did last month, when you headed up the compensation review project?" In some cases, you may have to provide team members with informal or formal training before they are ready to assume the additional responsibility. (More about that in the next chapter.)

Reality Check
Telling is not coaching.

—Wolf J. Rinke

Coach Like a True Professional

At this point, you may be saying to yourself: "Okay, coach, I've got it, but what specifically must I do if I want to coach one of my team members?" I'm glad you asked, because here are the specific stages that identify the coaching process:[12]

Stage 1: Agree on the Project

This is where you and your team member sit down and agree on the specific project that she is going to be responsible for. These stages, by the way, assume that it is a major project and that you are communicating face to face with your team member. It is also assumed that this project represents an area of strength for you and an area of weakness for your team member—something that would enhance your team member's competence and, once mastered by your team member, would take a load off your shoulders. Of course, traditional managers hesitate to provide this type of coaching because, according to them, they lack the time. Deep down they are really afraid that they will coach themselves right out of a job. Nothing, of course, could be further from the truth. In fact, coaching is an essential skill you need to master if you want to thrive in today's leaner and flatter organizations.

Stage 2: Mutually Identify the Goals and Outcomes Expected

I like to call this *defining a good job*. So often things don't go the way you expect because your team member didn't really understand the outcomes you wanted to achieve in the first place. When you are done with this stage, both of you should be very clear about the when, where, what, who and how. Let me emphasize that you should always set high expectations because that will help determine how successful your team members will become. The reason is that in the long run *you get the type and quality of performance you expect and accept.* Furthermore, most people can do far more and far better than others expect of them. Marty Edelston of *Boardroom Reports* reinforces this concept with the message printed on his notepads:

GOODBETTERBESTNEVERLETIT
RESTUNTILTHEGOODISBETTER
ANDTHEBETTERISBEST

(No, we didn't forget the spaces; that's exactly how Marty has it written.)

Winning Action Step

Do everything you can to create a climate that encourages team members to tell you and the other managers what to do.

Stage 3: Facilitate Self-Discovery

This is the stage that distinguishes coaching from delegating. It is probably the most difficult stage for most managers, especially those who are used to telling others what to do.

You can best facilitate self-discovery by:

- Listening actively—listen for the meaning, not just the words. This requires you to make your own mind quiet. It also requires you to talk far less than you are used to. Remember, there must be a reason that you were born with two ears and only one mouth. Maybe you were meant to listen twice as much as you talk, especially when coaching others.

- Helping your team members think through the process and consequences of their proposed actions—this means that *they* do the thinking. To ensure that this happens, you might ask: "What would be the consequences of you taking this action?" Remember, your role is to facilitate their thought processes, *not* think for them!

• Sharing your good and *bad* experiences—your team members will learn from both. Most managers hesitate to share how they have messed up. They feel they must maintain a facade of perfection. However, sharing what has *not* worked for you, especially your really bad goofs, is particularly helpful here. It makes you more human and gives your team members permission to be less than perfect—which is what you are anyway!

Winning Action Step

Do whatever you can to get off the pedestal. Make sure the next story you tell your team members describes how you've messed up.

Stage 4: Agree on the Boundaries

Most of stage 4 is already done because you now have mutually accepted boundaries in your organization. You don't know what I'm talking about? Time to go back to chapter 2! Remember your mission, vision, and core values? They represent the ultimate parameters, or gold standard, for you and your team members. Of course, you may need to verbally supplement them so that your team members know where your comfort zone is and where the danger zone begins. You may also want to define when you want to be briefed and what type of feedback you want, for example, whether you want it in writing or in person.

Stage 5: Authorize and Empower

To get the job done, team members must have authorization. I like to refer to it as giving your team members rope. By the way, that includes the appropriate spending authority to get the job done. And please don't be timid here. After all, if *housekeepers* at Ritz Carlton hotels have the ability to spend up to $2,000 to solve customer service problems,[13] what's your excuse? To make this work, you must also master the art of letting go. You see, it is virtually impossible to learn by doing if your team members have to check with you every time they need to make a decision or a change. They would spend all their time running after you, instead of taking care of business. In other words, you must tell your team members how far they can go without coming to you, and then you must stay out of their way and let them do their thing. This has been particularly hard for me because when I see something wrong, I instinctively want to correct it. The better way is to let the team members learn from their own mistakes. "But," you protest, "let them make a mistake, and not say *anything?*" Yup, pardner, that's what I mean. "All the time, regardless of the consequences?" No, that's why practicing *winning management* is an art first and a science second. You must do a risk/benefit analysis. That's what physicians are taught to do anytime they prescribe medication. They weigh the benefits of the medication against the risks associated with it. You must do the same thing when making a decision about how much rope you should give your team members.

That reminds me of a supposedly true story. It has been told that one of the young IBM vice presidents made a mistake in the stock market. In fact, it was no ordinary mistake because it would cost IBM about $10 million. Shortly thereafter, the young vice president was summoned to the office of the chairman of IBM, Tom Watson. Expecting to be fired, the young man was not very happy as he showed up in Mr. Watson's office. Bracing himself for the worst, he had his head hung low and listened somewhat defensively. As the conversation progressed, it became clear that Mr. Watson was talking about new opportunities, perhaps even a promotion. So the young vice president tentatively asked for clarification. When his initial perceptions were confirmed, he asked incredulously: "You mean you are not going to fire me?" Mr. Watson replied, equally startled: "Fire you? After we just spent $10 million training you?"

Winning Action Step

The next time someone makes a mistake or messes up, congratulate her for taking a calculated risk.

Stage 6: Summarize and Reality Test

The purpose of this stage is to enhance communication accuracy. If the project is critical, I would do some reality testing by having the team member state in her own words what, specifically, the two of you have agreed to. A good way to accomplish this is to say to your team member: "As you well know, Jane, this is a critical project for us. Please be kind enough to summarize for me what it is that you are going to do between now and the next time we meet." Assuming that at this point you are both singing from the same sheet of music, you'll be ready to move to the final stage.

Stage 7: Track and Follow-through

This stage is designed to make sure that nothing falls between the cracks. It is especially critical if you are coaching someone for the first time. In that case, you will want to be sure to put a note on your calendar or tickler file that will remind you of the date and time your team member promised to provide you with a report, update, or any other kind of feedback. Once that is achieved, stand back—yes, really stand back—and what ever you do, don't—let me say it again, *don't*—interfere! Now, watch your team members grow.

Having mastered the seven stages of the coaching process, you are now ready to learn some advanced coaching and empowerment strategies which will enable you to achieve extraordinary results with ordinary people.

Treat All Employees As Team Members

A sports analogy will illustrate this point. Although the coach appears to be the most important individual in the game, the fact is that each and every player is equally important. The coach, who has the overall perspective, is certainly more knowledgeable about the game plan and the particulars of the play. This enables him to direct the players in a way that builds on each team member's strengths, while exploiting the weaknesses of the other team. In spite of this broad perspective, high visibility, and extensive power, the coach is dependent on every member on the team. In other words, there is a *symbiotic* relationship between the coach and the team members.

A beautiful example of this interdependence was demonstrated in the 1980 Olympics by the U.S. ice hockey team. The U.S. team, headed up by Coach Brooks from the University of Wisconsin, consisted primarily of a bunch of college kids who did not even know each other twelve months prior to the game. On the other hand, the Russian team had trained together for many years. Yet the U.S. team, who according to the odds-makers were the underdogs, beat the Russian team. Why? Although I'm not an ice hockey expert, the primary reason seemed to be that the U.S. team played as a turned-on, tuned-in, determined team. Void of any superstars, each team member depended on every other team member to get the job done. When one team member got tired or was injured, the other members of the team pulled more than their weight. In short, nothing is more powerful than a turned-on, tuned-in, motivated team, which has all its energy focused on the attainment of the team's mission, vision, and core values.

That is the kind of power I would like you to be able to harness by empowering everyone who works with you on your team. Note I said *with* you, not *for* you. This is not just a matter of semantics to me. How you speak about your team members reveals your values and beliefs. I recommend that you make it a practice to say that people work *with* you instead of *for* you or *under* you. (Think about the latter. Can you really afford to say that in this day and age of sensitivity about sex discrimination?)

Let me make this a bit more concrete with an example. Let's say you are the general manager of a four-star hotel that prides itself on its outstanding cuisine. You even hired a high-powered (translate as expensive) European-trained chef who devotes a lot of effort to creating the finest meals. Although the chef is certainly a very important member of the team, every other team member is equally important. For example, what happens to customer satisfaction, which is your ultimate performance indicator, when even the most delectable meal is served on a dirty plate or by a grumpy server? The answer is obvious: You will not score, and if it happens often enough, you will be out of the game. So start right now to treat *all* your employees, especially those on the front line, as if they are the most important members on the team. *They are!*

Reality Check

The people who have the greatest impact on your organization, i.e., the front-line employees, typically are paid the least amount of money and receive the least amount of training and the fewest benefits.

—Wolf J. Rinke

There is another equally important reason for speaking and thinking well of your team members. No matter how long you've been in the business, *your team members know more about their jobs than you do!* Please don't protest too loudly. I know how you feel; I came up through the ranks also. Still, I stand by my assertion. They—not you, work those jobs five to six days per week, eight or more hours per day. At best, you haven't done the job for a while; at worst, you have never done it. In addition, your team members know how to make their jobs better and can save your organization a ton of money. But you've got to ask them, involve them, and empower them!

Here is an example of what I mean. This came from one of my hospital clients, who was under the gun to conserve, save, and, in general, do more with less:

As I made my rounds, I spent some time with one of the clean-up crew members; I think they referred to him as a sanitary engineer. Even though he seemed a bit slow mentally, I was impressed with how much he knew about his job, which was understandable since he had been at it for about ten years. At the same time, he knew virtually nothing about the bigger picture. He was barely aware that management was contemplating laying people off because of cost constraints. As we chatted, he volunteered several suggestions that had the potential to save a considerable amount of money. When I asked him whether he had given his suggestions to his supervisor or someone on the management team, he said no. When I asked him why, he shrugged and said, "Why should I? They don't care." When I asked how he knew that, he said, *"Well, I've been here almost ten years and no one has ever asked me my opinion about anything."*

This illustrates how we can miss out on a wealth of opportunities when we don't take advantage of the power and knowledge of *all* our team members.

Winning Action Step

Give your team members more authority than you think is wise. They will rise to the occasion—most of the time.

Build on Team Members' Strengths

Winning managers realize that there are no perfect people. So they use very little of their mental energy to attempt to make their team members perfect. (Of course, when you hire new team members, you should take extraordinary care and effort to find the absolute best people money can buy.) Building on people's strengths begins with catching people doing things *almost right* and goes on from there.

People come in all shapes, colors, and abilities. It is this diversity in people that makes management so exciting and challenging. It is diversity, not sameness, that makes teams incredibly innovative, a critical competence in this rapidly changing global economy. So whatever you do, get juiced by diversity and, most important, *quit looking for people who are like you!* To empower people in your organization, you must find out what people's strengths and weaknesses are and then appreciate them for *both* their strengths *and* their weaknesses. Too many of us waste too much time complaining about people's weaknesses instead of figuring out what they are really good at and then using them accordingly.

A look at history provides us with a memorable example. When President Lincoln needed a commander to lead the Union Army to victory, he needed a super soldier, kind of like "Stormin' Norman." He received lots of advice on who that should be. After extensive deliberation, he chose General Ulysses S. Grant, a man who was not highly regarded by many because he had not attended the "right" schools, was poorly mannered, did not come from the "right" social circles, and had a drinking problem. In spite of all this, Lincoln selected him because he *won battles.* Lincoln smoothed over his other deficiencies, appeased the politicians, and made sure that General Grant had what he needed in order to do what he did best. Lincoln used the same skills you need to use to empower your team members. Come to think of it, this perfectly describes the role and responsibilities of a *winning manager.*

Here is another example. Recently, I was consulting with an executive who was describing his management team to me. After he had given me a detailed description, he said, "I think that, overall, I have some great people, but I can't understand why they won't take responsibility for their departments." Upon encouraging him to give me more details, he finally said: "I can't understand why they don't manage the way I do." This executive, like so many of us, was using himself as the gold standard and was attempting to clone himself. By doing so, he became insensitive to the fact that there are as many different ways to get the job done as there are people. The important question was whether these managers got the job done, not whether they got it done exactly as the boss would have done it. Our subsequent discussion centered on the important *winning management* skill of being able to *accept people for who they are, not who they "ought to be."*

Winning Action Step

When you must evaluate one of your team members, ask yourself: "Am I using myself as the gold standard?" If you are, quit doing it!

This one critical realization has helped me to function as a *winning manager.* It has also helped me in my personal life. For years, I was unable to get along with my father, until I began to realize that we were continually attempting to make each other over in our own image. We each used our own beliefs and values as the gold standard, and if the action or behavior in question did not meet that, then we perceived it as "weird." Only after we accepted that neither of us could really change the other, and that both of us are okay the way we are, were we able to begin to communicate and get along.

This same principle extends to people in organizations. As a *winning manager,* you must completely buy into the belief that it is almost impossible to effect a lasting change in people's *basic* behaviors. Therefore, instead of reminding people of their weaknesses, you will get much better results from helping your team members figure out what they are good at and then putting them in situations and positions that will enable them to build on their strengths.

Reality Check

Of the 5.6 billion people on the planet Earth, there is not one perfect person.

—Wolf J. Rinke

Overlook Team Members' Weaknesses

At this point you might be saying: "Okay, coach, you've got me convinced, but what about my people's weaknesses?" My answer is: *Forget about them.* Let me qualify this a bit by sharing how you can dramatically improve the performance appraisal process—that dreaded activity that typically focuses on weaknesses—that you do with (or is it to) your employees about once a year. Instead of regurgitating all the things the employee did wrong over the past year, I recommend that you use this opportunity to grow people. One way to do this is to be future oriented. (Remember the spilled milk story?) Another is to put the team members in charge of this process by having them fill out their own evaluation. (Remember, you are treating your team members as adults, and most adults hate to be evaluated.) Also, be sure to encourage your team members to evaluate *you.* Ask them what it is that you can do to help them do their jobs more effectively. (That's called 360-degree evaluation.)

What about employee weaknesses? My recommendation is for you to ask your team members to make up a list of their strengths and weaknesses—weaknesses that compromise their ability to get the job done should receive an asterisk. Next to each asterisked weakness, employees should note an action strategy that will identify how they plan to address the weakness. Make up a similar list, and then sit down with the team member to review her performance appraisal and action plan. (The assumption is that you didn't forget my earlier advice and have already undergone a similar scrutiny of yourself.)

The two of you should compare notes, starting, of course, with accomplishments and strengths. Provided that you both agree on the major items, you begin by accentuating the positive accomplishments and emphasizing how your team member (let's call her Rosie) can build on her strengths. Next, take a look at what Rosie proposes to do about her *asterisked* weaknesses. Use these to help her set some realistic goals for the next twelve months. While you are at it, find out what you can do to help Rosie attain these goals and objectives. Then encourage her to *forget all the other weaknesses*. The outcome should be a personal action plan or, if you like, her road map to success, which will serve as the basis for her next performance appraisal. By the way, if you are wondering about how honest people are with themselves, I have found that generally there is an overlap between your evaluation and that of your employee. If there is a difference, it is usually because a team member is harder on herself than her supervisor is.

What about the really serious employee problems? (I knew you would not let me off the hook that easily.) First, let me emphasize that there should be no surprises during the performance appraisal. In other words, if the problem was that serious, Rosie should already have long known about it, and you should not be rehashing any past problems. Remember the hot-stove rule? If you don't, reread the section on how to punish effectively in the previous chapter. If the employee has far more weaknesses than strengths, she should never have been hired in the first place, and you may have to terminate her, as we discussed earlier.

Winning Action Step

Hiring and firing decisions can be simplified by visualizing a balance beam scale. Place the individual's strengths or contributions on one side and weaknesses or "costs" on the other. Check which way the scale tilts, and make your decision. Fire someone as soon as possible after it has been decided that the person's weaknesses far outweigh his strengths.

Help Employees Make It to the Top Faster

People represent one of the few resources that have the potential to *appreciate,* but only if you invest in them. One way to do this is by promoting from within. Although many organizations subscribe to this philosophy, few practice it as aggressively as Stew Leonard's Connecticut dairy store (better known as the "Disneyland of supermarkets"). He calls his promotion program the "ladder of success," a literal illustration of which is proudly displayed, together with the employees' photos, all over the store. Leonard maintains that the people who start at the bottom and work their way up are the backbone of his business because nothing motivates people more than to know that they have a chance at *any* job in the store. He also believes that those who work their way up are the true champions because they know better than anyone else what it is like to be on the firing line. This approach also has a positive effect on the bottom line because it ensures that people are not overcompensated as a result of automatic longevity increases. So the next time you are hiring, take extra time to find individuals who want to get ahead and then provide them with a career ladder worth climbing.

Winning Action Step
Do everything in your power to promote from within.

Get Rid of Rules and Regulations

Take a look at your policy manual. Go ahead; do it right now! Is it all neat and shiny? Then throw it away! What about if it is soiled, replete with grease spots, dog-eared pages, and looking outright raunchy? Keep it! But, I implore you, please do everything in your power to get rid of unnecessary and demeaning rules, regulations, and policies that stand in the way of people providing quality and delivering excellence.

Is this advice realistic? There is ample evidence of companies excelling because they are adhering to this philosophy. For example, Nordstrom, the often-cited retailer that has mastered the art of customer service, has a policy manual with only one rule:

Rule #1: *Use your good judgment in all situations. There will be no additional rules.*[14]

Can this work for you? The answer is a resounding *yes,* but you must be sure to satisfy the regulatory agencies. My advice is to do what you must to comply with all applicable federal, state, and local regulations but no more, because pretty forms and lots of neat-looking documents "doth not an excellent organization make."

Winning Action Step

During the next twelve months, reduce all rules, regulations, and procedures by 50 percent. Do this every year until you only have those required by the regulators.

Achieving Extraordinary Results with Ordinary People

The most effective way to empower people is to provide team members with the tools and confidence that enable them to be their own authority. As mentioned in chapter 1, companies that achieved extraordinary financial results—more than 15,000 percent increases in stock values during 1972–1992—achieved "competitive success through people... by working *with* people, not by replacing them or limiting the scope of their activities. It entails seeing the work force as a source of strategic advantage, not just as a cost to be minimized or avoided. Firms that take this different perspective are often able to successfully outmaneuver and outperform their rivals."[15]

But, you protest, how come U.S. corporate executives are literally overdosing on downsizing? And how come they are getting such incredible increases in the value of their stocks as a result of downsizing? Well, the results are not nearly what they are cracked up to be. Here is the real skinny, according to a University of Colorado study of ninety-one companies over a seven-year period. They found that the companies that downsized the most aggressively had "the thinnest profits over the long term. Three years after the downsizing took place, earnings at the downsized companies had almost doubled. But the earnings of the companies in *the same industries that hadn't downsized more than quadrupled."*[16] (My emphasis.) So why so much downsizing, you ask? Number one, it's the in-thing to do. Number two, it does make the balance sheet look better, often much better over the short term. And number three, it is super lucrative for consultants, according to management consultant Alan Downs, author of *Corporate Executions.*[17] (Just to set the record straight, I'm not a proponent of downsizing!)

Winning Action Step

Never pigeonhole people, e.g., "She is just a secretary." You don't know what people are capable of until you have given them the opportunity to show you their stuff.

So how can you do it better? Probably one of the best examples of how to do it right is Herb Kelleher, CEO of Southwest Airlines, who looks for employees who work well in a collegial atmosphere, have a sense of humor, want to excel, and are totally dedicated to customer service. According to Kelleher: "We don't care much about education and expertise, because we can train people to do whatever they have to do. We hire attitudes."[18] Such attitudes result in extraordinary performance by Southwest employees. Case in point:

> A Southwest reservations clerk in Dallas took a call from a harried fellow who was putting his 88-year-old mother aboard a flight to St. Louis. The elderly woman was quite frail, the fellow explained, and he wasn't sure she could handle the change of planes at Tulsa. "No sweat," replied the clerk, "I'll fly with her as far as Tulsa and make sure she gets safely aboard the St. Louis flight."[19]

Oh, before I forget, yes, these highly motivated, extremely productive employees, who represent Southwest's competitive advantage, are *all unionized.*

Has Kelleher's passion for his "family" (as he refers to his team members) and empowerment, and his commitment to create a place of work where "kindness and human spirit are nurtured," paid off? According to testimony from one Southwest team member: "At other places, managers say that people are their most important resource, but nobody acts on it. At Southwest, they have never lost sight of the fact."[20] Review Exhibit 4-3, and you will be convinced that Herb Kelleher's empowerment strategy has paid off in many ways. In fact, it has paid off so well that Southwest has won the triple crown (best on-time arrival, fewest lost bags, and fewest passenger complaints) three years in a row. None of their competitors has achieved this even one time!

Can you achieve these kinds of results in your organization? As you might expect, my answer is not only yes, but *hell, yes!* Why am I so sure that you can? Because you are acquiring the skills you need to make this happen for your organization in this book. All that remains is for you to take *action,* so that knowledge is transformed into reality and extraordinary results!

Winning Action Step

Starting tomorrow, treat every team member as if she were the most important member of your team. Do this as if your job depended on it. *It does!*

Exhibit 4-3: How Productivity Pays Off for Southwest[21]

	AA	Delta	Northwest	**Southwest**	UAL	USAir
Cost per available seat mile	8.9¢	9.4¢	9.1¢	**7.0¢**	9.6¢	10.8¢
Passengers per employee	840	1,114	919	**2,443**	795	1,118
Employees per aircraft	152	134	127	**81**	157	111

EMPOWERMENT IN ACTION

Talking about taking action reminds me of a specific example that exemplifies what happens when a team member has been empowered. I had been on a grueling speaking tour when, after an arduously long flight (I call it cattle herding), I checked into the Marriott Suites in Scottsdale, Arizona at 2:00 a.m. Because it was late I gave the car keys to a bellman so that I could get checked in and go to bed. The following morning I had an early engagement with a client. After breakfast I gave my claim check to an attendant. After waiting about five minutes, Everado, the bellman, came back and told me that my car would not start. "It appears," he explained, "that someone left the lights on overnight." Given that I had an appointment with a very important client, I started getting a bit nervous. "Not to worry, Dr. Rinke." (Those Marriott folks have figured out how important our names are to us—I just wonder why most other service companies haven't caught on.) "I'll just drive you to your appointment in our van and get you there in plenty of time." On the way over, he told me that he would contact the car rental company and make sure that they correct the problem or provide me with another car. (Mind you, he came up with that, I didn't ask for it.) "Also," he continued, "what time would you like me to pick you up?" I assured him that I would be able to get a ride back, but that I would be extremely grateful if he could make sure that the car would be fixed, since I would have little chance to do it myself. At the end of a full and demanding day, I returned to the hotel. I could hardly believe it when I found out that Everado had indeed taken care of everything. And to think, all I had given him was the name of the car rental company! Mind you, he did it all without being asked by anyone! Plus, he was incredibly cheerful and composed at all times. A front-line employee taking independent, autonomous action to do right by the customer regardless of effort, inconvenience, or cost. That's what I call empowerment in action!

HOW TO KNOW IF YOU HAVE ARRIVED

To find out how well you have empowered your team members, take this quick test. Observe your team members to see what they do when they are confronted with a problem or a decision. Empowered team members will routinely ask themselves the following four diagnostic questions. Is the action I need to take to resolve this problem:

- Good for our customers?
- Good for our organization?
- In agreement with our philosophy?
- Good for me?

If they can answer all four questions with an unequivocal yes, empowered team members will feel free to make the decision without checking with you, or any other manager, even if there is no policy that covers this particular action. I would go even further and say that if you have truly applied the principles in this book, team members will act in accordance with what is right for the customer, *even if at times they have to violate rules and regulations.* The flow chart in Exhibit 4-4 may help your team members visualize this process.

Exhibit 4-4: Empowerment Decision Flow Chart[22]

When you need to make a decision, ask yourself these four questions:

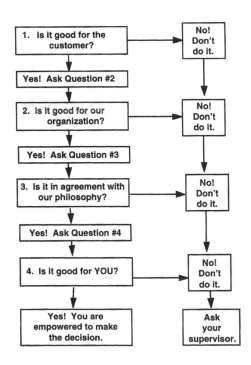

1. Is it good for the customer?
   No! Don't do it.
   Yes! Ask Question #2

2. Is it good for our organization?
   No! Don't do it.
   Yes! Ask Question #3

3. Is it in agreement with our philosophy?
   No! Don't do it.
   Yes! Ask Question #4

4. Is it good for YOU?
   No! Don't do it.
   Yes! You are empowered to make the decision.
   Ask your supervisor.

This important chapter emphasized that *winning managers* get in front of the power curve by coaching and empowering their team members so that they can be their own authority. At the same time, they tell their team members more than they want to know, which is the topic of our next chapter.

Winning Action Step

Get in the habit of pushing *all* decision making down to the lowest possible level.

SUMMARY

- People can be managed by fear or desire. Over the long run, desire results in greater performance, productivity, and profitability.
- The six types of power are:
  — Reward power
  — Coercive power
  — Legitimate power
  — Referent power
  — Expert power
  — Information power
- Employees who lack power:
  — Are vulnerable
  — Feel dependent
  — Avoid taking responsibilities
  — Feel overwhelmed
  — Are disillusioned
  — Feel helpless
  — Lack creativity
  — Are mistrusting
  — Lack motivation
  — Are activity focused instead of results focused
- Empowered team members believe that they can make a significant contribution to the organization and will help the organization deliver consistent quality.

- Effective coaches:
  — Guide people
  — Build confidence
  — Motivate
- The seven stages in the coaching process are:
  1. Agree on the project.
  2. Mutually identify the goals.
  3. Facilitate self discovery.
  4. Agree on boundaries.
  5. Authorize and empower.
  6. Summarize and reality test.
  7. Track and follow-through.
- You can empower your employees by:
  — Treating them like team members
  — Building on their strengths
  — Discounting their weaknesses
  — Helping them climb the ladder of success
  — Getting rid of rules and regulations
- You can best achieve extraordinary results with ordinary people by recognizing that a company is only as good as its people and then acting accordingly.
- Empowered team members are those who take independent actions after they have been able to answer the following diagnostic questions with an unequivocal yes.
  — Is it good for our customers?
  — Is it good for our organization?
  — Is it in agreement with our philosophy?
  — Is it good for me?

Winning Action Step

Count the number of women on your management team. Do everything in your power to increase their presence to slightly above 50 percent. You'll be glad you did because most women find it easier than men to practice *winning management*.

NOTES

1. Adapted from W. J. Rinke, *The Winning Foodservice Manager: Strategies for Doing More with Less,* 2nd ed. (Clarksville, MD: Achievement Publishers, division of Wolf Rinke Associates, Inc., 1990), pp. 224–226.
2. F. Herzberg, "One More Time: How Do You Motivate Employees?" in *People: Managing Your Most Important Asset* (Boston: Harvard Business Review, 1986).
3. N. Cole, "How Employee Empowerment Improves Manufacturing Performance." *Academy of Management Executive* 9, no. 1 (1995): 80.
4. Ibid.
5. Rinke, *The Winning Foodservice Manager,* p. 227.
6. Ibid., 228.
7. J. Batten, *Building a Total Quality Culture* (Menlo Park, CA: Crisp Publications, Inc., 1992), p. 78.
8. R. C. Ford and M. D. Fottler, "Empowerment: A Matter of Degree," *Academy of Management Executive* 9, no. 3 (1995): 22.
9. Ibid., 24.
10. Ibid., 23–24.
11. F. Shipper and C. C. Manz, "Employee Self-Management without Formally Designated Teams: An Alternative Road to Empowerment," *Organizational Dynamics* 20, no. 3 (1991): 48–61.
12. *The Helping Hand: Coaching Skills* (Chicago: Video Arts Inc., 1990), videocassette.
13. T. Peters, *The Pursuit of Wow* (New York: Vintage Books, 1994), p. 18.
14. B. Dumaine, "Who Needs a Boss?" *Fortune,* 7 May 1990, p. 54.
15. J. Pfeffer, *Competitive Advantage Through People* (Boston, MA: Harvard Business School Press, 1994), p. 16.
16. K. D. Grimsley, "The Ax That Cuts Both Ways," *Washington Post,* 5 November 1995, pp. H-1, H-4.
17. Ibid.
18. K. Labich, "Is Herb Kelleher America's Best CEO?" *Fortune* 129, no. 9 (1994): 50.
19. Ibid.
20. Ibid.
21. Ibid.
22. W. J. Rinke, *Exceptional Quality Service (EQS): How to Consistently Exceed Your Customers' Expectations* (Clarksville, MD: Wolf Rinke Associates, Inc., 1994), p. 98.

Winning Action Step

Always assume that people want to do things *right,* because they do!

Communicating

5

Sixty percent of all management problems result from faulty communication.

—Peter Drucker

Now that you've mastered how to coach and empower your team members, you're ready to tackle the Achilles' heel of empowerment and team building, communicating.

PREVIEW OF COMING ATTRACTIONS

Just as before, we'll start by finding out how good a communicator you are. Then, we'll take a look at the data that account for why we are such ineffective communicators and, more important, what specifically you can do to improve your communication effectiveness and achieve win-win outcomes and cooperation. Next, I'll convince you once and for all that you must tell your team members more than they want to know. I will also provide you with specific strategies to enable you to accomplish this goal. Then we'll briefly learn how walking your talk and practicing management by walking around (MBWA) will enable you to empower your team members faster.

Last, but not least, we'll look at the tough part of *winning management,* specifically, how you can implement a peer-monitored performance system in your organization and benefit from having peer pressure go to work for you by implementing measurement systems that support the use of multifunctional teams. Obviously this is an important chapter, so let's put on our seat belts, get ourselves in gear, and begin by finding out just how good a communicator you are.

SAY WHAT?

In my communication *fun*shops, I like to ask my attendees: "How many of you have difficulties with communication?" Consistently, virtually all hands go up. Why? I suspect the reason is that human beings are relatively poor communicators. This reminds me of the story of the husband who came home from a political rally:

Wife: "How was the rally?"
Husband: "Pretty good."
Wife: "Who spoke?"
Husband: "The governor."
Wife: "What did he talk about?"
Husband: "Umm—he didn't say."

Research tells us that people speak at about 125 words per minute. However, we think at about 400–500 words per minute. That means we only communicate at about 25 percent efficiency. As a result of that inefficiency, about 80 percent of information is lost in five transmissions. You can test this for yourself by cutting a brief paragraph out of your local newspaper. At a meeting, gather five volunteers. Ask four to leave the room. Ask the person left in the room to read the paragraph, and then put it away. Then ask one person at a time to come back into the room. Have the first person tell the second person what the paragraph said. Then call in the third person and have the second person tell the third person what the paragraph said, and so on until you get to the fifth person. What you will find is that with each transmission, the information accuracy will suffer dramatically. When the fifth person tells the rest of the group what the newspaper paragraph said, it will be dramatically different from the original.

COMMUNICATION: HOW GOOD ARE YOU?

But what about *you?* How well do you communicate? Complete Exhibit 5-1 and you'll find out.

Exhibit 5-1: Communication Self-Assessment Instrument

Instructions: Using the following scale, circle the number that most closely indicates the frequency each statement applies to you. (People have different preferences and opinions; therefore, there are no right or wrong answers.)

SCALE:
Always	Almost Always	Infrequently	Almost Never	Never
A	AA	I	AN	N

	A	AA	I	AN	N
1. I avoid giving employees, especially those with little education, information about the financial status of the organization.	1	2	3	4	5
2. I ask people to slow down when they speak too fast.	1	2	3	4	5
3. I tend to finish sentences for people, especially if they speak slowly.	1	2	3	4	5
4. I listen primarily for facts, rather than ideas, when someone is speaking.	1	2	3	4	5
5. When I am engaged in conversation, I tend to think about what I am going to say next.	1	2	3	4	5
6. I tend to tune out when a familiar topic is being discussed.	1	2	3	4	5
7. To avoid hurting someone else's feelings, I pretend to be listening even when I am not.	1	2	3	4	5
8. A person's credentials (e.g., Ph.D., M.D.) or their title (e.g., president) helps me determine the value of what they are saying.	1	2	3	4	5
9. I do everything in my power to delay giving my team members information that impacts negatively on them, such as pending layoffs, cost-cutting initiatives, etc.	1	2	3	4	5
10. I avoid asking questions when I don't understand something.	1	2	3	4	5

TOTAL: _____

Scoring Instructions: Score each item in accordance with the number you have circled, *except item 2,* which has to be scored by reversing the scale, so that 1 = 5, 2 = 4, 3 = 3, 4 = 2, 5 = 1. Then total the scores in the space provided.

Examples:

1. I avoid giving	1	2	3	4	⑤	= 5
2. I ask people...	1	2	3	4	⑤	= 1
3. I tend to finish...	1	2	3	④	5	= 4

Communication: What Your Score Means

47–50   You are a master communicator, period! Be sure to mentor others who are not as talented as you are.

43–46   Excellent—you really know how to communicate.

39–42   Very good—you are on the right track.

35–38   Good—however, you can do better. But you know that already. After all, that's why you are reading this powerful book.

31–34   Okay—but you have not even begun to maximize your communication skills. Get ready, get set—to learn and apply!

<31   Pay extra careful attention to this chapter. Help is on the way!

Winning Action Step

During your next staff—oops, I mean—"team" meeting (I dislike "staff" because it sounds like the microorganism that can make you sick), talk less, much less, and listen more, much more.

PEOPLE ARE TERRIBLE COMMUNICATORS

Things get even more complicated when you add nonverbal communication. For example, in an often-cited classic study, Mehrabian and Ferris[1] found that if you want to persuade another person, your words play a relatively minor role. (See Exhibit 5-2.)

Exhibit 5-2: What Will Change People's Attitudes?[2]

Verbal content of the message	7%
Vocal characteristics (tone of voice, rate of speech, etc.)	38%
Facial expressions	55%

In other words, people are much more influenced by nonverbal cues than by the words they hear. (That's what Marshall McLuhan meant when he said "the medium is the message.") Now, add to that cultural and gender differences[3] and the many communication barriers we encounter (one author counted 130 barriers in the communication research literature;[4] for a partial list, see Exhibit 5-3), and you'll soon conclude that communication is a very fragile and inexact process. No wonder Peter Drucker maintains that communication is responsible for 60 percent of all of our problems. You did read that, didn't you? If not, it's time to go back to the beginning of this chapter and pay attention. This one is just too important to skim!

Exhibit 5-3: Barriers to Communication[5]

1. *Perceptual selectivity.* People can understand only limited information at one time.
2. *Evaluating things and people as good or bad.* A tendency that can place others on the defensive.
3. *Implicit assumptions.* Beliefs the communicator holds without being fully aware of them.
4. *Language differences.* Words mean different things to different people.
5. *Inadequate receiving.* Too much sending, not enough listening.
6. *Excessive kindness.* Reluctance to express negative information for fear of damaging the relationship.
7. *Inadequate feedback.* Sender does not find out if message has been received, acknowledged, and understood.
8. *Loss or distortion of information.* Changes in meaning brought about through serial communication.
9. *Failure to consult.* Tendency to avoid the input of persons who will be affected by, or who are capable of, improving a decision.
10. *Geographic factors.* Distance between organizational entities.
11. *Task specialization.* Differences in jargon, training, and work focus that impair understanding.
12. *Status, power, and authority differences.* Social factors lead to mistrust between members and groups.
13. *Pressure.* Misunderstanding resulting from technological changes, demands for increased productivity, and competition for rewards.

We haven't even talked about written communication, which most people have even more trouble with! The following provides several humorous examples of just how poorly we do with written communication. They are supposedly taken from actual claims submitted to an insurance agency and ended up in my files, unfortunately without a reference, although my failing memory is telling me they were once reprinted by Ann Landers; however, I don't think that was the original source. They are so precious that they are worth sharing with you anyway. Enjoy!

"The accident happened when the right front door of a car came around the corner without giving a signal."

"I had been driving my car for 40 years when I fell asleep at the wheel and had an accident."

"The guy was all over the road. I had to swerve a number of times before I hit him."

"Coming home, I drove into the wrong house and collided with a tree I don't have."

The moral of all of this is that *human beings are terrible communicators*. Yes, that includes *you!*

HOW TO COMMUNICATE MORE EFFECTIVELY

To help you become a more effective communicator, I recommend that you start with yourself and improve your own communication skills. You can do this by learning how to keep the communication window wide open and by mastering the art of communicating like a *pro*.

Keep the Window Wide Open

One of the best ways to improve your communication skills is to master a powerful communications tool referred to as the *Johari Window*. Developed by Joseph Luft and Harry Ingham (Johari is a contraction of their names), it helps people improve their interpersonal effectiveness in both their personal and professional lives by improving their mutual awareness of how they give and receive information.[6] The model, which I have modified for this purpose (see Exhibit 5-4), identifies four different "windows" representing the information that you know about yourself and that others know about you.

Exhibit 5-4: The Johari Window

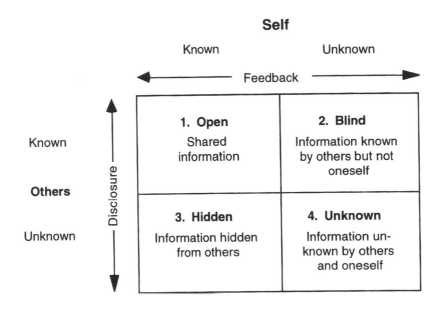

Window 1: *Open.* This represents information that is known to both you and others. If you are able to keep this window wide open by widely sharing information through disclosure and feedback, you tend to communicate very effectively with others. In fact, the larger the open window, the more effective the interpersonal relationship is likely to be.

Window 2: *Blind.* This represents information that is unknown to you but known to others. Your blindness could be a function of being kept in the dark or your inability or unwillingness to get to know yourself.

Window 3: *Hidden.* This represents the area that is known to you but unknown to others. Typically, this is the type of information that you may not be willing to share because it is personal, embarrassing, or private. Alternatively, it might be the type of information that you are not willing to share because it gives you the competitive advantage over others. Information in window 3 might embarrass you, make you feel vulnerable, or cause you to lose control or power.

Window 4: *Unknown.* This represents information that neither you nor the other party knows. It's important to recognize that even though neither party knows, the information can be discovered if both parties are willing to engage in freewheeling exercises such as brainstorming, the "what if" technique, or other creative exercises.

Communication effectiveness can be dramatically enhanced through self-disclosure (see Exhibit 5-5). The reason for this is twofold. First, self-disclosure legitimizes mutual disclosure. Once a person reveals closely held information to another, that person in turn will be more likely to share information that he previously hoarded. As a result, people get to know each other better, become more comfortable with one another, and are more likely to trust each other. All of these are key attributes if you want to enjoy a rich and rewarding personal and professional relationship and build an empowered team.

Exhibit 5-5: Disclosing Information Hidden to Others

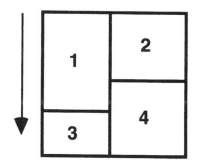

The second way that communication effectiveness can be enhanced is by increasing the level of feedback (see Exhibit 5-6). Feedback occurs when one person actively solicits information from another and demonstrates that she is willing to share information. Feedback encourages mutual disclosure, breaks down communication barriers, and promotes improved understanding and increased two-way communication.

Winning managers have mastered the art of keeping window 1 as wide open as possible by engaging in *both* self-disclosure and feedback

Exhibit 5-6: Providing Feedback to Others

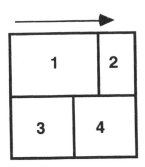

(see Exhibit 5-7). *Winning managers* conceal very little information and give extensive feedback. Their team members experience high levels of trust because there are few, if any, hidden agendas, closed doors, secrets, or unexpected surprises. Instead, there is lots of participative decision making, extensive collaboration, consensus building, and lots of open two-way communication. A side benefit of keeping window 1 wide open is that both you and your team members will develop more satisfying and rewarding relationships that lead to lower turnover, increased retention, improved performance, and higher productivity. Now that you know what it takes to keep the window wide open, let's take a look at what else you can do to communicate effectively.

Exhibit 5-7: Disclosing Information *and* Providing Feedback to Others

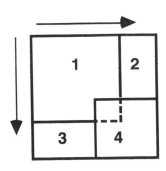

Communicate Like a Pro

The following nine specific strategies will enable you to communicate like a *pro*.

Utilize Adult Language

Eric Berne, author of *Games People Play*, and Thomas Harris, author of *I'm O.K.—You're O.K.*, popularized transactional analysis (TA), a useful model of interpersonal behavior and communication preferences. According to Berne, all of us have internalized three different "tape recordings" that represent our "ego states." These are the *child*, the *parent*, and the *adult*. These "tapes" have nothing to do with status, but rather refer to how we express ourselves in interpersonal communication.[7]

The *child* ego state refers to the behavior pattern, thoughts, and feelings that we learned when we were children. These include helplessness, blaming, and emotional expressions such as "I can't help it," "Don't blame me," "It's his/her fault," "I don't care," "Won't," "I don't want to," "Let's have fun," and "Let's show them." Nonverbal cues of the child ego state include whining, whistling, laughing, teasing, expressing dejection, pouting, nail biting, moving restlessly, and looking rebellious, excited, or sad.

The *parent* is the ego state that we develop by observing parents and other authority figures. When we are in a parent role, we tend to be very judgmental, critical, controlling, comforting, or nurturing. You know that you are using your parent tape when you use such phrases as "You can't do that," "You have to," "You should have," "Always," "Never," "You don't understand," "You are not listening to me," "Here let me show you," "We've always done it this way," "You are bad," and "Here, let me fix it for you." Nonverbal cues of the parent include finger pointing, looking at your watch while talking, finger tapping, pressing lips tight, grinding teeth, checking on others, scowling, sneering, patronizing, supporting, or expressing sympathy.

The third internal tape that we can play is that of the *adult*. An adult is a fact finder, information seeker, analyzer, and logical problem solver. When you use your adult tape, you ask why, what, when, where, who, and how. And you say such things as "I made a mistake," "I changed my mind," "I don't know," "I don't understand," "It is my opinion," "Let's check this out," and "What can we learn from this?"

When you are in this ego state, you tend to be clear, calm, and void of judgments. Your nonverbal expressions include straight but relaxed posture, comfortable eye contact, and a friendly face that says "I'm interested, alert, thoughtful, and attentive."

Generally speaking, communication effectiveness is dramatically enhanced when people express themselves in an adult ego state, especially when both parties are playing the same tape. Since it is difficult to change other people, I would strongly urge you to get in the driver's seat of your transactions by using adult language to express yourself.

Accept 111 Percent Responsibility for Your Communication

Most of us are experts at blaming other people. Have you noticed that when something goes wrong it is almost always the fault of the government, the boss, the economy, the weather, the traffic, or anything else, but seldom, if ever, *the person who is making the excuses!* To make this point, I love to ask someone who arrives late for something—one of my daughters for dinner, a student for class, or a team member for work—this question: "Would you have been on time if $1,000 were riding on this?" The answer is almost always "Of course!" Which demonstrates that most of us avoid taking responsibility for our actions! This has disastrous effects when we communicate because in order to have communication you must have at least one sender *and* one receiver. If either one is missing, there is no communication. Unfortunately, since you are unable to control another human being, you are left with only one person to blame if there is a communication breakdown: *you!*

This reminds me of an interesting experience. At one of my assignments at a large U.S. medical facility, a number of us shared a secretary (Maria) who spoke only broken English with a very heavy Spanish accent. (If I remember correctly she had emigrated from Venezuela.) One day, one of the English-speaking managers wanted to get a letter corrected. A lengthy and heated discussion ensued. Finally Maria said, in exasperation, *"Wat de madder wit you? Don you speek no Ainglish?!"*

To achieve dramatic communication improvement, I strongly recommend that you buy 111 percent into the following axiom: *If it is to be, it is up to me.* Here are several specific examples to help you translate this axiom into reality:

Instead of: Don't you understand?
Use: *Let me explain that a different way.*
Instead of: You make me so mad!
Use: *I feel angry when you do that.*
Instead of: You're not listening to me!
Use: *I must not be expressing myself clearly. Let me be more precise.*

Reality Check

We don't see things as they are, we see them as we are.

—Anaïs Nin

Listen Actively

Even though it's been said by Abraham Lincoln that "it is better to remain silent and be thought a fool than to speak out and remove all doubt," most of us are very good at removing all doubt most of the time. In other words, human beings are extremely poor listeners. One reason is that, as managers, most of us are very good at "talking and telling," instead of "listening and learning." Just as in sales "telling is not selling," in management "telling is not coaching," nor is it practicing *winning management.* The reason why this is a critical skill is because it's been estimated that managers spend approximately 75 percent of their time at work communicating, and about half of that time listening. That means that unless you have mastered this skill you will be ineffective about 37.5 percent of the time at work.

To become an active listener, remind yourself that *there must be a reason that we were born with one mouth and two ears* and adhere to the following guidelines:

- Stop talking, because when the mouth is engaged the ears are out of gear.
- Show the person speaking that you are listening actively, which you can do by removing all distractions. For example, hold your calls, make eye contact, lean slightly into the person, and acknowledge the message and the messenger.
- Demonstrate empathy by getting inside the other person's thoughts and feelings. This can be expressed by saying "I see,"

"I understand," "I follow you," "I'm with you," and so on.

- Take off your mask and be yourself. In the speaking profession we say: *The microphone is never off.*
- Before ending the communication, summarize and reality test.

Winning Action Step

Whenever you talk with anyone, listen actively by totally focusing on what the person has to say and do not think about what and how you are going to answer.

Reality Test

There is an old saying: "Don't assume anything; it makes an *ass* out of *u* and *me*" (ass-u-me). Unfortunately, most of us assume that words have meaning. They do not! The reality is that all of us speak a different language because we all have different values, beliefs, and life experiences that impact on how we interpret everything. In my opinion, it is accurate to say that no one can ever totally understand another! For example, what does the word "fast" mean to you? If you are an amateur photographer, you might be thinking of the speed of the film. If you are a dietitian or have been dieting a lot in your life, you might think of "not eating." If you operate a laundry or do a lot of laundry, you might think that it refers to how stable a color is. If you like to race, you might think of the speed of a vehicle. The list goes on. (In one of my seminars the attendees came up with more than thirty meanings for this relatively simple word!)

To improve your communication accuracy, I would like you to get in the habit of reality testing. Any time you communicate with another human being, especially in situations that are very important, I recommend that you summarize your communication with these powerful sentences: "Please tell me what you heard me say," or "Let me tell you what I understand we've agreed to." Avoid at all cost the useless question "Do you understand?" In most cases, admitting that you do not understand is analogous to saying "Hey, I'm stupid; explain it to me again."

Express Yourself in Positive Terms
When we speak, we can say things negatively or positively. For example, you can say, "I can't get it for you right now" or "I will get it for you in five minutes"; "Don't litter" or "Please put your trash in trash cans." In each case, both statements say the same thing. Which do you think is easier to understand and more effective? According to Walther, research has demonstrated that positively worded statements are one-third easier to comprehend than their negative counterparts.[8] The reason is that human beings are unable to move away from the reverse of an idea. Instead, we move toward that which we visualize in our minds. Don't believe it? Stop for a moment. Now *don't* think of a green dinosaur. What did you just think of? It was a green dinosaur, right? Take advantage of this phenomenon by taking just a little extra time to figure out how you can express yourself in positive terms. Avoid identifying what it is that you do *not* want. Instead, identify what you want to happen. (Remember the PIN technique; it works very well to help you think of the positive. So be sure to PIN it. Don't NIP it.)

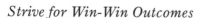

Reality Check
Say something positive or say nothing at all.
—Wolf J. Rinke

Strive for Win-Win Outcomes
Always remember that there is absolutely no one who likes to feel like a loser. So when you communicate with someone else, always be on the lookout for issues, trends, developments, or prospects that will be beneficial to both of you. For example, if you are talking with a consultant, ask: "Jane, what type of expertise do you have that my company might be interested in?" When talking with one of your team members, use the following powerful phrase: "How can I help you?" When you talk to one of your customers, instead of saying "According to company policy you have to…" use "What options can we think of that will…." This attitude shows that you are interested in helping the other party win. That person will then be more inclined to share empowering information with you.

Convey Integrity at All Times

People are sensitive to a variety of cues, so I recommend that you always tell it like it is, even though it shows that you are not omnipotent, or it may be somewhat uncomfortable for the other party. People prefer to communicate with people they can trust, rather than those they have to second-guess. Be aware of self-defeating phrases that some people use habitually without being aware of the implications. For example, avoid saying "Let me be absolutely honest with you." If you say that to me, I'm thinking: "What are you normally?" or "Is this the only time? Everything you've told me before has been a lie?" Here are four other phrases that are helpful to master. They will be painful to express until you get comfortable with your own fallibility, but they will enable you to thrive faster in these rapidly changing times.

- "I don't know."
- "I've made a mistake."
- "I changed my mind."
- "I need your help."

Reality Check

The communicator is the person who can make himself clear to himself first.

—Paul D. Griffith

Get to the Point

This one may not be a biggie, but in this hyperspeed world it is becoming ever more important, especially in your written communication. Forget the day when you assumed (there is that word again) that your professor put your paper on a scale and the heaviest got the A. In business it just isn't so! A great example is the Gettysburg Address, which has exactly 267 words in it. Most are extremely simple. There is no need to get a dictionary out to read this document and, believe it or not, there are only three words that have more than ten letters in them. Now, can you think of a more powerful document than the Gettysburg Address? I just printed it out and read it to count the words and to refresh my memory. It is *awesome!* So whatever you do, make it a practice to say it with the fewest and simplest words. Say things concisely and actively. For example, instead of saying "at the present time," say "now." Or instead of saying "that is something that I think we should explore," say "I will look into it." Remember: the shorter and simpler, the more powerful.

Make Them Glad They Communicated with You

To turbocharge your communication effectiveness, pretend that the person or persons you are communicating with have printed across their forehead a big bold sign that reads *"Make me feel important."* This phrase will remind you to always focus on the other person's needs. Effective communication is first and foremost a helping activity or, to put it differently, it is a win-win exercise. A way to keep tabs on yourself during the communication process is to ask yourself: What proportion of the time am I talking about myself? To get a handle on that count the number of times you use the words "I," "me," "my" during your conversation. As a rule of thumb, if you are spending more than 20 percent of the time talking about yourself, you have "I" disease. "I" disease is especially counterproductive when you are communicating with someone for the first time. Remember, most people like to talk about themselves. Let them. The more they do, the more you can learn about their needs. And if you can meet those needs, they will have your name and image positively imprinted in their mind's eye for many years to come.

Now that you know how to communicate like a *pro,* I would like to give you a little extra help by providing you with specific phrases that will help you express yourself more powerfully and achieve win-win outcomes (Exhibit 5-8). Exhibit 5-9 will show you how you can use blockbuster questions to improve communication and achieve cooperation.

Winning Action Step

Copy Exhibit 5-8 and use it for your next team meeting. (I know it's copyrighted; that's why I just gave you permission to copy it.) Then, enlarge it and put it in your meeting rooms, and use the principles to communicate more effectively with your team members.

Exhibit 5-8: Powerlanguage: How to Achieve Win-Win Outcomes

To persuade:	Use the feel, felt, found formula. "I know how you *feel;* Ms. Jones *felt* just like you do until she used our product and *found* that..."
To increase cooperation:	Ask: "Are you willing to...?"
To increase accountability:	Ask: "Can I count on you to...?"
To keep communication channels open:	Talk about how *you* feel: "I feel hurt when..."
To avoid justification:	Give an example: "I found it works to..."
To deflect hostility:	Express empathy: "I understand your point of view."
To achieve results:	Defeat the problem—not the person: "What specifically don't you like?"
To focus on goals:	Ask: "To do or accomplish what?"
To diffuse conflict:	Use "I" language: "I disagree" instead of "You're wrong."
To increase understanding:	Ask: "What specifically don't you understand?"
To get things done:	Focus on the outcome, not the process: "What stands in your way?"
To assume responsibility for communication:	Use "I" language: "I am not communicating with you."
To shorten conversation:	Use closed-ended questions: "Isn't this a great day?"
To lengthen conversation:	Use open-ended questions: "What do you think about this day?"
To communicate with precision:	Reality test: "What I heard you say is..."
To get to win-win:	Ask: "What can I do for you?"
To get a decision:	Take advantage of the "pregnant" pause.

Exhibit 5-9:

How to Use *Blockbuster* Questions to Improve Communication and Cooperation

Blocks	**Blockbusting**
Any block	Use the echo technique: Repeat the last few words as a question or agree with the blocker by saying:
	"I appreciate where you are coming from," or
	"I respect your point of view."
Universal blocks:	
— No one	"Has there ever been a time when…?"
— Everyone	"Isn't there someone who hasn't…?"
— Always/Never	"Has there never (ever) been a time when…?"
Generalizations:	
— Too much/many	"Compared to what?"
— Too anything	"What specifically is too…?"
Absolutes:	
— Can't	"What prevents you from…?"
— Have to	"What would cause you to…?"
— It's impossible	"What would happen if…?"
— Right/Wrong	"Right (wrong) for whom?"
Refusal	"What evidence do you need to have…?"
Impasse	"Why don't we come back to that later?"
Criticism	"I realize you think…"
	"What specifically don't you like about…?"
Anger	"Perhaps we should agree to disagree."
	"Perhaps we should talk about this later.

Winning Action Step

Prior to counseling an uncooperative team member, review Exhibit 5-9. Master the blockbusters, and you'll get more cooperation, more often.

Now that you have mastered specific strategies which will enable you to become a more effective communicator, let's shift gears slightly and find out what it takes to communicate more effectively with your team members. After all, communication is the fuel that makes empowerment work.

TELL TEAM MEMBERS MORE THAN THEY WANT TO KNOW

Imagine for a moment that it is early January; you and twelve other managers from your company have been assembled at an elegant beach resort in the Bahamas. After opening comments from the CEO, I am introduced. The COO tells you that I have a special project for you, and that as soon as that project is completed all of us get the rest of the day to do what ever we want... swim, sail, scuba dive, or whatever else your heart desires. Can you smell the ocean, hear the waves lapping on the shore, taste the ice-cold margaritas, see the sparkling crystal clear water? And, oh yes, it is an absolutely gorgeous day outside! After briefly energizing you, not that you need much of that after those remarks, I give each of you a big handful of puzzle pieces from a plastic bag. Then I tell you that, as a group, you have all of the pieces needed to complete the puzzle, and that just as soon as you have put it together we can frolic on the beach. What would you all ask for? If you said, "the box top from the puzzle," you would have given the same response I get from my audiences. What you need to get this done in a reasonable time is the box top! Now, let me have you pause and think about your team members. Are they asked, like employees in most organizations, to put the puzzle together—to accomplish their work—without the box top? Without the big picture?

Without a doubt, knowledge, especially knowledge of the big picture, empowers and motivates team members. In a management and labor study of Fortune 1000 companies conducted by Ernst and Young, it was found that 96 percent of the managers and 86 percent of the employees agreed that "employees would be more motivated if they knew more about how the work they do helps the company make money."[9] Yet, when visiting various companies, I never cease to be amazed at how few team members know about the big picture. When

I ask managers about this, I'm frequently told that "they don't care" or that "they don't understand." I disagree vehemently on both counts. *A caring attitude is created;* it does not happen by itself. If it is true that team members don't care, then the management team had better take a close look at their management practices and find out what can be done to modify them. The same is true if team members "don't understand" because somehow most employees manage to balance their personal budgets and understand whether they have money left over or are broke. What I'm saying is that it is your responsibility to put this type of information into words or, better yet, pictures (in the form of graphs, pie charts, etc.) that just about anyone can understand. Speaking for myself, I don't understand the national debt because I have no idea what $5 plus trillion looks like. But if you compare this year's debt to that of previous years and put the data in a bar chart, I will be able to immediately tell whether things are getting better or worse. You can use the same approach to give your team members the status of your budget and anything else they need to know in order to help you make things better.

Reality Check

You can't treat your employees like mushrooms—keep them in the dark and feed them crap—if you want them to do the right thing for the customer, the company, and you.

—Wolf J. Rinke

How to Kill the Grapevine

In this age of downsizing, rightsizing, reengineering, takeovers, and declining resources, managers are often faced with the question of whether they should share sensitive information with employees. For example, recently I was asked by an executive whether or not he should tell employees that the board of directors had made the decision to cut about 10 percent of the work force due to budgetary constraints. After determining that all other alternatives had been exhausted, my advice was: Tell your team members everything exactly the way you know it. Why? Because if you don't tell them, they will find out anyway through the grapevine. In the absence of a formalized communication network, your team members will get the news, wildly exaggerated and in a way over which you have absolutely no control, and in a way that is totally distorted. Once the grapevine gets hold of it, the impending 10 percent reduction will be magnified to "half the people will be laid off."

Another way that managers miss the boat is that they do not repeat information often enough with a wide variety of communication media. Recently I was to energize the management team of a high-tech company at a conference in Ocean City, Maryland. In interviewing the president of the company so that I could customize my presentation, I found out that he had floated the idea of inviting spouses to the conference but was undecided. During my interview I suggested that since Ocean City is a resort community, and since the event was not just a team-building but also a celebration event, it would be advisable to invite spouses. He agreed. When I arrived, I noticed that a number of team members had not brought their spouses. When I asked the project manager of this event what had happened, he said: "I sent them all a memo telling them that spouses were invited. People just don't read their mail anymore!" I agreed. They don't. Worse, we all process different information sources differently. As a result, Galpin suggested that "because of their 'filters' people are more likely to misinterpret a one time announcement from senior management."[10] They might not process the whole message or they might selectively focus only on those aspects that directly affect them. Therefore, an important message, such as an anticipated restructuring, must be communicated using multiple consistent exposures via meetings, memos, newsletters, e-mail, and any other mechanisms that will get the message out repeatedly. Only then will most of the people internalize the content of your message. (Notice I said most of the people. It's my experience that, no matter what you do, it's virtually impossible to reach all of the people all of the time.) Since information is a vital source of power, it is important that you, not the grapevine, use it, direct it, and make it work for you and your organization. In short, *if in doubt, tell your team members more, and more often, than you think they want to know.*

Winning Action Step

Find out where team members get most of their information. If it is from the grapevine, commit to destroying it by telling people more, and more often, than they want to know.

Communicate the Big Picture

A *winning manager* should spend more time communicating than doing anything else. In chapter 2, you learned that one of your primary responsibilities is to communicate the organization's philosophy to all team members and customers at least half a dozen times every day. Your message must be motivating, consistent, positive, simple, and direct so that it can serve as the rallying cry for the organization. Every team member should know how the organization and its various profit centers are doing, whether they are reaching the critical success factors, which areas are doing best, which need to do better, which targets are being attained, and which areas are falling behind. Without that knowledge, team members cannot be expected to serve the customer and help the organization prosper. Remember that only those team members who are informed become committed, and only *truly committed people can do anything.*

An example of *not* adhering to this strategy was demonstrated to me in what I thought was a very fine restaurant in Louisville, Kentucky. I had just finished a presentation and went to have some lunch. I was seated by the head waiter; shortly thereafter a server came to bring me water. Since I was in a hurry, I asked him what the soup of the day was. He said, "I don't know, you have to ask the waiter." When the waiter came, I found that he, too, did not know. He had to make a special trip to the kitchen to find out. To me, this was an example of how ignorance can lead to poor customer service. The impression I was left with was that they didn't care very much about their service. Such carelessness usually pervades the entire organization. After my food arrived, my initial negative impression was confirmed, possibly because it was a self-fulfilling prophecy. Of course, I not only remember this example of poor service but it has been passed along to many others. Talking about this reminds me of another story along the same lines, just a bit lighter: While dining at one of the major hotels in New York City, a customer asked the waiter—who appeared to be fairly new on the job—what the *soup du jour* was. The waiter indicated that he didn't know, but would check in the kitchen and be right back. After what seemed an eternity, the waiter returned with the answer: "Sir, the *soup du jour* is the soup of the day."

One service organization that clearly understands that knowledge empowers team members, and has mastered the art of telling people more and more often than they want to know, is the Disney organization. Part of its training consists of overeducating all employees, whom Disney refers to as "cast members," about all aspects of the theme park before they ever get to go "on stage." The underlying assumption is that customers, whom they refer to as "Guests" (note the capital *G*), will tend to seek information from the first employee they run into, whether or not it's that employee's job. The Disney management team wants to be able to capitalize on this golden opportunity to make an excellent impression. So they make sure that *every* employee knows all the information likely to be asked by guests, or that the employee can at least refer the customer to the nearest information source. The potential benefits in customer relations are obvious, but there is a hidden benefit. A knowledgeable employee is one who is not afraid to be in front of the customer. Such team members feel empowered because they *know* they can help.

Get People Started on the Right Foot

To me, the most underutilized opportunity for empowering team members is the employee orientation program. This is the golden opportunity when team members are the most impressionable. They are new to the organization, they want to make a good impression, and they represent the future of your organization. (Remember, even *you won't get a second chance to make a first impression.*) Your orientation program should help the new employee become familiar with the organization, team members, supervisors, key members of the management team, job, and your expectations. A formalized orientation program should be supplemented by an employee handbook. (Remember, if the information is important, you must use multiple sources.) Keep in mind that this initial period provides you with the opportunity to socialize the new team member into the team and to convert and indoctrinate—yes, I mean indoctrinate—the person with the organizational philosophy, goals, and objectives. (I'm assuming that he would not have been hired if there was not a good fit with your organizational philosophy.) No orientation program should ever be over before this indoctrination has been accomplished.

Winning Action Step

During your MBWA sessions, keep asking your team members: "How can I help you do your job better?" and "How can you help us with...?" Ask customers: "How can we better serve you? Then, act on the information you collected!

CONTINUING EDUCATION AND TRAINING

Getting people started on the right foot is a good beginning. But don't stop there, because in this rapidly changing world people must become voracious lifelong learners if they want to maintain the competitive advantage. So let's next focus on the importance of providing continuing education and training opportunities to your team members so that they can communicate smarter, not just harder.

Why Bother?

After all, many small and midsize organizations and corporations are doing just fine even though they do a dismal job of providing continuing education and training opportunities to their employees. In asking managers in a variety of organizations about their commitment to continuing education and training, I'm given answers like the following:

- "We don't have a budget for that!" "We barely have enough for necessities." (Tell me what is more essential than investing in people. After all, a company is only as good as its people.)
- "Our employees are too essential. We can't free 'em up for that."
- "We don't have any qualified instructors."

- "We are on shift work and can't get enough people together at one time."
- "We don't have facilities or equipment."
- "Our employees don't want to be bothered."
- "My employees work incredibly long hours. They don't have time for stuff like that." (Can you think of a better reason to provide them with education and training.)
- "My people can barely read and write." (Ditto from above.)

Reality Check

Less than half of all employers in the United States offer their workers the type of formal job skills training considered essential for improving productivity and higher wages.

—Robert Reich

I'm reminded of my oldest daughter's first job, as a hostess in an upscale local restaurant. (I'll omit the name to protect the guilty.) When she first reported to work, the manager gave her a schematic of the smoking and non-smoking sections of the restaurant, explained the seating procedures in three sentences or less, and concluded by asking, "Do you have any questions?" That was the extent of their orientation and on-the-job training program for someone who had never worked as a hostess before. And that is for a team member who because of her strategic position can make or break the profitability of this organization.

Although I am aware of the constraints mentioned above, providing inadequate training is shortsighted because the benefits of investing heavily in human capital far outweigh the costs. For example, providing continuing education and training, especially skill training, to all team members:

- Reduces labor turnover rates
- Enhances skills, proficiency, and competence
- Increases productivity
- Enhances a person's self-image
- Motivates and empowers
- Improves people's receptiveness to change

Think Education Is Expensive? Try Ignorance

But, you say: Does continuing education and training really pay off? Ask winning companies such as General Electric, which spends 4.6 percent of payroll on training; U.S. Robotics, which spends 4.2 percent; or Motorola, which spends 4 percent of payroll.[11] In the case of Motorola, that means mandating that every employee participate in at least forty hours of continued learning per year. Incidentally, Motorola is considering doubling that goal. Why? Because CEO Gary Tooker is foolish? No, because Motorola has been able to demonstrate that, as a result of education and training, the number of patents have increased by 20 percent and *employee productivity has more than doubled in about five years*. In fact, Motorola estimates that education and training has provided them with a return on investment of thirty to one.[12] Unfortunately, most U.S. companies have not yet seen the light; they only spend an average of 1.2 percent of payroll on training. How about your organization? How much are you investing in your most valuable resource?

What About the Payoff to the Bottom Line?

I'm glad you asked! According to a study reported by Work America,[13] investing in people boosts productivity at a greater rate than investing in more time on the job or new equipment. Specifically, they reported that a 10 percent increase in the average education of workers yields an average increase of productivity of 8.6 percent. In non-manufacturing establishments, the gain was 11 percent. Compare that to increasing the number of hours employees worked by 10 percent, which resulted in an average increase in productivity by 5.6 percent and to increasing investment in capital expenditures for new equipment, which only increased the productivity by 3.4 percent. Clearly education and training is a true win-win proposition that helps both the employee and the organization remain competitive in a rapidly changing world. In other words, you have absolutely no excuse not to invest in your team members. (My English teacher would turn over in her grave if she saw this double negative. But I wanted to be sure that you get this point!) And more importantly I would like you to take action *now!*

> ## Winning Action Step
>
> Have your accountant analyze how much you currently spend on continuing education and training for your team members. Then, budget half a percent more for the coming year, and increase this every year until you spend 4 percent of payroll on continuing education and training. You can't afford not to, because you and your organization are only as good as your people!

Education Is Learning to Think; Training Is Learning to Do

But what should those training programs focus on? I strongly recommend that you provide both education *and* training to all of your team members. What's the difference? Education is learning to think, and training is learning to do. In today's rapidly changing world, your team members need to be able to do both. Let me illustrate with a brief story.

A well-known fast-food chain (the name is omitted to protect the guilty) that prides itself on their excellent training program wanted to increase their sales with suggestive selling. So they taught their customer service representatives to consistently suggest a dessert with every order. In comes me, Mr. Customer, patiently waiting in line until it is my turn to place my order with a cheerful young lady named Debbie.

Debbie: Welcome to Mc (oops, I almost slipped). What would you like?

Me: (Impressed with her cheerful attitude.) I'd like a strawberry sundae and a medium cup of coffee.

Debbie: That's a Strawberry Sundae and a medium cup of coffee. Would you like a piece of our delicious apple pie with that?

Me: (Looking puzzled.) ????

Debbie: (Embarrassed.) Oops, you've already ordered a dessert. Sorry, but they are telling us to suggest a dessert with every order.

You see, that's what happens when a company relies only on *training*. People become like little robots instead of empowered and intelligent human beings who have the ability to think on their feet and make the right decisions on behalf of the customer.

> ## Reality Check
> Job skills training marks the dividing line between workers who succeed and those who are left behind, between work places that are productive and those that cannot compete.
>
> — Robert Reich

What Kind of Education and Training?

What specific programs should you offer to your team members? In addition to mandatory training required by your state and federal agencies, I recommend that you provide education and training programs that focus on personal development, customer service, team building, communication, diversity, skill training, and motivational programs.

Personal Development

Include such topics as building positive self-esteem, goal setting, developing effective interpersonal skills, stress management, and other instructions that help your team members feel good about themselves and the contribution they can make to the mission of the organization. But you might say, "I don't have time or money to provide my team members with personal enrichment programs." Consider this: *Individuals who do not feel good about themselves, the company they work for, or their boss, will not be able to consistently deliver exceptional quality service!* It is just not enough to tell your employees to "smile at the customers and be nice to them." Your team members have to feel good about themselves before they can succeed at practicing the venerable and increasingly rare art of *serving* the customer.[14]

Customer Service

All team members—yes, even those in support functions—must have an opportunity to internalize critical customer service standards and expectations unique to your operation. Include such topics as when and how to respond to customers, how to handle complaints, how to maintain control, how to meet customer expectations, how to empathize and understand the customers' needs, and how to handle confrontations and resolve conflicts.

Team Building

This is absolutely essential for your management and supervisory personnel. It should provide them with a comprehensive understanding of the organization's vision and philosophy, group decision making, conflict resolution, communication, and interpersonal skills.

Communication

This is one topic that probably you can never overdo. Provide team members with training in effective listening, enhancing perception accuracy, empathy, nonverbal communications, reducing communication barriers, mastering open-ended communication methods, and, for those who answer the phone, effective telephone techniques.

Diversity

No, you don't do it to comply with the regulations, you do it because it is a survival tactic. Succeeding in the next millennium requires constant innovation. The more diverse your work force, the greater the probability that you'll be able to take advantage of innumerable opportunities. No matter what others want you to believe, diversity is a strength, not a weakness. So set specific targets to achieve a rich variety of men, women, and minorities. Reward attainment of those targets and then provide lots of opportunities to learn, work, and socialize together. (The only people we don't like are those we don't know, or those who have been lumped together as a homogenous group, which is what stereotyping is all about.)

Winning Action Step

Count the number of ethnic minorities on your team, including your management team. Do everything in your power to increase it to about 20 percent. Over the long term, it'll be the best decision you've ever made.

Skill Training

Providing your team members with the skills they need to effectively do their job is essential for obvious reasons. However, it will also provide them with high levels of self-confidence in their own abilities to satisfy their internal and external customers all of the time. As a result, your organization will realize all kinds of positive outcomes, not the least of which is a positive impact on the bottom line.

Motivational Programs

Even though I left this one for last, it is just as important as all the others. Providing the above training will furnish your people with a proverbial battery. To keep that battery charged, you'll need to supplement your training efforts with motivational programs. These sessions are also needed to maintain your team members' pride in belonging to a winning team and a winning organization.

However, education and training is not enough. You must also put your money where your mouth is by walking your talk.

Winning Action Step

Commit yourself to letting every one of your team members participate in every possible continuing education and training program you can get your hands on. Don't use the excuse that someone can't go because you are short-handed. You will always be short-handed! Others will take up the slack once they see that they too have a chance to better themselves.

WALK YOUR TALK

To improve communication effectiveness and achieve 111 percent commitment to the philosophy and to empowerment, you, the *winning manager*, must be prepared to walk your talk. Walking the talk means that you must go beyond talking about the vision and values of the organization. You must buy into them with your head and your heart; you must live by them and consistently demonstrate the desired behaviors through role modeling and actual conduct. In short, this means that you have to practice what you preach.

Long before Peters and Waterman popularized the expression "management by walking around" (MBWA), Katz and others[15] conducted a study of supervisors to determine whether high-performing work groups were led by supervisors who had behaviors, attitudes, and values different from their less productive counterparts. The study was of insurance claim agents at the Prudential Insurance Company, and performance was measured by the number of insurance claims processed. After demographic differences had been accounted for, it was found that the high-performance group (let's call it Group A) was managed by supervisors who had a distinctly different management style than that used in the low-performance group (Group B). (See Exhibit 5-10.)

Exhibit 5-10:
Differences in Behavior Between Supervisors of High-Performing and Low-Performing Work Groups[16]

	Group Performance	
Supervisory Behavior	High (Group A)	Low (Group B)
Type of supervision	General	Close
Trust	High	Low
Time spent with employees	More	Less
Orientation	People	Production

In general, Group A supervisors did a lot more MBWA. While walking around, these supervisors visited with their team members and demonstrated a real interest in them, their families, and their personal concerns. The supervisors of Group B talked to their team members mostly about the work, giving detailed instructions, deadlines, and so forth. When it came to getting a raise for their employees, Group A supervisors were very up front with their team members and let them know whether or not they thought the employees deserved it. If they did not, the supervisors would not ask for the raise but instead talked about what each employee needed to do to upgrade his or her performance. Once that performance level had been reached, the supervisors would go forward and fight for their team member. The Group B supervisors, on the other hand, would ask for the raise, even when they felt the employee had not met expectations; get turned down; and then blame their lack of success on upper management.

Even though it sounds as if this came out of the most recent management best-seller, this study was actually conducted in 1947, proving again the old axiom that the more things change, the more they stay the same.

Winning Action Step

Starting next week, block out a half-day every week on your calendar for MBWA time. Schedule nothing else during that time. In six months, increase it to two half-days per week. Then keep it up and never go back.

What are the lessons to be learned from all this? To succeed, you, as the *winning manager* and coach, must learn to take care of, actively listen to, and be up front with your team members. That process starts with doing everything you can to help them do an excellent job. To do that effectively, you must get out of your office and practice MBWA by spending time with your employees and customers. Once your team members have gone the extra mile for you, you must see that they are appropriately recognized by, yes, you guessed it, tying rewards to performance. In addition, you must be genuinely concerned about your team members' personal lives. This interest must go beyond active listening. Although I am not saying that you should become your team members' baby-sitter, you should make every effort to help them learn how to help themselves. Examples include helping your team members find rides to work when they can't get there because of legitimate reasons, day care for their children, assistance for remedial education, and—if they have serious difficulties, such as drug, alcohol, marriage, or financial problems—counselors who will be able to help them solve their problems.

Although this list is not intended to be all-inclusive, the point is that, if you wish to instill a team spirit in your organization, you must take care of your own. There is more than enough evidence that high-performing organizations go far beyond the basics and are finding that it pays off on the bottom line.[17]

By the way, if you are saying, "That is fine for the Fortune 500 companies, *but* it can't be done in my company, because...," I would like to challenge you to get your "but" out of your mouth (have you noticed that *but* is an erasure word—it erases everything you've said prior to it). Seriously, though, it is not just possible in your company or organization, it is absolutely essential if you plan to attract and keep highly qualified team members in an ever-tighter labor market. My experience has been that the organizations that are winning in today's competitive global business climate have *learned to worry less about the work and worry more about the people who do the work.*

Reality Check
Your team members won't do it for the organization, but they may do it for you. How well have you treated them lately?
—Wolf J. Rinke

LET PEER POWER WORK FOR YOU

Contrary to what you might be thinking at this point, I am not advocating that running a winning organization consists only of warm and fuzzy strategies. There is a hard side to all this in the form of measuring, because what gets measured gets done. This emphasis on measuring should include collecting data about all critical success factors and related performance indicators. These include all the components in your philosophy statement, your goals, and the more mundane factors such as profits, time, and attendance. Now, you may be saying to yourself, "What's new about that? We do it now." What is different is how the information gets used. But first, let me briefly address another, related issue.

I Know It When I See It

When I talk about measuring the global components of a philosophy, I'm often confronted with blank stares. After all, how do you measure quality, customer satisfaction, value to the customer, taking care of all employees, innovation, and so on? Even though difficult, there are concrete ways to measure, or at least estimate, just about anything. For example, quality of service could be defined as a certain percentage or numerical score on your customer satisfaction survey, taking care of your employees could be defined as a certain rate of turnover, and innovation might be estimated by the number of suggestions implemented during a specified period. To make a long story short, if you can touch it, smell it, see it, or talk about it, you *can* estimate it.

Display Performance Data

"Okay, coach, I have figured out how and when to collect my estimates; I have even figured out how to summarize the data so that it makes sense to 99 percent of my team members. Now what?" Go public to engage the most powerful force in the organization: peer pressure. This is very different from the way such data is used in most organizations. Normally what is done is that management takes this data to the next lower level, usually the supervisor or project manager, who is always between a rock and a hard place. The supervisor or project manager in turn takes the data to the team members and tells them that they are not doing enough or that they have screwed up again. Besides the fact that this will not result in positive action, this type of communication will usually be received negatively or defensively. After all, employees are adults, and very few adults enjoy catching hell. (Do you?) Most don't even like to be told what to do.

A better strategy is to get people to want to do something. This can be accomplished by simply posting the data, in an easy-to-understand format (bar or line graphs are great), in a conspicuous place. For example, if you have summarized customer satisfaction data, attendance records, profit and loss statements, and so forth, put them on the employees' bulletin board so that everyone can "see how *we* are doing." If the data can be organized by teams (e.g., by shifts or departments, units, etc.), or if you can compare it to industry standards, peer pressure can go to work. Putting peer pressure to work is especially effective when every team has a roughly equal chance to succeed. Remember to recognize the winning team members in front of their peers in your next hoopla session. It will reinforce the positive behavior and further strengthen peer pressure. If the action is dramatic, you might even consider awarding prizes or rewards.

What about low or inadequate performance? To the maximum extent possible, you should let that be handled by self-imposed pressure or peer pressure as well. Either one is much more powerful than when team members are told by management what to do! (Have doubts? Who has a greater influence over your teenage children—you or their peers?)

Reality Check

Good leaders [and *winning managers*] must first become good servants.

—Robert Greenleaf

An Ounce of Prevention...

Going public with such data, especially the negative data, can be risky. So be sure to observe the following five rules:

- Make sure the data are correct. People get mighty upset if you do not give credit where credit is due. They get even more upset, even irate, when the data reflect negatively on them and are not accurate.
- Let the employees serve as their own standard, or let teams compete against others *outside* the immediate work area or against standards. Every time you have a winner, you have a loser. Losing repeatedly can lower people's self-image and contribute to destructive internal competition.
- Focus more on team achievements than individual achievements. Having individuals win is powerful; getting teams to win is even more powerful.
- Focus on the positive. For example, if going public with attendance records, highlight those team members who have come to work *on time* instead of those with a poor attendance record. One of my clients accomplished this by putting a star next to each employee's name for every day they made it to work *on time*. After only two weeks, the trends that team members had been aware of became obvious and peer power went to work on those who were *not* carrying their load.

- Tie rewards to performance. It is the most powerful management principle of all time. And the trend is clear. More and more companies are moving in this direction. According to one study, 20 percent of U.S. companies have already or are in the process of implementing variable pay plans. Another 26 percent are giving it serious consideration.[18]

Winning Action Step

Begin collecting and posting performance data now. Then stand back and let peer power go to work for you.

Build Measurement Systems That Empower

Meyer[19] suggested that multifunctional teams need new performance measurement systems to make sure they are empowered and can successfully deliver complete value-delivery processes that cut across several functional areas. Such systems must be:

- Designed primarily as a feedback system for the multifunctional team as opposed to a control system for management. Team members must have systems that will let them know when to take corrective actions. Management must have a system that lets them know when to offer assistance. Once managers use these systems to keep tabs on or control team members, empowerment ceases to exist and the measurement systems become counterproductive.
- Developed by the team. No one has a better understanding of what specifically must be measured and when than the team members who do the actual work. Managers should provide their input *after* the basic systems have been designed to make sure that they support the organization's strategy and long-term initiatives.
- Able to track performance across functional areas such as product development, order fulfillment, and delivery to ensure improvements in customer service.
- Kept to a minimum. Typically, too many measurement systems are implemented for the benefit of management, so they can be sure

they are not losing control in an empowered environment. Team members should focus most of their time on value-added activities that improve customer satisfaction, not majoring in minors. A review of the organization's critical success factors can help provide an answer for team members and managers as to which measurement systems should and should not be implemented.

- Supported by functional measures. Even highly effective cross-functional teams still need to rely on some old-fashioned functional measures. An example is tracking receivables. Without it, cross-functional team effectiveness will be rapidly impaired.[20]

Winning managers invest in their team members by telling them more than they want to know, empowering them, and providing them with the tools that will enable them to stay on track. As a result, they find out that *people can do anything they want to do when they want to do it badly enough.*

Winning Action Steps

Encourage your team members to design measurement systems that will help them stay on track.

SUMMARY

- Human beings are very ineffective communicators.
- Communication effectiveness can be dramatically improved by:
  — Utilizing adult language
  — Accepting responsibility for the communication process
  — Practicing active listening
  — Reality testing
  — Expressing yourself in positive terms
  — Striving for win-win outcomes
  — Conveying integrity at all times
  — Getting to the point
  — Making others glad that they communicated with you
- *Powerlanguage* and *blockbuster* questions will increase cooperation and lead to win-win outcomes.

- Telling team members more than they want to know is best accomplished by:
  - Making sure that they know about *all* aspects of the operation
  - Providing comprehensive orientation programs
  - Providing effective job-related continuing education and training programs
  - Keeping them informed of how well the organization is doing
- Leading by example (walking your talk) and practicing management by walking around (MBWA) will dramatically improve communication and your management effectiveness.
- The effectiveness of peer-monitored performance systems is enhanced by:
  - Making data public
  - Disseminating accurate data
  - Avoiding unnecessary internal competition
  - Focusing on team, instead of individual, accomplishments
  - Focusing on the positive
  - Tying rewards to performance
- Measurement systems will support cross-functional teams if they are:
  - Designed primarily for the benefit of the team
  - Developed by the team
  - Able to track across functional areas
  - Kept to the minimum
  - Supported by functional measures

Winning Action Step

Anytime you are in doubt about whether you should share negative or financial data with your team members, tell them.

NOTES

1. A. Mehrabian and S. R. Ferris, "Inference of Attitudes from Nonverbal Communication in Two Channels," *Journal of Consulting Psychology* 31 (1967): 248–52.

2. Ibid.

3. D. Tannen, "The Power of Talk: Who Gets Heard and Why," *Harvard Business Review* 73, no. 5 (1995): 138–148.

4. D. Fisher, *Communication in Organizations,* 2nd ed. (St. Paul, MN: West Publishing Company, 1993), p. 36.

5. Ibid., 36–37.

6. J. Luft, *Group Processes: An Introduction to Group Dynamics* (Palo Alto, CA: National Press Books, 1970).

7. E. Berne, *Principles of Group Treatment* (New York: Oxford University Press, 1964).

8. G. R. Walther, *Power Talking: Fifty Ways to Say What You Mean and Get What You Want* (New York: Putnam's Sons, 1991).

9. A. R. Carey and G. Lynn, "Knowledge Boosts Motivation," *USA Today,* 22 February 1996.

10. T. Galpin. "Pruning the Grapevine," *Training & Development* 49, no. 4 (1995): 31.

11. K. Kelly and P. Burrows, "Motorola: Training for the Millennium," *Business Week,* 28 March 1994, 159.

12. Ibid., 163.

13. "Investing in People Boosts Productivity by 8.6%," *Work America* 12, no. 6 (1995): 3.

14. W. J. Rinke, *The 6 Success Strategies for Winning at Life, Love and Business* (Deerfield Beach, FL: Health Communications, Inc., 1996).

15. D. Katz, N. MacCoby, and N. C. Morse, *Productivity, Supervision, and Morale in an Office Situation* (Ann Arbor, MI: University of Michigan Institute for Social Research, 1950).

16. W. J. Rinke, *The Winning Foodservice Manager: Strategies for Doing More with Less* 2nd ed. (Clarksville, MD: Achievement Publishers, division of Wolf Rinke Associates, Inc., 1990), p. 232.

17. J. Pfeffer, *Competitive Advantage Through People* (Boston, MA: Harvard Business School Press, 1994). Also see M. Huselid, "The Impact of Human Resource Management Practices on Turnover, Productivity, and Corporate Performance," *Academy of Management Journal* 38, no. 3 (1995): 635–672.

18. B. Wysocki, "Unstable Pay Becomes Ever More Common," *Wall Street Journal,* 4 December 1995, p. 1.

19. C. Meyer, "How the Right Measures Help Teams Excel," *Harvard Business Review* 72, no. 3 (1994): 95–103.

20. Ibid., 96.

Winning Action Step

Love—yes, I said *love*—your team members. They make you look great!

Customer Focused

6

There is no such a thing as service industries. Everybody is in service.

—Theodore Levitt

Right you are Ted Levitt: Everyone, including *you,* dear reader, is in the service business. According to President Clinton, even "the Federal Government must be customer driven."[1] After all, customers are the lifeblood of every business because it is the customers who generate your income regardless of what kind of business you are in. And that income can only be increased in three fundamental ways:

- By finding new customers
- By improving the profitability of your current customers
- By retaining more of your current customers for a longer period of time[2]

So, get ready, get set, and whatever you do, get excited because mastering this *C* will have an immediate, direct, and dramatic impact on your bottom line.

To get us started, I would like you to think of what you remember about the restaurants you dined at during the past two to four weeks. When I ask my Service Management seminar participants to do this, they consistently identify two extremes—kind of like the good, the bad, and ugly, I guess. They remember very bad experiences, (e.g., service was extremely slow, the server was rude, the place was filthy, and so on). And they remember extremely positive experiences, where the service was impeccable, the food was delicious, or they were brought a complimentary dessert because they had to wait before being seated. At this point you might be saying to yourself: That's what I remembered, too, but so what? Here is the so what! *If you satisfy your customers*—that is, you merely meet their expectations—*you'll likely be out of business soon.* That's right, if all you do is *satisfy* the customer, you have a high probability of not surviving in this highly competitive world. Why? Because your customers will forget you! Your organization will become persona non grata; you'll be gone from their consciousness. And if they don't remember you, they won't be back, and worse, they won't tell their aunts, uncles, brothers, sisters, or their friends about you. To get them to remember your company, your service providers must *exceed* the customers' expectations. Only if you exceed their expectations will you turn customers into advocates, or better yet, into your own high-powered PR agents, to the point that they will do your advertising for you. Advertising—that is, word-of-mouth—that actually works. That's why I want you to get excited about this chapter!

PREVIEW OF COMING ATTRACTIONS

In this chapter you will learn how you and your team members can take advantage of the ultimate strategic imperative by delivering service that is fast, imaginative, and customized. First you will find out about a powerful metric, the American Customer Satisfaction Index (ACSI); then you'll have a chance to find out how customer focused you and your organization are right now by completing the Customer Focus Audit. That will be followed by providing you with specific data about what your customers want. Next you'll discover why you must manage services different from products, and I will do my best to convince you that everyone in your organization has a customer. That will be followed by specific costs and benefits associated with poor and excellent service. Last, but not least, I will provide you with eight specific steps that will enable you to implement a highly effective exceptional quality service strategy, one that turns customers into advocates.

CUSTOMERS CAN'T GET NO SATISFACTION

"Not me, not my customers. We're doing our customer surveys and, with some minor exceptions, our scores are excellent." That's what I hear from many of my clients. If so, how come the statistics don't support it? Here is what I mean. In 1994 the University of Michigan and the American Society for Quality Control conducted a large-scale, comprehensive, and systematic study of customer satisfaction in more than two dozen manufacturing and service industries, as well as several public sector functions such as mail delivery, garbage collection, and the Internal Revenue Service. The purpose of this study was to provide the United States with a reliable economic indicator, an index, that takes into account both quality and service. After all, customer satisfaction is every bit as important to the health of the economy as productivity and price.

That index, the American Customer Satisfaction Index (ACSI), was released for the first time in the fall of 1994 and again in the fall of 1995.[3] The latter provided the United States with a year-to-year comparison for the first time. And the news is simply not very good for most industries. In fact, there was an overall decline in customer satisfaction. Rated on a scale from 0 (no satisfaction) to 100 (maximum satisfaction), the national average for 1995 was a miserable 73.7, 1.1 percent lower than in 1994. Although the decline appears small, it does represent a warning sign, especially since productivity as measured by the gross domestic product (GDP) increased by a robust 3.3 percent during the same period. Yet quality and customer satisfaction, as measured by the ACSI, was down in service industries, up only in manufacturing, and steady in all other sectors.[4]

Dole, a food processing company, better recognized as the "pineapple company," tops the list with a score of 90. Scores go down dramatically from there with, you guessed it, the Internal Revenue Service being on the bottom of the list with a score of 54.[5] (Now it's a fact, Internal Revenue *Service* is an oxymoron.) During this period the greatest gains in product categories, albeit very small, were made by fast-food restaurants (+1.4 percent) and automobile manufacturers (+1.3 percent). The biggest losses? Newspapers (-5.6 percent) and personal property insurance (-6.2 percent).

What about the individual quality and service gainers? Would you believe the leader of the pack was the U.S. Postal Service? That's right—satisfaction with first-class mail delivery and counter service increased by a whopping 13 percent, although it is still miserably low at a score of 69. Certainly very far from a passing grade. The biggest individual loser? Gannett, the folks who own *USA Today,* dropped 12 percent in 1995 to a score of 66, which is the same score Americans gave to their suburban police forces.[6] An analysis of the scores revealed that, in general, the more contact a company had with its customers the lower the scores tended to be. Hence hotels, department stores, restaurants, and airlines all scored below average. The ACSI results indicate that U.S. businesses have made three critical errors in their attempt to deliver customer satisfaction. They have:

1. Viewed customer service as a cost instead of an investment
2. Underestimated and/or are unaware of the customers' rising expectations
3. Been unable to link customer satisfaction to financial results[7]

Findings from the ACSI should have alerted you to the realization that quality and service are indeed the business imperative for the next millennium. In addition to managing service, we must also manage quality. Hence I use the term *exceptional quality service* to identify the service system that *winning managers* must master if they want to take advantage of the business imperative of the next millennium.[8]

Winning Action Step

Grab your calendar right now and assess what proportion of your time was spent with either your internal or external customers during the past five working days. If it is less than 50 percent, make up an action plan that will get you to spend 5 percent more of your time with your internal and external customers during the next week. Each week thereafter, increase it another 5 percent until you spend 70 percent your time interacting with the people who have the potential to help you succeed.

CUSTOMER FOCUS: HOW WELL ARE YOU DOING RIGHT NOW?

Let's get started by having you complete Exhibit 6-1.

Exhibit 6-1: Customer Focus Audit

	Yes	No
1. Are you measuring and tracking:		
a. Customer satisfaction?	___	___
b. Customer loyalty?	___	___
2. Do you know:		
a. Why customers are satisfied?	___	___
b. Why customers are dissatisfied?	___	___
c. Why customers defect?	___	___
3. Do you obtain customer satisfaction data from:		
a. Surveys?	___	___
b. Mystery shoppers?	___	___
c. Focus groups?	___	___
4. Do you know what proportion of your revenue stream comes from:		
a. Loyal customers?	___	___
b. Referrals?	___	___
5. Do you measure and review customer satisfaction data at least every six months?	___	___
6. Do your employees have the authority to independently fix customer complaints regardless of costs?	___	___
7. Do you measure and track:		
a. Employee satisfaction?	___	___
b. Employee turnover?	___	___
c. Employee productivity?	___	___
8. Are employee selection criteria tied to what managers *and* customers believe is important?	___	___
9. Do you measure and track employee satisfaction data at least every six months?	___	___
10. Do you conduct employee exit interviews?	___	___
11. Is employee recognition tied to customer satisfaction?	___	___
12. Is employee compensation tied to customer satisfaction?	___	___
13. Does your organization have a customer focused mission/ philosophy statement that virtually all employees know by heart?	___	___

14. Do you:
   a. Spend 70 percent of your time with customers
       and employees?   ____ ____
   b. Have a 100 percent unconditional money back
       guarantee?   ____ ____
   c. Have a service recovery strategy?   ____ ____
   d. Plus up service failures?   ____ ____

Add all *yes* responses and *no* responses.   ____ ____
Multiply *yes* responses by 4 to compute your total score. ____ x4

TOTAL _____

What Your Score Means

91–100 You have figured out how to take advantage of the business impera-
        tive of the next millennium and are likely to experience continued suc-
        cess regardless what business you are in.

81–90   You have built a strong foundation for delivering consistently excellent
        service. This chapter will provide you with specific strategies to do
        even better.

71–80   You have mastered some of the strategies needed to be customer
        focused, and you will learn new tricks of the trade in this chapter.

<71   Time to get serious! You must master lots of new customer service
        strategies if you want to survive in this competitive service-driven
        economy.

Now that you have a better idea how customer focused you are,
let's begin this journey by finding out what is important to your
customers.

Winning Action Step

This week, call your own company or organization and pretend you
are a customer. Answer the following question candidly: Based on the
initial impression, would I want to do business with this company or
organization?

WHAT DO CUSTOMERS REALLY WANT

To be 111 percent customer focused, it is imperative that you and every one of your team members knows what every customer does and does not expect during a service encounter. (See Exhibit 6-2.)

Exhibit 6-2: Customer Expectations

Customers want:	**Customers don't want:**
• To be acknowledged	• To be ignored
• To feel important	• To feel bad about themselves
• Undivided attention	• To feel like they are interrupting
• To be listened to	• To be talked *at*
• To be treated like an individual	• To feel like a number
• Solutions	• Problems
• To be appreciated	• To feel like they are a bother
• Their needs met	• To feel frustrated
• To be satisfied	• To be pressured

Now that we know what every customer expects, let's get a bit more specific and find out what customers perceive service quality to be. To gain an understanding of that question, more than one thousand nine hundred customers of five large, well-known U.S. service companies were surveyed by Berry et al. What they found is that customers utilize five broad service dimensions—reliability, responsiveness, assurance, empathy, and tangibles—to judge service quality. Of these, customers consistently rated reliability as the most important dimension. (See Exhibit 6-3.)

In other words, no matter how friendly, apologetic, or empathic your service providers are, your customers will take their business elsewhere if they cannot count on you to be dependable and accurate.

Reality Check

The best way to drive your competition crazy is to make your customers happy.

—Guy Kawasaki

Exhibit 6-3: What Is Important to Your Customers?[9]

Dimension	Percent of Customers
RELIABILITY. 32%	
The ability to perform the promised service dependably and accurately.	
RESPONSIVENESS 22%	
The willingness to help customers and provide prompt service.	
ASSURANCE 19%	
The knowledge and courtesy of employees and their ability to convey trust and confidence.	
EMPATHY. 16%	
The caring, individualized attention provided to customers.	
TANGIBLES 11%	
The appearance of physical facilities, equipment, personnel, and communication materials.	

To find out why customers switch from a familiar service provider to a new one, Susan Keaveney and her team of researchers at the University of Colorado utilized a critical incident technique, which involves analyzing stories told by dissatisfied customers to identify the critical incidents that precipitated the switch to another service provider. Incidents were broken down into eight categories. Findings revealed that the largest category, 44 percent of customers, switched because of "core service failures" such as "service mistakes, billing errors, and service catastrophes." The second largest category, 34 percent of customers, switched because of "service encounter failures." These failures came about because service providers exhibited conduct that was "uncaring, impolite, unresponsive, or unknowledgeable." The third largest cause of switching, 30 percent of the respondents, was "price," which was further subdivided into four subcategories: "high prices, price increases, unfair pricing practices, and deceptive pricing practices." The remaining five categories were: "inconvenience, employee responses to service failures, attraction by competitors, ethical problems, and involuntary—failures beyond the control of the service providers."[10] Of interest was the finding that six of the eight factors that caused customers to switch were under the control of the service providers, and that even customers in relationship-intensive services, such as physicians, switched just as often as those frequenting restaurants.

What's clear from both studies is that service providers play a critical role in satisfying and keeping customers. That means that your front-line workers and service providers—the individuals who typically get paid the least, receive the least amount of education and training, and generally are perceived to be on the bottom of the totem pole—have the *largest* impact on the customer's perception of service quality. I hope this finding is ringing your alarm bells! Are you saying to yourself, "Maybe I need to begin to see my front-line employees in a different light! Maybe it's time for me to treat them like customers! Maybe I need to treat them like kings and queens!" You certainly should! Because according to Exhibit 6-3 their actions are responsible for at least 57 percent of your service quality!

Winning Action Step

Randomly select a dozen employees and invite them to a "Breakfast with the Boss" session one day next week. During breakfast ask them the following questions: What one thing could I do or provide you that would let you do a better job or make your job easier? What, if anything, irritates you when you are at work? Why do you work here? What do you wish we would do or provide you that we do not do or provide you now? Summarize that data and act on it now. Then provide feedback to the employees you interviewed. Now repeat this process once a month.

WHY MANAGE SERVICES DIFFERENT FROM PRODUCTS?

Most existing management models are based on a production model. These models have served us very well in the past in such industries as manufacturing, mining, farming, transportation, and construction. Productivity in these industries has increased at an annual rate of 3 to 4 percent for the past 125 years. That means we have experienced a forty-five-fold expansion in overall productivity in these industries during that time.[11] In fact, in farming the results have been even more impressive. Those good old days are, however, coming to a screeching halt. Why? Because we have become *too* productive in these industries. (It's harder to get better when you are operating at peak performance.)

At the same time, there has been virtually no increase in the productivity of service workers. One reason is that we throw old manufacturing management solutions at a radically changed economy. For example, according to Drucker,[12] we are finally beginning to realize that capital cannot be substituted for labor (people), and new technology often does not generate anticipated increases in productivity in a predominately service-oriented economy. One of the reasons for this is that services are different from products in several ways:

- Services cannot be produced and inspected in advance.
- Services cannot be stored.
- Services are "produced" and "consumed" simultaneously.
- Services are intangible.
- Services cannot be demonstrated in advance.
- Service quality is a perception that is unique to the person who is experiencing the service.
- Services cannot be passed on from one person to the next.
- Services almost always require human interfaces.
- Service quality is difficult to measure.
- Quality control can only occur at the time of delivery.

These, as well as other attributes of services, require us to manage differently in a service environment. What needs to happen is that the pyramid needs to be flattened and turned upside down. (See Exhibit 6-4.)

Winning Action Step

Next month, mystery shop your own company/organization. In the event that most service providers would recognize you, utilize a friend you trust or, better yet, hire a mystery shopper. The insights you gain about your own organization will blow you out of the water. Repeat this process at least once a year.

Exhibit 6-4: Exceptional Quality Service Organization Chart

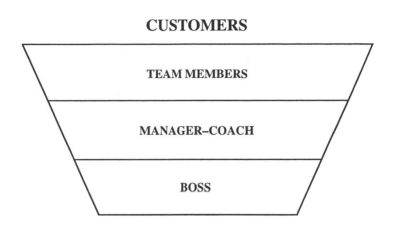

CUSTOMERS

TEAM MEMBERS

MANAGER–COACH

BOSS

Exhibit 6-4 is intended to remind everyone in the organization that the customer is the one who is really the boss. It is the customer who pays everyone, and since the customer pays your bills, everyone in the organization better be 111 percent focused on satisfying the customer. It is also designed to sensitize you to the fact that the more layers you have, the slower and more error prone your delivery systems are going to be and the less likely you'll be able to take care of your *internal* and *external* customers.

Everyone in every organization has a customer. At this point, you are probably saying, "That's not true. Many of my team members, such as order processors, bookkeepers, production personnel, housekeepers, etc., do not have a customer." You're right in that they do not have an *external* customer. They do, however, have an *internal* customer. Someone on the inside of the organization depends on them to get their job done correctly so that they, in turn, can deliver quality service to the external customer. Does that include the people on the bottom of the proverbial totem pole, like a receptionist? Well, let's say that you've gone the extra mile to empower your team members to take extraordinary care of your customers. A customer calls your organization and the phone is answered in a tired, bored, slurred, unintelligible tone of voice—the kind of answer that to this date I still get from at least seven out of every ten calls I make to companies and organizations. (Test your own organization frequently by calling yourself at random times and see how well you do. Or better yet, use a mystery caller.) Will your customers believe that you care about them? Of course not!

Reality Check

Where do you go to complain about the Complaint Department?

—Laurence J. Peter

CUSTOMER SERVICE: WHAT'S IN IT FOR YOU?

Most managers assume that delivering good service is expensive. They perceive customer service as a cost instead of an investment. I have been told "That's the best we can do because we can't afford to pay higher salaries to attract a more competent service staff." (That's like the old saw, "We don't have time." In fact, have you ever noticed how people often don't have time to do it right the first time, but always have enough time to do it over again?)

The Cost of Poor Service

Here are some statistics to keep in mind the next time you think that you can't afford to deliver exceptional quality service:[13]

- Customers are dissatisfied with about one in every four purchases. Depending on the product or service category, this can go up to 65 percent of the time.
- Most disgruntled customers (96 percent) do not complain to the business that made them unhappy. The reason? They feel it is not worth their time or effort. This means an actual complaint represents just the tip of the iceberg because for every complaint received, there were twenty-six others you did not receive.
- Consumers do, however, make up for it when they complain to others, because the average customer who has experienced a problem tells about ten other people. Some 13 percent of disgruntled customers tell as many as twenty other people.

- To make matters worse, about two out of three customers who had a complaint that was not resolved will not come back to do any more business with that establishment.
- What about when everyone in your organization does a good job? A job that meets the customer's expectations? Well, customers are apparently not nearly as generous with spreading the good word because they will only tell about three other people.

These findings have withstood the test of time. For example, Hart et al. reported "that customers who have bad experiences tell approximately 11 people about it; those with good experiences tell just 6."[14] Another study that evaluated why customers switch to a new service provider found that "75% of [customers who switched] told at least one other person and usually several other people.... Only 7%, in contrast, told the original service provider."[15] Similarly, the Forum Corporation reported that more than two-thirds of customers no longer do business with certain service providers "because they find service people indifferent or unhelpful."[16] This last observation reminds me of a bit of humor that, unfortunately, is not very funny because it is too real:

Customer complaining to clerk at checkout counter: "How come you didn't say 'thank you' when I paid?"
Clerk: "Don't you see it's printed on your receipt?"

You certainly do not have to be a mathematician or an economic genius to figure out that poor service will cost your organization lots of money. If you are dependent on repeat business (and who isn't), you will lose megabucks, because bad news travels like wildfire. For example, Domino's Pizza has estimated that a regular customer is worth more than $8,000 over the life of a ten-year franchise. Stew Leonard, the owner of the Disneyworld of food stores, estimates one customer to be worth $50,000 over the same period; and Carl Sewell of Sewell Cadillac estimates that every customer has a lifetime sales potential of $332,000.[17]

Plus long-term customers are worth more to your organization. First of all, they are relatively cheap to keep. (You've heard that it costs five times as much to acquire a new customer as to keep an old one.) They buy more—after all they are already familiar with you and know what you have and what they can expect; they are willing to pay more; they are much less likely to be lured away to the competition by discounts; and they create less bad debt.[18] Is that enough motivation to get serious about delivering consistently exceptional quality service?

Reality Check

Most service failures are not failures; they have been designed into the system.

—Leonard A. Schlesinger

The Cost of Poor Service in Action

Still not motivated enough? Let me share a brief story that demonstrates the cost of poor service. We live near a small town about halfway between Baltimore and Washington, D.C. The town has only one laundry. The laundry was convenient and fairly reasonable, so my wife used it for all of our laundering. One day I put on a freshly cleaned shirt and noted that it had small tears all over the front. Since the shirt was virtually new, we knew that the damage could not have been done by us. Besides, the tears had a pattern, making it appear that the shirt had gotten stuck in a piece of equipment. I called as soon as I discovered the condition of the shirt. The owner's wife answered the phone and then put her husband on the phone for me to speak to. He told me to bring the shirt in for him to see because "our machines don't damage clothing." (Notice he had already made up his mind and really didn't want to be bothered with the facts.)

When I brought in the shirt, with the laundry tag still attached, the owner said that he didn't think that he damaged the shirt but he would be willing to send the shirt to an independent "research institute" for a determination. I reminded him that I had been a steady customer and had never had a problem before. I also pointed out that it would save them money to just take my word and refund the cost of the shirt rather than spend more to have a research institute check it out. I also suggested that if they did not replace the shirt, they would lose our business, and that as far as I was concerned the findings from the research institute were not relevant to me. The facts were: We gave him a fairly new shirt totally undamaged and it came back to us torn. How it got that way was academic. I then explained that perhaps he did not want to alienate a $20-a-week (or about $1,000/year) customer over a $40 shirt. The owner, however, would not budge. He insisted on having the shirt tested. Several weeks later my wife inquired again. We received an evasive answer. We persisted several times until we made one more trip and were told by the wife that they did not damage the shirt and therefore were not willing to pay us for it. We thanked her, walked out, and have never done business with them again.

Now think about it: a $40 shirt for about $12,000 worth of business. (That's $1,000 per year over twelve years, the average number of years Americans live in one location.) To top it off, it would not have cost them even $40 if they had mastered the magic service recovery phrase: What can I do to make it right for you? You see, we might have suggested that he give us $40 worth of laundry coupons, which at most would have presented a real cost of approximately $5 to him. Give up $12,000 for $5? That's what I mean by the cost of poor service.

Winning Action Step

Tomorrow, randomly select a dozen customers and ask them the following questions: What one thing could we do to serve you better? What, if anything, irritates you when you interact with us? What do we do, sell, or provide that you value more than anything else? Why do you buy from us? What do you wish we would do or have that we do not do or have now? Summarize that data and act on it now. Then provide feedback to the customers you interviewed. And don't forget to give your customers a small token of appreciation for taking the time to speak to you. Now repeat this process once a month.

Bottom-Line Benefits of Exceptional Quality Service

According to Zeithaml et al., businesses that rank in the top third on relative service quality sell their products and services, on average, at prices 5–6 percent higher than those in the bottom third.[19] Even more startling, Reichheld and Sasser[20] found that companies can increase their profits by 25–125 percent (not a typo) by retaining just 5 percent of their defecting customers. And Xerox Corporation discovered that customers who rated their service encounter a 5 on a 1–5 scale, with 5 being an "A," were six times as likely to do business with Xerox again, compared to those customers who rated it a 4 or "B." (Please note that many service companies are satisfied with a B rating. Are you?) For impact on a greater scale, Wharton professor David Larcker found that companies ranked highest on the ACSI significantly outpaced lower-ranked companies in the stock market. How much? "While the S&P 500 rose 2.7% over the six months beginning in August 1994, the companies in the top quartile of the satisfaction index rose 5.3%."[21] In other words, customer satisfaction not only has an impact on the bottom line, it also has an impact on how well stocks perform.

The other major benefit we discovered in chapter 3 was the customer–employee satisfaction connection. You may remember that establishing a strong exceptional quality service culture leads to dramatic increases in customer satisfaction *and* equally strong improvements in employee satisfaction. In turn, such organizations experience higher employee retention and productivity, and incredible increases in revenue growth and profitability.[22]

Winning Action Step

In the event your customers don't recognize or remember your organization when you call them, get busy and develop a memorable *unique selling proposition* (USP). This is the single identifiable attribute that sets your organization apart from the competition in the customers' mind. It could be price (although I don't recommend you compete on price—it's too tough to do), service, logo, jingle, company name, or anything else that the customer associates with you. If you don't have a USP, start to develop one *now!* It will be one of the best investments you've ever made.

HOW TO IMPLEMENT AN EXCEPTIONAL QUALITY SERVICE STRATEGY

Now that you recognize that delivering consistently exceptional quality service is not an option but, rather, a survival strategy, let's see what you must do to become a totally customer-focused organization. We begin this journey, as you begin any journey of a thousand miles, with a single step. Let's call it Step 1.

Step 1: See the World Through Your Customers' Eyes

The tough part of any customer service business (remember that's any business) is that customers' expectations are not static. Actually, their expectations rise all the time. So if you want to do this right, you must start with a diagnosis of where the customer is right now. Can you imagine seeing your physician with a stomachache and being told not to bother to take your clothes off because "it is obvious you need your appendix removed"? Can you imagine being told that *before* you've had a chance to explain your symptoms? Before being examined? Would you get worried? Would you seek a second opinion? You bet! I would! Yet frequently we make changes in organizations just that way. To prevent that type of malpractice, I strongly recommend that you begin with a detailed assessment of your current organization. Such an assessment should consist of interviews with your external and internal customers and a review of your current organizational structure, policies and procedures, compensation systems, and operational systems. For this to be effective, I highly recommend that a neutral third party conduct these assessments. If you are part of a large organization, this could be someone from another department, such as human resources (HR) or personnel. If you are in a relatively small company, it would be best if you relied on a consultant or someone else from another company who is skilled in organizational effectiveness (OE) or human resource development (HRD). If you run your own company or are basically a one-person organization, enlist the help of a colleague who may be interested in trading services. The reason for using a neutral third party is that it is highly unlikely that someone within your organization can establish enough trust to get accurate data.

Your assessment should start with the most important group, the external customers. There are several methods for you to find out what your customers really want (read: what they are willing to pay for) as opposed to what you think they want. Let me emphasize at this point that these two perceptions are likely to be very different, especially if you have been in business for some time. The first assessment is a one-on-one interview with randomly selected customers. We typically like to interview about 1–3 percent of the client's customer base. A relatively simple but highly effective format we like to use for this purpose is shown in Exhibit 6-5.

Exhibit 6-5: Customer Survey[23]

1. Name of Company: _____
2. Compared to similar companies, how would you rate this company on a scale of 1–10 (10 best)? _____
3. What makes this company a # _____?
4. If you had to describe this company with one or two words, what would they be?
5. If you could make one recommendation to this company on how they could improve their products or services, what would that recommendation be?

Other ways that you can find out how your customers perceive your service and obtain recommendations on how you can improve that service include customer comment cards (more about those later), suggestion boxes, e-mail, computer touch screen surveys, telephone follow-up calls, interviews, and customer focus groups. In addition, two of the best ways to get feedback about the quality of your service is to simply ask your customers and to use mystery shoppers.

It is also extremely revealing and informative to assess your customers' moments of truth so that you can experience the service experience through the customers' eyes. A *moment of truth,* as coined by Jan Carlzon,[24] is the quality of the interchange between a customer and a front-line employee. These are the moments that define the customer's perception about your operation, organization, or company. In other words, they create your customer's reality. To assess this reality, it is suggested that you assemble a small group of service employees and several of your customers and ask them to identify all the possible moments of truth involved in the critical services that your organization provides. That means that you want to be very thorough about finding out with whom, where, and how the customer comes in contact with your employees, or anyone else who might be perceived as one of your employees. This process can be very illuminating because we tend to focus on the obvious and forget about the most important points of contact.

For example, let's assume you are the owner of a gourmet restaurant. Who is responsible for the first moment of truth? The wait staff? No. In fact there are many others who precede them: the person who answers the phone when the customer calls for a reservation, the person who parks the car, the person who greets the customer at the door, the person who offers to check the customer's coat. Yet most restaurateurs totally overlook these first critical moments of truth. That means that your customers will likely have formed their impressions about the restaurant long before they ever speak to the wait staff, let alone get their food.

Remember that each one of these contacts results in the customer forming either positive or negative opinions about your organization. These opinions are your customer's reality. Whether they are rational or irrational does not matter since perceptions are always correct to the individual who holds them. Also keep in mind that the first and last impressions are always the most persistent. Unfortunately, these impressions are usually shaped by the people who are paid the least and who often receive the least amount of training.

Winning Action Step

If I walked into your office right now, would you be able to tell me how satisfied your team members and customers are? How those scores compare to the benchmark in your industry? The trend of those scores during the past two years? If you have no idea, put a system in place that will give you that kind of data within the next three months.

After you have identified all of the moments of truth, you must next figure out how you can manage each moment of truth, even those you are not even directly responsible for. For example, assume a customer calls your organization during non-business hours. Whoever answers that phone, even if it is the cleaning person, will create that moment of truth. Managing the moments of truth will mean that you measure, monitor, and track the level or quality of service for critical moments of truth, especially those that leave a lasting impression on your customers.

The next customers you must assess are your employees, the people who often create the moments of truth. As you learned in chapter 3 (see Exhibit 3-4), research has demonstrated that there is a very close link between employee satisfaction and customer satisfaction. Hence, it is critical that we see the world not only through our customers' eyes but also through the employees' eyes. Although there are a variety of instruments you can use to assess the employees' level of satisfaction with their jobs, the one we have developed for this purpose is shown in Exhibit 6-6.

Exhibit 6-6: Consultation Needs Assessment[25]

1. Name of Co _____ Yrs w/Co _____ Today's date _____
2. Name _____ Title _____ Mgt ___ Empl ___
3. On a scale of 1–10 (10 best), how would you characterize this company as a place of work? _____
4. What *specifically* is good about this company?
5. If you had to describe this company with one or two words, what would they be?
6. If this were your company, what *one change* would you make immediately?
7. If a relative came to work here, what would you tell him/her that he/she needs to do to get ahead in this company?
8. Please tell me this company's mission.   N/A   Knows Y N _____ %
9. Please tell me this company's vision.   N/A   Knows Y N _____ %
10. What seems to be important to the senior manager (values)?
11. What are the most important problems employees are concerned with?
12. How can customers be served better?
13. What can be done to increase sales?
14. What can be done to save money?

Once you have analyzed and summarized the data from these two instruments (Exhibits 6-5 and 6-6), you will have a much better understanding of both your external and internal customers' expectations.

Winning Action Step

Do you provide incentives to new customers? If yes, make sure that the incentives to your long-term customers are at least as valuable.

Step 2: Document How You Are Doing *Before* You Do Anything

Be sure you hold onto the data you collected in step 1. It can serve as extremely valuable baseline data. This is important because otherwise how can you tell if what you have done has resulted in any positive outcomes, or if in fact your intervention has made things worse? The second reason for collecting this ammunition early is to help you figure out what your exceptional quality service strategy should be. After all, this data will tell you where you are doing well right now and where there is a need for improvements. That means that you will be able to prioritize your efforts. Plus you'll know when things start to improve and when to give your team members positive reinforcement. It will also point out where you need to place the most emphasis, so you can get the most bang for your buck from this intervention process.

Before I forget, let me remind you that just because you have always done something a certain way should not be a reason for you to continue it. Similarly, don't forget to look at the service strategies that *appear* to be working well. The old adage "if it ain't broke, don't fix it" simply does not serve us well in an increasingly complex and rapidly changing business environment. Instead we must learn not only to accept change, but exploit it. (More about how to do that in the next chapter.) So be sure to look very carefully at the tried-and-true and don't hesitate to shoot a sacred cow once in a while. (Sacred cows make great hamburgers.) It will help keep your organization young and full of vitality.

Here is a specific example of what I'm talking about. Most hospitals serve *three* meals per day during *scheduled* times. Why? Well, I don't know, but I bet in most cases it is because they have always done it that way. Soliciting information from patients might reveal that they prefer to receive meals on demand, and that they would be willing to pay extra for such a service. In addition, on-demand schedules might also have all types of other benefits, such as improving the nutritional status of the patients because they now get the food when they are ready to eat, instead of when they are in X-ray. This, in turn, may reduce the number of late trays, increase profit margins, lower plate waste, and increase patient satisfaction. The last may dictate which hospital patients choose the next time they have to be admitted to a hospital, and in the long run increase hospital revenues.

Reality Check
Meet customers' expectations and you may survive.
Exceed customers' expectations and you *will thrive*.
-Wolf J. Rinke

Step 3: Think Strategically About Service

This step should already be completed! You did develop your mission, vision, and core values in chapter 2, didn't you? Since we are talking about being customer focused, let's take a moment and go back to your philosophy and make sure that it is aligned with what your customers' wants and needs are! How do you know that? That's right, you go back to the data you collected in step 1, and ask some additional basic questions.

Customers: The What
A great way to start is to get a group of about 7–15 employees and managers together and have them answer this question: What does the term *customer* mean to us? L. L. Bean's definition of a customer is shown in Exhibit 6-7. My definition of a customer is: the king or queen who provides us with our daily bread.

Customers: The Who
After you have defined the term *customer,* you must next figure out who your customers are. Hold on, I can hear you moan all the way

over here. Yes, they are the people who walk through your front door, but what are their characteristics? You see, that is not nearly as obvious as it seems. Are they primarily young or old, blue or white collar, low, middle or upper income? This discussion will have a tremendous impact on your mission and also on your service strategy. For example, if you own clothing stores, you may find that customer demographics may be different in residential neighborhoods than in a business district.

Exhibit 6-7: What Is a Customer?

Customers are the most important people ever in this organization... in person or by telephone.

Customers are not dependent on us... we are dependent on them.

Customers are not an interruption of our work... they are the purpose of our work. We are not doing them a favor by serving them... they are doing us a favor by giving us the opportunity to do so.

Customers are not someone to argue or match wits with. Nobody ever won an argument with a customer.

Customers are people who bring us their wants. It is our job to handle them profitably—to them and to ourselves.

Of course, in some cases you will have several major groups of customers, which makes your mission and your marketing strategy a lot more complicated. Marketing research can identify your customer demographics. If you can't afford to get that sophisticated, you can do some of it on your own. You already found out in step 1 just how much information your customers are willing to provide if you just take the time to ask them. You will need some sort of survey to get at the information, and I would recommend that you get some professional help with that. That should be fairly inexpensive, as long as you are willing to collect and analyze the data yourself. If you can't afford to do that, go to your next best source, the people who know the most about your customers, your employees. Often just the process of thinking this through gets you on the right road.

How to Find Out What Your Customers Really Want

Now that you know who your customers are, you are ready to find out what *your* customers really want. For example, if you look back at the information collected in step 1, you may already know what your customers value (meaning that they are willing to pay for it). Are they primarily interested in high quality? Do they want to be served rapidly? Do they want low cost? Do they prefer self-service? Or do they want convenience? Now that you have a better idea who your customers are and what they really want, reevaluate your philosophy statement and make sure that it is customer focused. If not, change it!

Winning Action Step

Collect customer turnover data. Benchmark your data against the leader in the industry. Cut turnover by 10 percent this year and every year after until you are below the industry leader.

Step 4: Establish Service Standards

In addition to a service-focused philosophy, you must also have specific service standards. They will help you and your team members translate your philosophy into action, and allow you to measure how well you are accomplishing your critical success factors. This is important because, remember, what gets measured gets done. These standards should be derived from your philosophy, which in turn integrated what is important to your customers, as we found out in step 1. Setting these standards should involve your team members, the "managers" of the moments of truth. Your specific standards will be unique to your organization. Here are several examples to get you started.

Waiting Time for Service

Example: No customer will wait more then five minutes in line. If the wait exceeds five minutes, another line will be opened. If a customer waits longer than five minutes, the customer will receive an apology from the service provider.

Handling of Phones

Example: Phone calls will be answered on the first or second ring. The person answering the phone will thank the customer for calling, identify herself with a first name, and ask how she may be of service. (Example: "Thank you for calling Wolf Rinke Associates. This is Gail. How may I help you?") Every phone call will be concluded with a positive greeting such as: "Thanks for calling" or, better yet *"Make it a great day."*

Handling of Customer Compliments/Complaints

Example: Each team member is empowered to resolve customers' complaints to their satisfaction, provided the cost does not exceed $1,000 per customer. Expenditures in excess of this amount must be approved by the general manager.

Follow-up of Customer Compliment/Complaint

Example: All customers who register a compliment/complaint will be asked to provide their name and address so that they can receive a follow-up call from a manager within twenty-four hours.

Use of Service Provider's Name

Example: All service providers will wear name tags at all times while serving customers and introduce themselves by their first name.

Use of Customer's Name

Example: Service providers will use the customer's last name, preceded by Mr. or Ms., whenever possible throughout the service encounter.

You may wish to share the Exceptional Quality Service Code of Conduct with your team members to reinforce your service standards (Exhibit 6-8).

Exhibit 6-8: Exceptional Quality Service Code of Conduct

- The customer is the person who pays your salary—treat him accordingly.
- You are dependent on the customer—the customer is not dependent on you.
- The customer is why you come to work—the customer is not an interruption.
- The customer does you a favor when she does business with us—you are not doing the customer a favor by serving her.
- Just like you, the customer has feelings, emotions, prejudices, and biases—so be forgiving.
- Always, always, always agree with the customer—winning an argument with a customer means that you won the battle and lost the war!

- Just like you, the customer is an imperfect human being—so be generous.
- The customer deserves the most courteous and attentive treatment you can give him.
- Customers don't like to complain. So when they do, treat them like royalty. They are giving you information that will allow us to improve and make more money.
- A frown on a customer's face represents the loss of one year's salary. How many years of salary are you able to do without?
- The customer is the lifeblood of our organization/company—without her, we will be out of business, and you will be out of a job!

You may also want to share Exhibit 6-9 with your service providers so that they can communicate more effectively with your customers and achieve dramatic improvements in customer service.

Exhibit 6-9:
Fifteen Ways to Communicate More Effectively with Customers

BAD

	BETTER
1. We don't have that.	We have...
2. What's your problem?	Tell me how can I make it right for you.
3. Is that all?	Would you like a _____ to go with that?
4. Why didn't you...	Let me correct that.
5. It's not my department.	I'll take care of that right now.
6. We don't do that.	We offer...
7. You can't...	You can...
8. We can't...	We can...
9. You should have...	I can...
10. You have to...	May I suggest that...
11. I only have two hands.	I'll be happy to take care of that.
12. Follow me.	Allow me to take you to...
13. I'll try.	I will.
14. That's our policy.	We'll do whatever it takes...
15. No.	Yes.

Step 5: Back It Up with an Ironclad Service Guarantee

An example of an ironclad service guarantee is Bugs Burger Bug Killers (BBBK), a Miami-based pest extermination company. Their guarantee to their clients (hotels and restaurants) is as follows:

- You don't owe one penny until all pests on your premises have been eradicated.
- If you are ever dissatisfied with BBBK's service, you will receive a refund for up to 12 months of the company's services—plus fees for another exterminator of your choice for the next year.
- If a guest spots a pest on your premises, BBBK will pay for the guest's meal or room, send a letter of apology, and pay for a future meal or stay.
- If your facility is closed down due to the presence of roaches or rodents, BBBK will pay any fines, as well as all lost profits, *plus* $5,000.
- In short, BBBK says, "If we don't satisfy you 100%, we don't take your money."[26]

Effective service guarantees represent a self-fulfilling prophecy, because they promise quality and deliver it. The reason? They define for the customers and your team members exactly what they can expect in advance. Provided the service guarantee is accompanied by an effective feedback loop that is monitored and provides for ongoing correction of the service delivery system, it will pay for itself many times over. For example, BBBK charges up to ten times more than its competitors,[27] and an owner of four restaurants in Seattle reported that his service guarantee resulted in an increase in sales of 25 percent and a doubling of profits.[28] To be effective, a service guarantee has to be:[29]

1. Unconditional—an example of a well-known unconditional service guarantee is mail-order merchant L. L. Bean's "100% satisfaction in every way."

2. Easy to understand and communicate—this means that the customer knows exactly what to expect. *Example:* "We will provide you with service within twenty minutes or the meal is on us."

3. Meaningful—in two different ways. First, it guarantees what is important to the customer. For example, fast service may be important

to a customer who enters a fast-food restaurant, but probably not to customers who dine in a gourmet restaurant. Second, it is fair in terms of compensation when the guarantee is not met. The best example is Domino's Pizza. Originally they promised a free pizza if it was not delivered in thirty minutes. What they discovered, however, was that customers found that guarantee unreasonable and did not invoke it on a regular basis, therefore depriving Domino's of valuable feedback. Once it was changed to $3 off, customers perceived it to be meaningful and began asking for it. Of course, now Domino's has been forced to give up their service guarantee altogether because of increased expenses associated with litigation due to driver accidents.

4. Easy and painless to invoke—if the guarantee is not met, the customer should not have to go through a lot of effort or feel guilty about invoking the guarantee. This is particularly important since the customer already has been inconvenienced.

5. Easy and quick to collect—ideally the payout should be awarded on the spot with relatively little effort on part of the disgruntled customer.

To achieve total recovery, I recommend that you "plus up" disgruntled customers. Plussing up customers means that you correct the problem as soon as possible. Then you add an additional and unexpected bonus to compensate customers for their inconvenience. For example, if a customer returns a defective product, you replace it immediately with a new one of his choice. Then you offer the customer a complimentary coupon or a free valuable gift to compensate him for the trouble and inconvenience. Another example of plussing up the customer is from BBBK: "If your facility is closed down due to the presence of roaches or rodents, BBBK will pay any fines, as well as all lost profits, *plus* $5,000."[30]

Winning Action Step

Analyze your database to determine which customers have not done any business with you during the past twelve months. (If your database does not tell you that, change it.) Send these customers a valuable incentive that's hard to refuse and invite them to do business with you again.

Step 6: Measure, Monitor and Evaluate

To find out how customer focused you and your team members are, you have to measure, monitor, and evaluate. This can be accomplished by various means that, depending on your budget, can vary in sophistication. Regardless of how little you can spend, it is important that you measure, monitor, and evaluate at least one key indicator or criterion for each critical success factor. One of the most popular methods is the customer satisfaction survey. Exhibit 6-10 shows a relatively simple survey.[31]

Exhibit 6-10: Customer Comment Card

How Are We Doing?

1. **How would you rate your overall experience?**
Hated it   Loved it
1   2   3   4   5   6   7   8   9   10
2. **How would you rate the product quality?**
Hated it   Loved it
1   2   3   4   5   6   7   8   9   10
3. **How was our service?**
Hated it   Loved it
1   2   3   4   5   6   7   8   9   10
4. **How would you rate our responsiveness?**
Hated it   Loved it
1   2   3   4   5   6   7   8   9   10
5. **What one thing did you especially like?**
_____

6. **What is the one thing you would like us
to improve?**
_____
_____

Your name and address (optional):
_____
_____
_____

Thank you for your time.

As you can see, this type of instrument does not have to be very sophisticated to give you quality data. For other types of rating scales that you can use to construct your own satisfaction surveys, see Exhibit 6-11. A problem with the customer survey forms used in most hotels and restaurants is that the customer initiates it. That, unfortunately, will give you skewed data. Basically, you'll get information from customers who are very upset or very happy. However, these customers are usually not representative of the majority.

Exhibit 6-11:
Types of Scales for Rating Customer and Employee Satisfaction

101-Point Scale

0% 100%
Complete   Complete
Dissatisfaction   Satisfaction

5-Point Scales

•	•	•	•	•
Excellent	Good	Satisfactory	Fair	Poor

•	•	•	•	•
Very Satisfied	Satisfied	Neutral	Dissatisfied	Very Dissatisfied

•	•	•	•	•
Much Better	Better	About the Same	Not as Good	Much Worse

10-Point Scales

1	2	3	4	5	6	7	8	9	10
Not Important at All									Extremely Important

1	2	3	4	5	6	7	8	9	10
Poor									Excellent

So how can you do it better? Administer the surveys during a specified but random and representative period of time. Representative means that if most of your sales are made Monday through Friday from 1:00 to 5:00 p.m., do the study during that time, not on Saturday morning. And during that specified time ask *everyone!* This will give you a snapshot of customer satisfaction, one which is much more indicative of how your customers feel than the passive system. (This method will also ensure that you don't get a case of information overload.) If you find that you are having a tough time getting *everyone* to respond during the specific date and time, consider using a prize, or a chance at a prize, to induce customers to return the survey to you. One way to do this is to tell your prospective respondent that all responses will be eligible for a drawing. The winner might win one of your products or services, or a weekend trip for two, donated by a travel agent interested in relatively inexpensive advertising. Another way to get high response rates is to have a contest with prizes, rewards, or money going to the service providers who achieve the highest proportion of returns. Even if you spend some money to accomplish this, it is still the cheapest and most effective market research you can do. You will have a thousandfold return on investment, assuming, of course, you *act* on your customers' recommendations.

Other survey methods include personal or telephone interviews, suggestion boxes, mystery shoppers, and customer focus groups. Also, don't forget to query the people who spend more time with the customers than anyone else: your employees—your managers of the moments of truth. What you measure is really more important than how you measure. To find out what to measure, you need to get back to the data you collected in step 1, which defined what is important to your customers. If, for example, you found out in step 1 that the customer values quality, then you have to monitor return rates, repair rates, down time, and other measures that are indicative of quality. If, on the other hand, the customer values speed, then you might want to conduct a queuing study to provide you with the average time it takes to serve your customers. Whatever you do, be sure to remember the good old KISS principle (keep it simple, sweetheart) because less is better whenever you implement measurement systems.

Winning Action Step

If you have not conducted a comprehensive customer satisfaction survey during the past twelve months, conduct one during the next month. Address any unsatisfactory ratings immediately. Then let customers know what you have done to address their concerns. Get aggressive about consistently exceeding your customers' expectations by repeating this process every six months thereafter.

The reason I want you to keep it simple is that I have seen too many measurement systems where the system has become the end in itself, instead of a means to an end. Most people are so enamored with measuring (I guess because bean counting is easy to do) that they collect so much data they experience a bad case of information overload. Unfortunately, the symptoms of this disease are anxiety leading to inaction, also known as "paralysis by analysis."

But what to do with the collected data, you ask? I know you already have the answer to that question. If it is positive, you are going to save it for your next hoopla session so that you can publicly celebrate the service heroes and provide them with meaningful rewards. (More about that shortly.) What about the negative data? Post it where everyone can see it so that you can let peer pressure go to work for you. That's all? Well, yes, unless there are some very serious deficiencies that require immediate remediation. In that case, you might have to get all the managers of the moments of truth together to find out what *they* plan to do about the problem.

Evaluating is the other aspect of this step. This simply means that you must do more then just collect and monitor the data; you must also chart it so that you can analyze it for trends. This is called *trending,* which, if you cut away the fluff, simply means that you take a look to see if you can find any patterns. Are there repetitions that indicate a serious problem? For example, if service time has increased an average of one minute over the past month, you might not consider it a problem. But if the service time has increased by three minutes over each of the past five measuring periods, you should be concerned because a pattern is unfolding before your eyes. In this case, even though the service time might still be within acceptable standards, it would be indicative of an impending problem that should be fixed before it becomes a serious problem.

One more important comment before I leave this step. When collecting data, remember that the two most valuable sources of information are your customers and your team members. In either case, nothing beats firsthand information, which is best attained by asking, "What can I do to serve you better?" or "What can I do to help you serve the customer better?" In each case, they know and will be delighted to tell you, if you just take the time to ask!

Let me remind you that you must create a similar measurement, monitoring, and evaluation system for each one of your critical success factors. Also, if you are contemplating skipping this step altogether, *don't*. How will you know how you are doing—whether you are getting better, getting worse, or standing still—unless you have some parameters that are monitored and evaluated on an ongoing basis? Worse than that, how will you know what to fix and, most important, how will you tie rewards to performance?

Reality Check
If it's fun, it gets done.

—Wolf J. Rinke

Step 7: Reward and Re-energize

This step is what makes or breaks the whole exceptional quality service strategy. What I mean is that you can have the best customer service program, but if your service providers cannot see the connection between what they do and specific outcomes that are important to them, their level of motivation will be short lived.

I remember talking to an exercise physiologist who was attending a health promotion conference. After some discussion, I found out that he had bought a restaurant in San Francisco. Having grown up in the restaurant business, and also having spent twenty years in health care, I know that it is much easier to make a living as an exercise physiologist than a restaurateur. So I just could not help but inquire as to what had motivated him to make this decision. To make a long story short, I found out that he not only enjoyed the restaurant business, he was actually making very good money in it. When I asked who was minding the store while he was attending this expensive meeting (it was in Lake Louise, Canada), I found out his secret to success: profit sharing. Everyone—yes, everyone including the dishwasher—in his restaurant was financially tied directly to how well the business was doing.

In other words, the key is to give every one of your team members a piece of the rock. This can be in the form of profit sharing, employee stock ownership programs (ESOPs), gain sharing, or any other method that, as closely as possible, connects levels of performance to levels of rewards and gets every one of your team members to feel like an owner. The closer the connection, the better the performance. Good examples of this compensation principle in action are sales people who get paid on a commission basis.

A poor example is the buyout by employees of United Airlines, which included everyone except (are you ready for this?) the flight attendants. Now let me ask you, based on what you have learned in this chapter, who manages the greatest number of moments of truth when you fly, and who leaves the greatest impact on the customer's perception? Of course, it's the flight attendants. I guess that's why they were left out.

Reality Check

Managing well is common sense. The problem? Common sense is not very common.

—Wolf J. Rinke

At this point you might be saying: "Okay, coach, that sounds great, but I manage in the public sector and don't have the ability to give monetary awards." First of all, from my experience of working twenty years for the Army Medical Department, you probably *can* give monetary rewards; it just takes a lot of work. Besides that, there are so many other ways to reward people: time off, a pat on the back, employee recognition programs, service awards, team-member-of-the-month awards, complimentary letters, displaying employee photos in a conspicuous place, plus many other hoopla activities that recognize team members for a job well done.[32] Basically, finding rewards for your valuable managers of the moments of truth is limited only by your and your team members' imaginations. Remember, however, to get the most bang for your buck: go public whenever you can. People love hoopla and rah-rah. If in doubt, just attend a sales meeting of some of the winning sales organizations such as Mary Kay, Shaklee, Frito Lay, or Tupperware. That reminds me: Do visit and benchmark yourself to successful companies so that you can learn from the masters. Success in business is *no* magic! Just find out what the winning companies do, have the guts to do it just a little bit better, and your company or organization will be successful too!

Another method to keep your team members and the system energized is for you to be personally involved in the critical performance components of your service system. Talking about getting personally involved reminds me of Sam Walton, who made it a point to visit virtually all of his stores at least once every year. During his visits, Sam himself would greet customers and provide his team members with pep talks. Now let me ask you, what message would you get if you were working at Wal-Mart? I'm sure there would be no question in your mind that you and your customers are very important!

And so it goes with your critical performance indicators. It is not enough to tell people what is important; you must get personally involved and practice what you preach! No matter what basic innate abilities your team members have, never underestimate them. All people are street smart, and they will see you as a fake if you say one thing but practice another. They also will not comply, at least not for long, because your actions always speak much louder than your words. If you are not deeply committed to a service philosophy, you might be better off to give someone else the responsibility and authority to handle it, or you'll be forced out of business soon.

Winning Action Step

During your next "all hands" team meeting, celebrate three service champions by telling everyone in visual detail how they exceeded customers' expectations. Reward the service champions in front of everyone. Make sure that the reward matches the act. Now repeat the process at every one of your team meetings.

Step 8: Provide for Continuous Exceptional Quality Service Improvement

Continuous improvement, better known as *continuous quality improvement* (CQI), and by many other abbreviations resembling an alphabet soup, is an important part of the exceptional quality service strategy. In fact, I believe it is imperative that you establish a system that harnesses the energy of all your team members to improve everything all of the time on an ongoing basis. How you do it is really not that important. You can accomplish it with TQM, CQI, quality circles, problem-solving teams, cross-functional teams, or even structured suggestion programs.[33] What is important is that regardless of which process you choose, you must:

- Actively involve team members.
- Permit, even encourage, team members to make mistakes.
- Publicly celebrate team members' victories, no matter how small.
- Tie rewards to team members' improvements and performance.
- Stick with it for at least one to three years.

SERVICE RECOVERY

At this point, you're probably saying, "okay, coach, I'm with you; I'm ready to commit to an organization-wide service strategy; I'm even ready to involve all my team members in continuous improvement. But what about when we mess up?" Good question. Messing up is okay because, remember, people are not perfect. The bigger issue is, what are you going to do about it when it happens? Actually, there is lots of good news in this section. Let's see what the research says about service failures:[34]

- Between 54 and 70 percent of customers who experience a service problem will come back if the complaint was resolved. In addition, if it was resolved quickly, up to 95 percent of all complainers will do business with you again. Not only that, the customer whose complaint was resolved quickly will tell about *five other people about the "good" experience they had.*
- But what happens if you are unable to resolve the customer's complaint? Here comes the really good news: Those who complain are more likely to do business with you again, *even if the problem was not resolved to their satisfaction,* than those who have a problem but don't bother to complain.

Please don't take the previous sentence too literally. Next thing I know you'll tell your team members to screw up on purpose. Instead, impress upon them the importance of taking care of the complaint as fast as they know how. In addition, these statistics also suggest that you should treat complainers like royalty because they are sufficiently interested in telling you how you can get better. Not only that, they are also providing you with extremely valuable and hard-to-come-by information for free. (Remember that you only hear from about 4 percent of your unhappy customers. That means for every four complainers, ninety-six dissatisfied customers are walking out without saying a thing.) Since complainers provide you with very valuable and inexpensive advice, I recommend that you make it worth their while. If nothing else, with courtesy or, better yet, with something tangible like a gift certificate or anything else that lets them know just how much you appreciate their interest. (Yes, I recommend that you do that even if they are obnoxious!) The implementation of just this one principle is worth one hundred times the price of this book, especially if you are dependent on repeat customers. (If you don't think *you* are, think again!)

Winning Action Step

Do you know what percentage of your customers are repeat customers? If you don't, start collecting that data now and begin to treat those customers better than your new customers.

Here is what you must do to make your service recovery system work for you:[35]

- Encourage and make it easy for your customers to complain.
- Respond personally and with lightning speed.
- Develop and aggressively utilize a problem resolution system that ensures that virtually every complaint is resolved *before* your customer has a chance to tell anyone else.

When your service providers do mess up, what specifically can they do to ensure that your excellent service reputation is not permanently eroded? I recommend that every one of your service providers master the seven specific steps shown in Exhibit 6-12.

> ## Winning Action Step
> Check the level of spending authority your team members currently have to take care of customers. If it is less than 150 percent of the current costs of remedying your most frequent service breakdowns, change it right now!

Exhibit 6-12: Service Recovery in Seven "Easy" Steps

Customer: "Your service stinks! What kind of place is this that can't deliver the right model!?!"

Step 1: *Calm yourself.* Angry or excited people shut down their ability to communicate effectively. Take a deep breath. Tell yourself that this is not personal.

Step 2: *Reality test.* Find out what is really wrong, and what the customer's expectations are—what the customer wants done to make it right. Speak in a low, calm voice.

Example: "Sir, I'm sorry that we have not met your expectations. Please tell me what is wrong, and what I can do to make it right for you."

Step 3: *Apologize.* This should be done as soon as possible after the infraction. The apology should be stated in the first person by the individual who is aware that the customer has been mistreated. Use calming language such as:
- "I will..."
- "This is important to you and..."
- "This is not the kind of service we want to give and..."
- "Your business is important to us and..."
- "I apologize..."

Example: "I apologize that we delivered the wrong model."

Step 4: *Fix it.* This involves getting things back to the status quo. It is important to demonstrate to the customer that you have his best interest at heart.

Example: "Let me check on this right now. I will personally make sure that the right model is delivered today."

Step 5: *Express empathy.* Unlike sympathy, empathy shows compassion for the person who feels wronged.

Example: "I know how you feel. Just last week I..."

Step 6: *Plus up.* The customer feels wronged or has been inconvenienced. You must compensate him for the inconvenience you have caused him.

Example: "To make up for your inconvenience I would like to offer you a special coupon that entitles you to take 10 percent off your next purchase."

Step 7: *Follow up.* This is the icing on the cake. Do this as soon as possible after correcting the service failure. The purpose of this step is to reverse any remaining negative perceptions.

Example: The evening of the delivery, call the customer at home to make sure the right product was delivered. Again thank the customer for his patience and his business.

Reality Check

Sign seen at the entrance of the *Silver Diner,* a chain of diners committed to service excellence and total customer satisfaction: *"The answer is YES, now what's the question!"*

Getting every one of your team members to live in accordance with this kind of service attitude will assure that you are well on the road to delivering quality service and consistently exceeding your customers' expectations.

SUMMARY

- Overall level of customer satisfaction in the United States is unsatisfactory.
- Quality and service are the business imperatives for the next millennium.
- Of the five broad service dimensions—reliability, responsiveness, assurance, empathy, and tangibles—customers consistently rate reliability as the most important.
- Services must be managed with a service, as opposed to a production, management paradigm.
- Everyone in every organization has a "customer."
- Delivering consistent excellent customer service is an investment, not a cost.

- An exceptional quality service strategy can be implemented by:
  — Seeing the world through your customers' eyes
  — Documenting how you are doing now
  — Thinking strategically about service
  — Establishing service standards
  — Backing it up with a service guarantee
  — Measuring, monitoring, and evaluating
  — Rewarding and re-energizing
  — Providing for continuous exceptional quality service improvement

Winning Action Step

Analyze your database to find answers to the following questions:

— What percentage of our target market does business with us?
— What percentage of customers purchase more than one thing when they place orders?
— What percentage of our customers are repeat customers?
— How long do our customers do business with us?

If you don't have this data, get it! If you do have it, implement strategies that have the potential to increase each one of the above.

NOTES

1 "Putting Customers First. Serving the American Public: Best Practices in Telephone Service," *Federal Consortium Benchmark Study Report,* February 1995.

2. A. W. H. Grant and L. A. Schlesinger, "Realize Your Customers' Full Profit Potential," *Harvard Business Review* 73, no. 5 (1995): 59–72.

3. T. A. Stewart, "After All You've Done for Your Customers, Why Are They Still Not Happy?" *Fortune* 132, no. 12 (1995): 178–182.

4. Ibid., 180.

5. J. Fierman, "Americans Can't Get No Satisfaction," *Fortune* 132, no. 12 (1995): 186.

6. Ibid., 186–190.

7. Stewart, "After All You've Done for Your Customers," 180. For additional details or the complete ACSI, contact the American Society for Quality Control, 611 East Wisconsin Avenue, P.O. Box 3005, Milwaukee, WI 53201-3005, (800) 248-1946.

8. W. J. Rinke, *Exceptional Quality Service (EQS): How to Consistently Exceed Your Customers' Expectations* (Clarksville, MD: Wolf Rinke Associates, Inc., 1994).

9. L. L. Berry, A. Parasuraman, and V. A. Zeithaml, "Improving Service Quality in America: Lessons Learned," *Academy of Management Executive* 8, no. 2 (1994): 33.

10. T. Richman, "Why Customers Leave," *Harvard Business Review* 74, no. 1 (1996): 9–10.

11. P. F. Drucker, "Boosting Productivity Will Be Vital," *Baltimore Sun Maryland Business Weekly*, 6 April 1992, p. 4.

12. Ibid.

13. The Technical Assistance Research Programs Institute, *Consumer Complaint Handling in America: An Update Study*, Contract HHS-100-84-0065, 1986.

14. C. W. L. Hart, J. L. Heskett and W. E. Sasser Jr., "The Profitable Art of Service Recovery," *Harvard Business Review* 90, no. 4 (1990): 153.

15. Richman, "Why Customers Leave," 10.

16. L. A. Schlesinger and J. L. Heskett, "The Service-Driven Service Company," *Harvard Business Review* 69, no. 5 (1991): 71–81.

17. J. L. Heskett et al., "Putting the Service–Profit Chain to Work," *Harvard Business Review* 72, no. 4 (1994): 164–174.

18. Stewart, "After All You've Done for Your Customers."

19. V. A. Zeithaml, A. Parasuraman and L. L. Berry, *Delivering Quality Service* (New York: Free Press, 1990).

20. F. F. Reichheld and W. E. Sasser, Jr., "Zero Defections: Quality Comes to Services," *Harvard Business Review* 67, no. 5 (1990): 105–111.

21. Fierman, "Americans Can't Get No Satisfaction," 192.

22. Heskett et al., "Putting the Service–Profit Chain to Work."

23. For more information regarding how to measure customer satisfaction, see Richard F. Gerson, *Measuring Customer Satisfaction*, Crisp Publications, 1200 Hamilton Court, Menlo Park, CA 94025, (800) 442-7477.

24. J. Carlzon, *Moments of Truth* (New York: Harper and Row Publishers, 1987).

25. For a variety of assessment instruments and training materials contact Pfeiffer and Company, 8517 Production Ave., San Diego, CA 92121-2280, (800) 274-4434.

26. C. W. L. Hart, "The Power of Unconditional Service Guarantees," *Harvard Business Review* 66, no. 4 (1988): 54.

27. Ibid.

28. T. W. Firnstahl, "My Employees Are My Service Guarantee," *Harvard Business Review* 67, no. 4 (1989): 28–34.

29. Ibid., 55–56.

30. Ibid., 54.

31. Gerson, *Measuring Customer Satisfaction*.

32. B. Nelson, *1001 Ways to Reward Employees* (New York: Workman Publishing Company, Inc., 1994).

33. M. Edelston and M. Buhagiar, *"I" Power* (Fort Lee, NJ: Barricade Books Inc., 1992).

34. The Technical Assistance Research Programs Institute, *Consumer Complaint Handling in America: An Update Study.*
35. Hart, Heskett, and Sasser, "The Profitable Art of Service Recovery."

Reality Check

Most people spend too much time getting ready to get ready.

—Wolf J. Rinke

Change-Driven

7

Every organization has to prepare for the abandonment of everything it does.

—Peter Drucker

Wow! Did you read Drucker's quote? Did you reflect on it? Did you get nervous? Are you sweating? If not, you're in trouble! One reason, Peter Drucker is relatively conservative! Another reason, you're out of touch with reality—the reality that "change" is an understatement par excellence. The more accurate word is "revolution." Because that's exactly what we are right in the middle of! But you probably knew that already. Especially if you are a middle manager, you—more than anyone—have been affected by reengineering, layoffs, downsizing, rightsizing, or whatever the current euphemisms may be. The bigger question: What are you doing about it?

PREVIEW OF COMING ATTRACTIONS

In this exciting chapter you will first take a look back at the future and become aware that you are in the middle of a revolution, a revolution that will not only impact how you manage others but also the speed of change you can anticipate in the future. That review will make you very sensitive to the need to constantly reinvent yourself and your organization. After this wake-up call, you will again have a chance to do a bit of self-diagnosis by completing the change self-assessment instrument. Next I will introduce you to several unique aspects associated with every change process so that you can anticipate and deal effectively with these attributes. The individual change model that follows will acquaint you with seven specific stages that individuals tend to go through when they are confronted with change. Recognizing those will enable you to take advantage of the next section, which will outline specific things you can do to overcome resistance to change. Switching from an individual perspective, we will next look at a four-phase communication process model that will make it easier for you to communicate significant changes to your team members. Next you will learn how to prime the proverbial change pump by building a learning organization. You will even discover what system of learning likely will be the most effective for your organization. This chapter will conclude by providing you with specific strategies for achieving a lasting organizational transformation. First the macro perspective and then the specific action steps that are required to make change stick for you, your team members, and your organization.

Reality Check

To be scared out of your senses is sensible. To be comfortable is suicidal.

—Tom Peters

ARE YOU READY FOR A REVOLUTION?

Change can be perceived as evolutionary or revolutionary. Total Quality Management (TQM), the change process that Drs. Deming and Juran exported to Japan (which in turn exported it back to us), sees change as continuous small incremental improvements at the margin—an evolutionary process. Unfortunately, the world that you and I live in is changing at such a rapid rate that evolution will no longer cut it. What is required instead is a revolution, and that is exactly the stage we are in.

The previous revolution, which occurred at the turn of the century, was fueled by the internal combustion engine. This one is fueled by a much quicker engine—a microprocessor, or the chip. It is the chip that is making everything faster, much faster, and is increasing productivity in virtually all industries by leaps and bounds. Let me give you an example. Have you been to a card store recently and noticed those new cards, the ones that actually play a "Happy Birthday" tune when you open them up? According to one estimate, that one card "holds more computing power than existed on earth before 1950."[1] As if that were not enough, it's been estimated that the computing power in the world is doubling every eighteen months. And is continuing to do it at ever-cheaper rates. For example, in 1991 (in terms of data processing that's eons ago) it cost close to $100 to process one million instructions per second on a mainframe computer. In 1995 that cost was down to $20. The same dramatic reductions have been achieved in storing and distributing of information.[2] That is good news, because U.S. industries "have been spending more on computers and communication equipment than on all other capital equipment combined."[3] As a result, the United States has once more become the worldwide productivity leader.[4]

One more shocker to give you a taste of revolution. This one probably will hit a bit closer to home since it may have affected you. Who is the nation's biggest private employer? Did you say GM, IBM, or Xerox? It's none of the above. It's Manpower! In fact, Manpower employs six hundred thousand people, a third more than the next largest, GM, and almost twice as many as venerable IBM.[5] This trend, by the way, is anticipated to accelerate so that by the year 2000 half of all working Americans will have joined the ranks of the "contingency work force."[6]

Why share this with you? To get you juiced by the prospect of change or, better, by the prospect of revolution because, make no doubt about it, it will affect *you!*

Reality Check

Rewarding success is easy, but rewarding intelligent failure is more important. We don't judge people strictly by results, we try to judge them by the quality of their efforts.

—Charles P. Holt

ARE YOU REINVENTING YOURSELF AND YOUR ORGANIZATION?

Individuals and organizations that will be able to compete in the next millennium are those that are constantly reinventing themselves. Individuals and organizations that take the same hum-drum stuff and turn it on its head are the ones that will thrive beyond their wildest imagination. Take the hum-drum of retailing. Sears had it all figured out. After all, they had been at it longer than anyone else and had mastered whatever there was to master. Or had they been asleep at the wheel? Not really! They were practicing incremental improvements while an unknown upstart by the name of Sam Walton looked at what everyone else was looking at and saw something different— different merchandising strategy. Different customer service focus. Different ways of ordering. Different use of information. Different use of technology. And voila, the rest is history.

Or take languid Taco Bell. Nothing but the samo, samo fast food. Okay, it was different; it was Mexican. But that's not where the difference is. The difference is in reinvention! Not doing business as usual, but rather radically changing *all* aspects of the business and taking advantage of chip technology to increase the efficiency and effectiveness of all aspects of their business. For example, by moving sophisticated information technology from headquarters to every store has saved managers fifteen hours of paperwork each week while at the same time provided them with real-time performance data regarding customer and employee satisfaction and costs. Similarly, instead of being in the food *production* business with large kitchens, Taco Bell has shrunk back-of-the-house space dramatically by outsourcing much of the preparation work. Now they see themselves as food *distributors* who are totally focused on creating value-added products that are important to customers. (Remember our discussion about the importance of knowing what business you're really in? If not, re-read chapter 2.) As a result, kitchen space has shrunk, customer service areas have increased, costs have been reduced, and an average of fifteen hours of food manufacturing time has been saved in each unit per day. Time that now can be used to focus on serving the customer. Has it worked? In a flat to declining fast-food market, Taco Bell's profits have grown 25 percent per year, compared to 6 percent for McDonald's U.S. restaurants.[7] Instead of resting on those laurels, Taco Bell has kept on reinventing itself by using technology to redefine who their customers are and what they really want. By conducting an in-depth study of their customer base, referred to as *high-frequency fast-food users,* CEO John Martin found out that Taco Bell has really two distinct segments of customers, *penny pinchers* and *speed freaks*, who each have distinct purchase preferences represented by the name they were given. They also found out that these two groups accounted for more than 70 percent of Taco Bell's volume. By repositioning their entire organization and reengineering their core processes to better serve the speed freaks, Taco Bell has been able to increase their peak hour capacity by 54 percent and reduce waiting time by 71 percent. To better serve penny pinchers, Taco Bell dramatically reduced prices on its core menu offerings to 25 percent below the prices in effect in 1982. By reinventing themselves in this manner, Taco Bell increased their sales from $1.6 billion in 1988 to $3.9 billion in 1993. At the same time, earnings rose from $82 million to $253 million.[8] Not bad, considering they are selling 59-cent, 79-cent, and 99-cent tacos.

Winning Action Step
Do everything in your power to become a leader in your industry.

Or let's really get radical and talk about that little upstart company, Netscape, that was trying to compete with Goliath—Mircosoft. Netscape had developed a software program that would dramatically simplify how users could navigate the Internet. If their strategy had been to find out what Microsoft is doing and do it better, they never would have been able to get a foot into the marketplace. After all, they simply did not have the capital or know-how to produce, market, and distribute their product. Instead they looked at what Microsoft was doing and did something radically different. They put information about their Web browser on a Web site on the Internet and announced that users could download the software (are you ready for this?) *free*. Users were requested to pay Netscape only *after* they had tried it out and found it to be useful. Did it work? Let's just say that after just a few short months more than six million copies of the software had been downloaded. But, you say, did people pay? Remember our discussion earlier? Regarding trusting all people, including customers, all of the time until they prove you wrong and you will be right about 97 percent of the time. That's exactly what happened to Netscape. Enough people paid to make it a $5-billion-company after only one year! (By the way, "billion" is not a typo). How could that be possible? Here is what James Clark, company cofounder and chairman of Netscape Communications, had to say about it:

> It took a lot of courage to initially give away our Web browser and to let people download it for free. Most business people would have resisted, wondering how that could ever be profitable. But you've got to recognize the Internet for what it is—a distribution channel. So we threw a lot of seeds into the electronic wind, and they took root in organizations all over the world. That established Netscape as an instant brand name—perhaps faster than any other in history.[9]

Of course they also didn't have to worry about nor pay for warehouses, duplication, shipping, distribution, advertising, and the myriad of other costs involved in doing business the old fashioned way. Every dollar that came to them was almost pure profit!

The reason I shared these examples with you is to stimulate you to think about how you can reinvent your organization, how you can break the rules by taking advantage of technology to achieve a competitive edge. In other words, I truly believe that the future does not belong to those individuals, organizations, or companies that compete. *The future belongs to those who reinvent themselves by taking advantage of new technologies.*

Winning Action Step

Don't compete—reinvent yourself! Find out what the competition is doing, and do something different.

WHAT IS YOUR CHANGE QUOTIENT (CQ)?

Now, let's find out how ready you and your organization are for doing business in the new millennium.

Exhibit 7-1: Change Self-Assessment Instrument

Instructions: Using the following scale, circle the number that corresponds to your level of disagreement or agreement with each statement. (People have different preferences and opinions; therefore, there are no right or wrong answers.)

SCALE: Strongly Disagree   Disagree   Neutral   Agree   Strongly Agree
              SD   D   N   A   SA

	SD	D	N	A	SA
1. The more often individuals are subjected to change, the more likely they will accept change.	1	2	3	4	5
2. Changes in our organization occur primarily because we need to catch up with the competition.	1	2	3	4	5
3. Our company's strength comes from innovation and growth.	1	2	3	4	5
4. Getting employees to look for new ideas in unrelated industries is a waste of time.	1	2	3	4	5
5. We use technology to continually reinvent ourselves.	1	2	3	4	5
6. A good portion of my time at work is spent on maintaining the status quo.	1	2	3	4	5
7. The change process can be enhanced by utilizing a change action team that represents the key stakeholders.	1	2	3	4	5
8. We pride ourselves on breaking the rules.	1	2	3	4	5
9. When confronted with change, I think first of what I will gain from the change.	1	2	3	4	5
10. Our management team spends a lot of time focusing on improving policies and procedures.	1	2	3	4	5
11. When I propose a change to my employees, they recognize that we are all in it together.	1	2	3	4	5
12. I believe that trust in the change agent and acceptance of change are unrelated.	1	2	3	4	5
13. The best way to overcome resistance to change is to embrace it.	1	2	3	4	5

14. I tend to feel uncomfortable with change.   1 2 3 4 5
15. We operate in accordance with the axiom: 1 2 3 4 5
    If it ain't broke, fix it anyway.
16. Creating and communicating a compelling   1 2 3 4 5
    vision is not necessary when undertaking an
    organizational transformation.
17. Sometimes you have to make the change process   1 2 3 4 5
    appear beneficial even when it is not.
18. Most fundamental organizational changes take   1 2 3 4 5
    three to eight years.
19. The best way to get people to change is to   1 2 3 4 5
    involve them in the change process.
20. I believe that education and training help build 1 2 3 4 5
    skills but have no impact on people's ability to
    be receptive to change.

                                          TOTAL: _____

Scoring Instructions: Score each item in accordance with the number you have circled, *except items 2, 4, 6, 10, 12, 14, 16, 17, and 20,* which have to be scored by
reversing the scale, so that 1 = 5, 2 = 4, 3 = 3, 4 = 2, 5 = 1. Then total your score
in the space provided.

Examples:

1. The more often individuals are subjected .... 1 2 3 4 (5)= 5
2. Changes in our organization.......................... 1 2 3 (4) 5 = 2
3. Our company's strength comes from........................ 1 2 3 (4) 5 = 4

Change: What Your CQ Score Means

95–100 *Super*—you are a veritable change machine. I bet not much grass
        grows under your feet.

85–94   *Excellent*—you have mastered a critical *winning management* skill.

75–84   *Very good*—get ready, get set to learn powerful new skills that will
        enable you and your team members to change more effectively.

65–74   *Good*—but you can do better. Let's get serious about change.

55–64   *Okay*—but you need to change. (Pun intended.) So read carefully and
        learn what it takes to achieve effective organizational transformations.

<55   Whoa! You are in luck! Few people will benefit as much from this
        chapter as you will!

Now that you have a better sense of where you are, let's next turn our attention to several unique attributes that accompany every change process so that you can manage it more effectively in yourself and your team members.

Winning Action Step
Banish the following sentiments from your thoughts and all of your meetings starting today: "We've always (never) done it that way"; "It's not invented here"; "It can't be done"; etc.

UNIQUE ATTRIBUTES ASSOCIATED WITH THE CHANGE PROCESS

Change, when it comes, gets most of us to behave in strange and mysterious ways. Here are several behavior patterns that you need to be aware of so that you can anticipate and manage them when they come your way.

- People will focus on what they must give up—virtually all change is first and foremost perceived as a loss as opposed to a gain. This in spite of the fact that much change over the long term results in dramatic improvements for most of us, in spite of the media generally portraying it otherwise. For example, during the period from 1945 to 1995, of thirteen "quality of life" measures, eleven dramatically improved, including life expectancy, per-capita income, level of education, households with phones, TVs, and other amenities that make our lives more pleasant, and the poverty rate. The two measures that worsened during this time were the divorce rate and children born out of wedlock.[10] Even when we get fired (that's a pretty traumatic change), most of us end up with a better job than before.[11]

- People prefer the status quo—this is true even when the new represents a dramatic improvement. A great example is the QWERTY typewriter keyboard. This highly inefficient keyboard layout was first introduced in 1873 to slow down typists so that the keys would not jam. Even though the original reason behind the

QWERTY system has long passed (that's a conservative statement), virtually every high-power computer you buy today continues to be delivered with the highly inefficient and unproductive QWERTY system. (During this time, speed of communication increased about ten million times.) Stop and think for a moment: The level of productivity we are foregoing—it's got to be in the billions—and all because typewriter keys were sticking more than one hundred years ago! That's what I call incredible!

- People perceive that they are in it alone—this perception tends to be true even if an entire team or company is undergoing change. Verify this for yourself. When the stuff hits the fan, most of us become quite self-centered and begin to worry about how it is going to impact us and our family.

- People tend to resist change more when they do not trust or like the change agent—President Ronald Reagan found the American people more receptive to change than Presidents Carter or Clinton.

- Every person will accept change differently—models of change are useful only as a guide because people are at different levels of readiness for change. To make matters even more complicated, the same person will accept change differently at different times.

- People tend to feel inadequate, awkward, ill equipped, and uncomfortable as a result of change—these feelings can be minimized (how in next section).

- People tend to revert to old behaviors—once the pressure for change has been removed. This holds true unless they have made the new behavior a habit, have found that the new behavior resulted in dramatic improvements, or that the old behavior is accompanied by lots of pain.

Winning Action Step

Starting right now, make it a practice to look for the *good* in every change.

INDIVIDUAL CHANGE MODEL

Even though we all react to change differently, researchers have identified that individuals tend to go through seven specific stages when confronted with change. These seven phases will help you diagnose where your team members are during a change process so that you can facilitate change. The seven transition stages are as follows:[12]

Stage 1:

Uncertainty—people typically feel unsure, overwhelmed, and fearful at this stage. They long for more information, so they can decide whether to buy in or stall. Unfortunately people tend to be somewhat paralyzed at this stage, so that even though they long for more information, they may not necessarily take the initiative to get it.

Stage 2:

Delusion—the assumption at this stage is that this too shall pass. (Remember how your felt when TQM was introduced in your company?) Because people tend to delude themselves, typically morale actually improves moderately in this stage.

Stage 3:

Introspection—in this stage people tend to look inward and begin to question their ability to deal with the change. Their sense of self-worth decreases dramatically, and their morale and mood are impacted negatively.

Stage 4:

Letting go—once people let go of the past and commit to make the change work, their morale and sense of self-worth begins to improve.

Stage 5:

Commitment—once people implement the new process or procedures and are beginning to get encouraging results, they become committed to make it work. As a result, they become even more positive and energized.

Stage 6:

Continuing learning—commitment leads to wanting to figure out how to make this process work even better. As a result, people become curious and seek additional information, training, and continuing learning, which in turn leads to increased self-confidence, high morale, and an improved sense of self-worth.

Stage 7:

Habit formation—in this stage the individual has fully adapted the change process and has developed new habits that will continue to be a part of her behavior pattern unless it is extinguished or another new transformation takes its place.

Winning Action Step

Put a sign behind your desk that reads: Every rule around here can be broken, except this one!

HOW TO OVERCOME RESISTANCE TO CHANGE

Given that change is so traumatic for most people, here are six specific strategies that you can use to overcome resistance to change. They are listed in order from least to most effective.[13]

1.   Explicit and implicit coercion—this is right from the old Theory X manual. Want something changed? Tell people about it. If they don't want to do it, threaten them with reduction in pay, termination, transfer, etc.

Advantage: Fast (that's about all it's got going for it).

Disadvantages: Too many to list. Don't use it unless you have an incredibly important reason that something must happen extremely fast!

2.   Manipulation and co-optation—manipulation occurs when information is selectively withheld and events are contrived to make the change process appear beneficial, even when it is not. (Reminds you of politics, doesn't it?) Co-optation is make-believe participation. It's when the boss asks people for their input *after* the decision has been made.

Advantage: Fast.

Disadvantages: Will very likely lead to increased resistance the next time a change process is introduced. Also increases cynicism and lowers morale. (Makes you wonder why it is used so much, doesn't it?)

3.   Negotiation and agreement—this is when you exchange something of value to achieve agreement and cooperation. This strategy is

useful when there is a clear-cut win-lose proposition, especially when the losing party has considerable power.

Advantage: May represent the path of least resistance.

Disadvantages: May lead to other power plays and be expensive.

4. Facilitation and support—this is when you provide training, counseling, and time off to help team members deal with fear and anxiety. Useful in a crisis such as the Oklahoma City bombing, or in high-stress change or adjustment situations that can't be avoided, such as moving offices.

Advantage: Ideal for adjustment problems.

Disadvantages: May be time consuming and expensive.

5. Participation and involvement—this is when team members play an active role and are truly involved in the design and implementation of the change process. This is an incredibly powerful strategy to overcome resistance to change, especially in situations where those who are proposing the change do not have all of the information to successfully design and implement the change, where resistors have considerable power or are critical to the success of the change process. Evidence indicates that there is an inverse relationship between participation and resistance: the more participation, the less resistance.

Advantage: It works! People who participate become stakeholders who are committed to make *their* change effort a success.

Disadvantages: Critics would say that it is time consuming and expensive. (Note: you either pay a little up front or you pay a lot later.)

6. Education and communication—this is where you create a learning organization and tell people more than they want to know. (See chapter 5.) These strategies are absolutely essential if you want to survive during a revolution. The reason? It makes change a normal state of affairs, as opposed to something unusual that must be avoided at all costs. It represents preventive medicine as opposed to surgery. It is driven by the observation that people can do the "how" once they understand the "why."

Advantage: It works! It does more than that—it is a competitive survival tactic for these rapidly changing times!

Disadvantages: Same as above.

Note that even though the last two strategies are clearly the most advantageous, the others may have a merit in certain situations. Also remember that all resistance to change is *not* bad. It serves as a check-and-balance system to make sure that management does not go off half-cocked into the wrong direction. Something you would never do, or would you? Maurer[14] goes one step further. He suggests that the *only* effective way to deal with resistance to change is to seek it out and embrace it.

Reality Check

Social systems, including organizations, work best when there are opposing views.

—Wolf J. Rinke

IMPLEMENTING CHANGE

Let's say that you manufacture a highly popular gardening tool. You have been in business for two years and have found out that your manual plant just can't keep up with demand. As a result, the management team has decided to automate the plant. The majority of your employees are highly skilled, extremely loyal, and committed to you and your company. In fact, many have been with you since you built this company from scratch. You are interested in keeping many of your productive and qualified team members, especially those with hard-to-find specialized skills. On the other hand, you know that there will have to be layoffs. You have hired a consultant to practice damage control. She has recommended that you use the following four-phase model to communicate the automation to your team members:[15]

Phase 1: Create awareness
Scope: Corporatewide
Purpose: To tell people what is happening
Specifics: In this phase you will want to:
- Provide information about the anticipated automation
- Stress senior management's involvement and support in the changeover
- Reaffirm the organization's core values
- Tie in the automation with the strategic goals and objectives
- Listen and respond to concerns

Phase 2: Project status
Scope: Organization specific
Purpose: To tell people where you are going
Specifics: In this phase you will want to:

- Demonstrate management's commitment
- Identify and respond to issues and concerns
- Explain the big picture
- Reaffirm the purpose of automation and how it is aligned with strategic plans
- Disseminate information from pilot tests

Phase 3: Roll-out
Scope: Project specific
Purpose: Explain what it means to your team members
Specifics: In this phase you will want to:

- Demonstrate management's continued commitment
- Provide specific information about how automation will affect them
- Provide training in new methods, techniques, and skills
- Listen and respond to issues and concerns

Phase 4: Follow-up
Scope: Team specific
Purpose: Explain how you will make it work
Specifics: In this phase you will want to:

- Demonstrate management's continued commitment
- Reaffirm organization's core values and strategic goals
- Listen to and act on suggestions
- Streamline and refine the automation process

To make this or any other change effort work, I suggest that you provide for two-way communications throughout the change process. Continue to be personally involved, and tie the change into the organization's core values and strategic goals. As mentioned in chapter 5, if in doubt tell people more than they want to know, tell it more often than you think is necessary, and use as many media as possible to get the message across. You might also find it helpful to utilize a communication-strategy matrix to make sure that the concerns of all stakeholders are considered and addressed (see Exhibit 7-2).

Exhibit 7-2: Communication-Strategy Matrix

Stakeholders (who)	Objectives (why)	Key Messages (what)	Vehicles (how)	Timing (when)	Accountability (ownership)
Middle Management	• buy-in • understanding • new skills	• new roles • new methods • personal impact	• meetings with the CEO and executives • training	• kickoff: week 1 • kickoff: month 1	• CEO and other executives • training dept.
Employees	• buy-in • understanding • new skills	• new roles • new methods • personal impact	• meetings with managers • training	• kickoff: week 1 • kickoff: month 1	• managers • training mngrs.
Customers	• information • awareness	• new methods • service impact	• meetings with sales reps	• kickoff: week 1	• sales reps
Shareholders	• information • awareness	• service impact • financial impact	• written information from CEO and CFO	• kickoff: week 1	• CEO and CFO
Community	• information • awareness	• service impact • financial impact	• news releases	• kickoff: week 1	• CEO

Managing a winning organization will require all team members to be change-driven. To do this you must build an organization "where people continually expand their capacity to create the results they truly desire, where new and expansive patterns of thinking are nurtured, where collective aspiration is set free, and where people are continually learning how to learn together" by building a learning organization.[16]

Reality Check

The rate at which individuals and organizations learn might become the only sustainable competitive advantage.

—Ray Strata

BUILDING A LEARNING ORGANIZATION

A learning organization "is an organization skilled at creating, acquiring, and transferring knowledge, and at modifying its behavior to reflect new knowledge and insights."[17]

Variety Is the Spice of Learning

Learning organizations have mastered the ability to learn from:[18]
- Systematic problem solving
- Experimentation
- Past experiences
- Other people's experiences
- Benchmarking
- Transferring knowledge and information

Systematic Problem Solving

This strategy is an outgrowth of the scientific method and has been popularized in business by the quality movement. It emphasizes that problems, or what I like to refer to as *opportunities,* should be solved by utilizing scientific methods such as the hypothesis testing approach used in scientific studies, or the "Plan, Do, Act Cycle" advocated by the late Dr. Deming. This approach, also referred to as *fact-based management* relies on data instead of gut feelings to make business decisions. Typically decisions are made only after the data have been analyzed and organized using statistical techniques such as Pareto charts, cause-and-effect diagrams, histograms, and correlations. Typical of this approach is the sophisticated six-step problem-solving process developed and utilized by the Xerox Corporation:[19]

Step 1: Identifying and selecting the problem. Discussion centers on what needs to be changed and, if at all possible, the "desired state" is described in observable and measurable terms.

Step 2: Analyzing the problem. Team members explore what stands in their way of reaching the desired state identified in step 1. Critical causes are identified, verified, documented, and ranked.

Step 3: Identifying potential solutions. A variety of idea-generation techniques are used to identify as many potential solutions as possible. These are clarified and a tentative solution list is generated.

Step 4: Selecting and planning the implementation of the solution. In this step a variety of criteria and metrics are identified to track and monitor the solution's effectiveness.

Step 5: Implementing the solution. In this step the solution is put into place, and team members make sure the plan is implemented as agreed upon.

Step 6: Evaluating the solution. This step involves looking back to make sure that the plan did indeed work the way it was expected. In the event that the plan did not solve the problem, the cycle is started all over again.

Winning Action Step

Install a suggestion box with a commitment to provide feedback within twenty-four hours and with a built-in profit-sharing plan.

Experimentation

This strategy involves a systematic search and trying out of new knowledge so that an organization can expand its opportunities and explore new ventures, procedures, and systems of accomplishing work or serving its customers. Like systematic problem solving, experimentation relies heavily on the use of the scientific method described above. The motivation, however, is what's different. Whereas systematic problem solving is motivated by an organizational problem, experimentation is driven because a company is seeking new opportunities or attempting to find new ways of achieving the competitive advantage. Experimentation consists of two basic strategies: ongoing programs and demonstration projects. Ongoing programs consist primarily of incremental learning derived from such well-known approaches as the continuous quality improvement (CQI) methods.

Successful ongoing programs share several common characteristics. They:

- Generate a steady stream of new ideas. New ideas are the fuel that make experimentation run; without them it will cease. To avoid becoming stale or getting into a rut, I suggest that you send team members to mystery shop the competition, or send them on a sabbatical to other industries or academic institutions so that they can bring back hot new ideas.

- Provide incentives for calculated risk taking. Team members will simply not experiment unless they know that they are safe. The way one of my clients has provided team members with this sense of security is via the use of a special award, the *GUP* or Goof Up award. It is awarded monthly to the individual that has made the biggest goof as a result of taking a calculated risk.

- Provide intensive training in the use of statistical techniques, graphing skills, and creativity techniques. Both managers and team members must be able to master skills that will enable them to design and evaluate experiments, redesign and analyze work processes, as well as harness the brain power of many people to come up with innovative ideas.

Demonstration projects are similar to ongoing programs, except that they involve system change projects that are designed to develop new organizational capabilities. Typically these large-scale projects are initiated from scratch with the intent of developing new organizational models and capabilities. An example of a large-scale demonstration project is the Saturn Division of GM. Unique attributes of demonstration projects include:

- Lots of learning by doing
- Driven by highly effective multifunctional teams
- Limited impact on the parent organization during the development phase
- Establishment of new norms and new ways of doing business
- Potential "roll out" to the parent organization after a successful model has been established

Winning Action Step

Have your team members visit the competition and bring back a list of what your competitors are doing better than you.

Past Experiences

This is an organized retrospective approach that is achieved from self-analysis and reflection. This approach utilizes case studies or post-project reviews and encourages team members to widely share what and how they have learned from both successes and failures. An example of this was demonstrated by the Boeing Company, which had extensive problems with the 737 and 747 planes. To make sure the problems would not be replicated, Boeing established a learning team called "Project Homework." This team was charged with comparing the development and production processes of the 737 and 747 with those of the 707 and 727, two of Boeing's successful planes. After three years of study and reams and reams of recommendations, members of the Project Homework team were assigned to the startup teams for the Boeing 757 and 767. Learning from past experience in this way helped Boeing introduce the most error free and successful new planes in the history of Boeing.

Reality Check

Those who cannot remember the past are condemned to repeat it.

—George Santayana

Other People's Experiences (OPE) or Other Organizations' Experiences
I refer to this as "BS" (borrow shamelessly), Tom Peters calls it "creative swiping," and textile giant Milliken refers to it as "steal ideas shamelessly" (SIS). Whatever the terminology, every company and organization must overcome the crippling "not-invented-here" (NIH) syndrome. All team members must be encouraged to constantly look for new ideas and innovative practices, especially in industries other than their own. Better yet, in other countries. Every time I travel abroad, I'm startled by how many innovative ideas and practices I discover that solve very specific problems we have in this country. All that is required is to adapt, modify, and implement—and voila, another "brand-new" idea is born. Other sources, of course, include your current internal and external customers who have very specific, functional solutions to 95 percent of all of your current problems. After all, they struggle with your products or services all of the time. To get these solutions, all that you have to do (are you ready for this astounding revelation?) is ask! Ask, observe, solicit, and cajole—via such methods as surveys, focus groups, mystery shoppers, critical incident techniques, and so on. Another approach I have used with a variety of clients is to have service team members shop the competition. To make this work, have team members bring back only positive practices. Negative practices may only be reported if your organization is currently engaging in the same negative practices. Otherwise, team members will come back with comments such as: "You won't believe how stupid the competition is." "You should have seen how they mistreated their customers." "I can't believe how much better we are." None of these observations, unfortunately, will teach anyone anything. Worse, they will reinforce how good you are, and how little you have to learn and change. (Not the attitude of a learning organization.) The reality? Every competitor can teach you something, but you must force yourselves to look for it!

Winning Action Step

Reward your team members for taking calculated risks, even when they fail. Remember, what gets rewarded gets done!

Benchmarking

Benchmarking, an integral process of applying for the Malcolm Baldridge Award, requires you to find out who the "leaders" are in your and your related industries, referred to as "best in class," observing how the leaders get the work done via site visits, interviews, and studies; comparing those practices to your own; and then making changes as necessary to match or, better yet, exceed best-in-class practices. It's important to recognize that best in class does not have to be in your own industry. For example, one corporate cafeteria client I worked with benchmarked the Ritz Carlton's service standards.

Transferring Knowledge and Information

Learning organizations are "boundarylessness." Knowledge and information, unlike other commodities, have a very short shelf life, which means that their maximum power is derived from being shared quickly. Transferring of knowledge can be achieved via reports, visits, training, education, newsletters, bulletins, meetings, and job rotations. Written communications are vastly expedited via electronic systems, such as e-mail and faxes. One of the most powerful ways to achieve a lasting transfer of knowledge can be achieved from job rotations. Obvious as it may appear, the best learning occurs when we do something. A wise Chinese philosopher long before our time figured that one out when he said: *"What I see, I believe; what I hear, I understand; what I do, I remember."* To take advantage of this, I recommend that you institute an aggressive job rotation program at all levels of the organization. In addition to facilitating lasting organizational learning, you will also find that job rotations significantly improve job satisfaction (most people enjoy variety), improve productivity (multiple skilled team members reduces the number of people needed to get the job done), enhance communication (once I have traveled in your moccasins I can *really* understand what you do), and increase profitability (fewer team members equals lower labor costs). It's important that job rotations be accomplished at the highest level of the organization. For example, a president of a business unit (BU) who has demonstrated his turnaround expertise by dramatically improving the fiscal health of his BU is a natural for a job rotation to another BU that is suffering from fiscal woes.

All of these approaches to learning must be supported by measurement systems to assure that the learning does indeed result in a change in organizational behavior, as well as improvements in performance, productivity, and profitability.

Reality Check

If you are not uncomfortable several times every day, you're not pushing the envelope enough.

—Wolf J. Rinke

Different Strokes for Different Folks

At this point you might be saying, "Okay, coach, I've got it. Building a learning organization is critical to me and my company's success in the next millennium. But what system of learning will work best for my organization?" Great question, and I have the answer for you, based on a comprehensive study conducted by a consortium of researchers from the University of Michigan, Florida International University, and the Center of Executive Development in Cambridge, Massachusetts. Based on interviews with 1,359 managers, in-depth case studies, and a review of the literature, they identified four basic types of organizational learning:[20]

- Continuous improvement—these organizations practice incremental learning by mastering each step in a process before moving on. This was the most frequently reported system of learning. Of the 1,359 organizations studied, 461 companies identified continuous improvement as their dominant learning system.
- Competence acquisition—these organizations learn by cultivating new capabilities in individuals and teams and by demonstrating a commitment to finding a better way to get the job done. Learning is an integral component of their way of doing business. Three hundred and forty respondents identified competence acquisition as their preferred system of learning for their business.
- Experimentation—these organizations are focused on learning by trying out new ideas and methodologies. Their competitive edge is to be a market leader by being the first to introduce new

products or processes. Of those studied, 281 respondents identified this system of learning as their dominant approach.

- Boundary spanning—these organizations scan other companies and competitors on an ongoing basis. Learning primarily is achieved by benchmarking their progress against industry leaders. Of those studied, 207 identified boundary spanning as the primary system of learning.

Which system of learning was the most effective? According to this study: experimentation had the greatest impact on an organization's competitiveness and ability to change, followed by competence acquisition, continuous improvement, and then boundary spanning.

Does that mean that you should adopt experimentation as *the* system of learning for your organization? No, not really. The most effective system of learning for your organization depends on your organization's culture and philosophy. For example, if you are managing a highly structured organization, such as a government agency, continuous improvement might work best for you. On the other hand, if you are in an organization that considers learning a competitive advantage, such as a research and development firm, you may want to chose competence acquisition as your dominant learning model. In an entrepreneurial, change-driven type of organization, such as a technology company, you might wish to rely on experimentation as your learning methodology of choice. Finally, if you are operating in an extremely competitive environment, such as a service company, you may want to rely on boundary spanning as your dominant mode of learning. Better yet, you may want to pick and choose from all four styles depending on the needs of your customers, the inherent capabilities of your team members, and your mission, vision and core values.

Winning Action Step

At least three out of five times have lunch or get together with people you have never met before or who think, act, and behave differently than you do.

ACHIEVING LASTING ORGANIZATIONAL TRANSFORMATIONS

Turnaround, TQM, reengineering, downsizing, delayering, rightsizing, virtual corporations, and the list goes on. Today organizational change seems to be the rule, not the exception. Yet, for the most part, change processes do not work. Even Michael Hammer, the father of reengineering, has admitted as much.[21] What is a *winning manager* to do? Not change? Hardly! Unless you want to commit hara-kiri! What you need is a change process that works over the *long term*. (Note the emphasis.) To assist you with achieving lasting change in your organization I would first like to share a macro paradigm, the *Organizational Transformation Process* (OTP). Once you understand the big picture, I will provide you with nine specific steps that you can take to achieve a fundamental and lasting change in your organization.

The Organizational Transformation Process (OTP)

The OTP is a framework I've developed to help a management team figure out what they want their organization to be when it grows up so that we can develop specific action strategies to help them get there faster. The process, which is customized to meet the specific needs of an organization, consists of the following ten phases:

Phase 1:
Committing. You, and other members of the management team, must be willing to make a total commitment to the transformation. Without a commitment, the process will fail.

Phase 2:
Assessing. Managers, employees, and customers are interviewed (ideally by an external consultant) to determine the *real* needs of the organization and its members. These findings are used to structure phases 3 and 4.

Phase 3:
Visioning. A facilitator helps the management team create the future of the organization by facilitating the identification of the mission, vision, core values, and critical success factors. (Given that you've completed chapter 2, this phase is already done.)

Phase 4:
Planning. Cross-functional teams develop preliminary action plans. These plans identify how the organizational systems, operating procedures, learning programs, and communication systems must be changed to support the transformation.

Phase 5:
Developing. Learning experiences are provided to develop the skills and competencies needed to transform the organization and make the mission, vision, and core values a reality.

Phase 6:
Implementing. A facilitator is utilized to facilitate consensus and ownership of the master action plan and create linkages to the organization's strategic goals, resources, and continuing learning programs.

Phase 7:
Reinforcing. Positive reinforcement strategies and measurement systems (metrics) are identified to keep the transformation on track.

Phase 8:
Monitoring. Monitoring systems are developed and implemented and collected data are made public to create positive reinforcement and peer pressure.

Phase 9:
Evaluating. Intervention strategies and learning experiences are evaluated to ensure that the critical success factors are attained.

Phase 10:
Improving. Continuous improvement strategies are initiated to ensure that the organization maintains its competitive advantage. After phase 10, the process starts all over again, as illustrated in Exhibit 7-3.

Winning Action Step

Make sure that you spend more time in your "uncomfortable" zone than your comfort zone. Expect the same from your team members.

Exhibit 7-3: The Organizational Transformation Process (OTP)

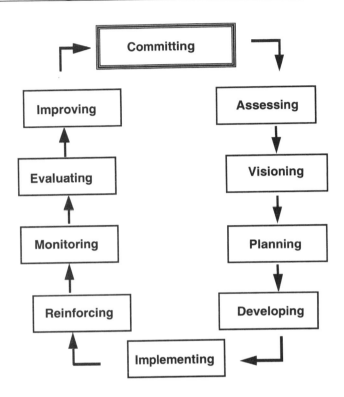

Winning Action Step

Pursue new product innovations that feel right in your or your team members' gut, even if your customers never asked for it. They didn't ask for CNN, minivans, or Walkmans either.

Making Change Stick

Now that you have the big picture of organizational transformation, let's roll up our sleeves and master nine specific steps that will help you achieve a lasting change in your organization:

Step 1: Mobilize Commitment by Creating a Powerful Sense of Urgency

This step seems the easiest but by all indications is the step that is most often messed up. In fact, Kotter maintains that about 50 percent of all companies fail in their change efforts because they fail to create a sufficient sense of urgency.[22] Let's face it: Most of us would rather deal with what we know, even if what we know is bad news, rather than chart the course of unknown territories. The reality is that fundamental change, the kind of change that most organizations must pursue in order to stay competitive, can not be accomplished incrementally. Or as Goss et al. have suggested: "[Companies] don't need to change what is; they need to create what isn't."[23] Fundamental change will only come about if virtually all of the management team and most stakeholders feel a sense of urgency and are motivated to change because not changing has greater negative consequences than maintaining the status quo. To accomplish that level of urgency requires a real or imagined crisis or a major opportunity that, if not taken advantage of, has the potential to challenge the survival of the organization and its members. My experience has been that step 1 requires critical mass of about 80 percent of the management team and about 66 percent of stakeholders, especially the team members who make things happen. Once most stakeholders are convinced that doing nothing has greater costs than making the change, and once about 66 percent of the stakeholders have made a commitment to making the change, critical mass has been achieved and you're ready to go on to step 2. Caution: Taking shortcuts with step 1 will likely lead to failure!

Reality Check

People do everything in their power to move away from pain and toward pleasure.

—Wolf J. Rinke

Step 2: Tailor the Change to Fit the Situation

It may be obvious, but I need to say it anyway: Every person is unique! Therefore, it stands to reason that every organizational entity is unique. After all, organizations are nothing but a whole bunch of people put together under one umbrella. Even within one and the same company, the change process that worked for one division may not work for another. Therefore, it is highly unlikely that intervention in company A will work in company B. It is critical that the change process be structured so that change occurs at a rate that is compatible with an organization's ability to assimilate change. Several rules to consider to guide your customization:

Rule 1: Team members' willingness to change is positively correlated with the anticipated benefit or the perceived severity of the personal loss. In other words, the greater the perceived benefit or crisis, the greater the willingness to change.

Rule 2: The more often individuals are subjected to change, the greater their acceptance of change. This rule makes a strong case for implementing some sort of change on an ongoing basis, provided, of course, that the change does not reduce your competitive posture.

Rule 3: Individuals are more tolerant of change that they have had an opportunity to understand and/or participate in. This rule provides you with lots of incentive to involve people in the change process.

Caution: Utilizing off-the-shelf change approaches or consultants who utilize the same approach with every organization likely will lead to failure.

Winning Action Step

Use specific examples to demonstrate to team members that most change has a silver lining.

Step 3: Assemble a Powerful Change Action Team

The senior executive must assemble a change action team that represents all of the key stakeholders and those who are passionate about the change. I recommend that at a minimum this team be led by the organization's leader (president or CEO if the change affects the entire company, division general manager if the change affects only one division, and so on) and consist of key members of the senior executive team, board representative(s), employee representative(s) (head of the union and/or other employee opinion shapers regardless of rank), and customer representative(s). The size of the team depends, of course, on the size of the organization. As a guideline, however, this team should be big enough to represent stakeholders who have the ability to smooth or sabotage the implementation of the change process. On the other hand, it should be small enough to be functional. Research regarding group size has established that the ideal group consists of five individuals. As the size of the group increases, communication becomes more complex. For example, three-member groups have nine possible communication links. That number jumps to seventy with five-member groups. In addition to communications becoming more complex, members in larger groups have less chance to participate, resulting in less satisfaction and a lower sense of cohesiveness.[24] In addition, the larger the group, the greater the possibility that cliques and factions will form. Caution: Delegating responsibilities for leading the change action team will likely lead to failure.

Step 4: Create a Vision of the New Future

Sorry, I know you are getting tired of hearing this, but here is that vision thing again. Much like our discussion in chapter 2, a vision that is simple, easy to understand, compelling, and able to communicate a clear picture of the new future is absolutely critical to the success of this intervention. Caution: The change action team needs to get back to the drawing board if your vision consists of more than three sentences, takes longer than two minutes to explain, and does not result in excitement and passion by front-line team members.

Reality Check

Concerns for the future, a sense of where opportunities lie, and an understanding of organizational change are not the province of any group; people from all levels of a company can help define the future.

—Gary Hamel and C. H. Prahalad

Step 5: Communicate the Vision and Identify WIIFM

To accomplish this step, look back to chapter 5, as well as the four-step communication model described in the earlier part of this chapter. A critical component of this step is to have every team member be very clear about *what is in it for me* (WIIFM), good and bad. P. T. Barnum was incorrect; you *cannot* fool most of the people most of the time. So be up front and tell it like it is. Also, be sure to personally communicate with the front-line supervisors who, according to Larkin and Larkin,[25] are the most critical players in any change effort. They recommend that managers spend most of their time, money, and effort communicating face to face with these supervisors. If things will get better for certain people, let them know that. By the way, the change must result in improvements for at least half the stakeholders, otherwise your change effort likely will fail! If others will be laid off, or otherwise be impacted negatively, let them know that too. But also let them know what assistance they can expect to get. Be sure to provide as much assistance as you possibly can without running the company into the ground because *negative* critical mass will assure the death of any intervention effort. Also, it is absolutely essential that you, the senior management team, and members of the change action team walk your talk! Remember, people will hear actions much, much louder than words! This is so critical that any member of the management and the change action team who is unwilling or unable to commit to the change effort must be removed from the organization either permanently or, if the organization is large enough, for the duration of the change process.

This reminds me of a long-term health care client who was desirous of implementing a TQM process. After having worked with the client for about six months and having made real advances, the awards team decided on a summer picnic to build esprit de corps and reinforce the message that all team members are critical to success. The management team blessed the event, and everything came together like a charm—except that on the day of the picnic only four of the nineteen members of the management team showed up. By not walking their talk, the management team not only wiped out the six months of progress, their lack of commitment put us further behind than the day we started. In fact, it raised the level of cynicism, skepticism, and mistrust to an all-time high. Caution: If you are not using *every* possible communication medium to talk about the new vision until you are sick and tired of it, you probably are not talking about it enough.

Step 6: Find the Energy to Build Powerful Coalitions

Every organization has what are referred to as *early adapters;* these are the folks who love change. Every organization has highly committed team members who are very willing to carry the ball (they represent energy), as well as opinion leaders. Use the change action team to identify these folks to become disciples of the change effort so that they can carry the message and their passion to the late adapters. Caution: Ignoring the late adapters can scuttle your change initiative!

Reality Check

Some people are like frogs. If you drop a frog into a pan of hot water, the frog will react immediately and jump out of the water. If you instead place the frog in a pan of lukewarm water and raise the water temperature gently and gradually, the frog will accept that change and stay in the water until he is boiled to death. Don't behave like a frog!

—David Mahoney

Step 7: Empower Everyone to Make the Vision a Reality

All team members and stakeholders must be empowered to do whatever it takes to make the vision a reality. This includes removing obstacles, be they policies, procedures, systems, or employees who are undermining the achievement of the vision. Everyone must be encouraged to use their initiative, energy, and power to help move the organization toward the attainment of the new vision. This does not mean that conflict should be squelched. Just the opposite. Conflict should be harnessed utilizing conflict resolution strategies. It is important that all team members recognize that conflict is good, since conflict—appropriately channeled—represents energy, energy that can be used to initiate creativity and innovation, the force that is needed to make the new vision a reality. Suppression of conflict and excessive controls, on the other hand, results in dramatic reductions in commitment, risk taking, and learning. This stage requires managers to be generous in giving their power away, encouraging team members to take calculated risks, and stimulating unconventional behaviors and actions. In short, managers must act like a coach, not a cop! Caution: Not letting go, *really letting go,* and excessive controls—other than the new vision being the only thing that is not optional—will stall the change process.

Step 8: Celebrate Incremental Victories
Most fundamental organizational changes take three to eight years to achieve. Yes, you read right, three to eight *years!* Few people will be able to maintain high levels of energy and commitment for such a long time. Hence it is critical that *achievable* goals and objectives be identified in six- or twelve-month increments. Attainment of these goals and objectives should be celebrated in a big way, with bonuses, public recognition, and other public promotions that will let everyone know that the organization is moving in the right direction. Caution: Change without positive reinforcement will extinguish the newly acquired behavior.

Winning Action Step

Offer a $1 million award, in the form of lottery tickets, for creative and weird ideas.

Step 9: Anchor the New Vision in the Corporate Culture
Let's face it: When the pressure is off, human beings and organizations tend to revert to old and comfortable behaviors. Behaviors that support the new vision must be continually reinforced until they become the norm. New team members and managers must be selected on the basis of how well they believe and support the new vision. Policies, systems, and organizational structures—especially reward and compensation systems—must be continually reevaluated and realigned to support and anchor the new vision so that it becomes the accepted modus operandi. Changes in the management team can lead

to rapid reversals and, therefore, new managers should be chosen on the basis of how well they can buy into and support the new vision.

A case in point is a health care client I had worked with for the purpose of implementing an empowerment program. After about eighteen months, team members finally began to take positive and independent actions on behalf of patients. All customer-service indicators began to point in the right direction. Complacency began to take place; after all, the perception was that the intervention effort had been completed. At about that time a new executive director was being hired. The board of directors took independent actions to search for a new director. Only after some cajoling did the board agree to involve the management team members. At that point, however, the board had already selected a candidate and only accommodated the management team's request in order to appease them. The individual who was selected had never worked in an empowered environment before and lacked the ability and/or the willingness to change. It took only about three months for the entire organization to revert to its prior autocratic behavior. Caution: Declaring victory before the new vision has been internalized as "the way we do business around here" will cause the change process to self-destruct.

Winning Action Step

Right now, initiate an action plan that will ensure that your work force, including management, will consist of 50 percent women and 20 percent minorities.

SUMMARY

- We are in an era of hyper-accelerated change that will require you and your team members not just to be able to accept change but to thrive on it.
- Most people confronted with change:
  — Will focus on what they must give up
  — Prefer the status quo
  — Perceive that they are in it alone

- — Will resist change more when they do not trust or like the change agent
- — Accept change differently
- — Tend to feel inadequate, awkward, ill equipped, and uncomfortable
- — Tend to revert to old behaviors
- Individuals tend to go through seven specific stages when confronted with change:
  1. Uncertainty
  2. Delusion
  3. Introspection
  4. Letting go
  5. Commitment
  6. Continuing learning
  7. Habit formation
- Resistance to change can be overcome by:
  - — Explicit and implicit coercion
  - — Manipulation and co-optation
  - — Negotiation and agreement
  - — Facilitation and support
  - — Participation and involvement
  - — Education and communication
- Change can be facilitated by using a four-phase communication process model:
  1. Create awareness
  2. Project status
  3. Roll-out
  4. Follow-up
- Learning organizations have mastered the ability to learn from:
  - — Systematic problem solving
  - — Experimentation
  - — Past experiences
  - — Other people's experiences
  - — Benchmarking
  - — Transferring knowledge and information

- The ten-phase Organizational Transformation Process (OTP) provides a macro perspective of organizational change.
- You can make change stick by implementing the following nine steps:
  1. Mobilize commitment by creating a powerful sense of urgency.
  2. Tailor the change to fit the situation.
  3. Assemble a powerful change action team.
  4. Create a vision of the new future.
  5. Communicate the vision and identify WIIFM.
  6. Find the energy to build powerful coalitions.
  7. Empower everyone to make the vision a reality.
  8. Celebrate incremental victories.
  9. Anchor the new vision in the corporate culture.

Winning Action Step

Do something unexpected every time you get together with your team members.

NOTES

1   T. A. Stewart, "Welcome to the Revolution," *Fortune* 128, no. 15 (1993): 38.
2. T. A. Stewart, "What Information Costs," *Fortune* 132, no. 1 (1995): 119.
3. J. Huey, "Waking Up to the New Economy," *Fortune* 129, no. 13 (1994): 36.
4. R. Hamrin and J. Jasinowski, *Making it in America* (New York: Simon and Schuster, 1995).
5. J. Fierman, "The Contingency Work Force," *Fortune* 129, no. 2 (1994): 31.
6. Ibid., 30.
7. L. A. Schlesinger and J. L. Heskett, "The Service-Driven Service Company," *Harvard Business Review* 69, no. 5 (1991): 71–81.
8. A. W. H. Grant and L. A. Schlesinger, "Realize Your Customers' Full Profit Potential," *Harvard Business Review* 73, no. 5 (1995): 59–66.
9. J. Clark, "Striking It Rich on the Net," *U.S. News and World Report,* 15 January 1996, 51.
10. R. J. Samuelson, "Great Expectations," *Newsweek,* 8 January 1996, 24–33.
11. W. J. Rinke, *The 6 Success Strategies for Winning at Life, Love and Business* (Deerfield Beach, FL: Health Communications, Inc., 1996).
12. J. D. Adams and S. A. Spencer, "People in Transition," *Training & Development* 42 (October 1988): 61–63.

13. R. Kreitner, *Management*, 5th ed. (Boston: Houghton Mifflin Co., 1992), pp. 494–496.

14. R. Maurer, *Beyond the Wall of Resistance* (Austin, TX: Bard Books, 1996).

15. T. Galpin, "Pruning the Grapevine," *Training and Development Journal* 49, no. 4 (1995): 32.

16. P. M. Senge, *The Fifth Discipline* (New York: Doubleday, 1990), p. 1.

17. D. A. Garvin, "Building a Learning Organization," *Harvard Business Review* 71, no. 4 (1993): 78–91.

18. Ibid.

19. Ibid., 81.

20. H. Rheem, "The Learning Organization," *Harvard Business Review* 73, no. 2 (1995): 10.

21. J. Mathews, "The Little Reengine That Can't Always," *Washington Post* 9 March 1995, B-10.

22. J. P. Kotter, "Leading Change: Why Transformation Efforts Fail," *Harvard Business Review* 73, no. 2 (1995): 59–67.

23. T. Goss, R. Pascale, and A. Athos, "The Reinvention Roller Coaster: Risking the Present for a Powerful Future," *Harvard Business Review* 71, no. 6 (1993): 98.

24. P. Yetton and P. Bottger, "The Relationship Among Group Size, Member Ability, Social Decision Schemes, and Performance," *Organizational Behavior and Human Performance* 32 (1983): 145–159.

25. T. J. Larkin and S. Larkin, "Reaching and Changing Frontline Employees," *Harvard Business Review* 74, no. 3 (1996): 95–104.

Winning Action Step

There are enough suggestions in this chapter alone to help you become a *winning manager* who is able to assemble a turned on, tuned-in team that is totally dedicated to building a high-performance organization. What are you waiting for?

The Beginning

8

After all is said and done, more is said than done!

—Unknown

I bet you thought that this would be the end. No, it really is the beginning, because this is where you take over—where you get in the driver's seat of your management career.

ACHIEVE AND MAINTAIN THE COMPETITIVE ADVANTAGE

To make sure you do not join the ranks of management dinosaurs, and instead continue to thrive, I would like to suggest that you master seven competitive strategies for a brave new management world.

Take Charge of Your Career

The days when your employer looked out for your career are gone and won't be coming back. *Fortune* magazine referred to this as "a brave new Darwinian workplace," a world where seven out of ten people agree with the statement: "I'm the one in charge of my life."[1] Take advantage of the following specific strategies to put yourself in charge of your management career:

- Pick your place of work carefully. Exercise considerable care to
  find the right place of work. After all, most of us spend at least
  one-third of the best years of our life at work. That is why you
  need to find a place of employment that has a positive organizational climate. Here are a couple of easy things to look for: How
  are people talking to each other? Are they upbeat, positive, ener-
  getic, and generally positively inclined toward the management
  team, their co-workers, and the organization as a whole? Check
  for negatives by noting how many signs tell employees what they
  are *not* supposed to do, how thick the policy manual is, and how
  many policies identify things that are not allowed. During your
  interview, ask the person conducting the interview to show you
  the corporate vision, philosophy, or mission statement. If the
  interviewer does not know what you are talking about, forget it.
  Such an organization does not know where it is going and, in that
  case, you cannot help get it there. If there is a philosophy statement, see what it says about the organization's commitment to
  developing its human resources. If nothing is said, it is very likely that the organization does not value its people, the only
  resource that has the potential to appreciate. Also look for an
  organization that is willing to pay you in accordance with how
  you *per*form instead of how you *con*form, that is committed to
  innovation and calculated risk taking, and that provides ample
  opportunities to people who want to succeed. Perhaps most
  important, find employment where you can build clusters of skills
  that are readily transferable across many different organizations,
  such as project management skills. This is especially important if
  you have previously specialized. You may also want to pick your
  industry carefully. Unless you are a thrill seeker, you may want to
  stay away from the following industries since they will likely face
  incredible turmoil: banking, media, entertainment, retailing,
  telecommunications, and utilities.[2]
- Pick your boss carefully. Part of finding the right place of work is
  finding the right boss.[3] The right boss is a person who, first and
  foremost, is interested in *your* personal and professional development, knows how to practice the double win, and is on her way
  to the top. Great bosses are also excellent mentors: they tell it like

it is, provide you with straight advice, use their abundant mental energies to catch you doing things *almost right*, are intent on making *you* look good, are committed to helping you succeed, and can take you along to the top. (If you are working for such a person now, I suggest that you nurture that relationship. It is worth its weight in gold.)

- Keep your résumé floating. Even if you have found a great job and a great boss, you should still be scouting for new and challenging positions. Keeping your résumé floating is especially important if you are no longer being challenged and growing in your current job. Remember, the day you get too comfortable in your job, you are vulnerable, and it's time to look for something else because it means that someone who gets paid less than you will be able to do your job cheaper, faster, and more effectively than you are.

Winning Action Step

Grab the Yellow Pages and call the six biggest head hunters. Ask if they have you listed in their database. If not, get busy to become known in the marketplace.

Invest More in Yourself Than in Your Job

Some managers are operating under the assumption that learning is only valuable when it relates directly to their specialty or when it is paid for by their employer. Unfortunately, that will no longer suffice in this brave new world, where learning may be the only sustainable competitive advantage. In a knowledge economy, information represents *the* system for wealth creation. To succeed in such an economy, you must invest in the most important resource you will ever own: yourself. You must be infinitely curious, be a voracious lifelong learner, and continually force yourself to get out of your "box." One way to do that is to get in the habit of reading outside of your professional specialty for at least half an hour every day.

What if you don't have the time? Do what I do—listen to educational audiotapes in your car. It will enable you to learn without taking away from your precious discretionary time. This new habit will keep you on the cutting edge, provide you with all kinds of new entrepreneurial venture ideas, and help you stay motivated even on days when you experience a temporary slump.

> ## Winning Action Step
> Analyze how much you currently spend on your personal and professional development. Increase your investment by half a percent every year until you reach 5 percent of your annual income.

Think Contribution, Not Position

In the good old hierarchical days, some managers were more concerned about position titles than results. In today's flat organizations, however, the primary determinants are results and outcomes, i.e., what specific effects do your services have on customer service, the bottom line, and other specific *measurable* outcomes? The new employer–employee contract can perhaps best be summarized as follows:

> There will never be job security. You will be employed by us as long as you add value to the organization, and you are continuously responsible for finding ways to add value. In return, you have the right to demand interesting and important work, the freedom and resources to perform it well, pay that reflects your contribution, and the experience and training needed to be employable here or elsewhere.[4]

To make this work for you, I recommend the following:

- Think projects. Old organizations were organized by departments and position titles. Today, most work gets accomplished by projects. To thrive in a project environment, recognize that work gets done primarily by three distinct specialties.[5] First there are the resource providers; these are the folks who develop and supply talent or money. Your human resource manager and financial officer would fit into this category. Next are the project managers. They are responsible for making sure that the talent and resources are organized in such a way that the project gets done.

Next is the talent. These are the people who have the skill to get the job done, such as plumbers, physicians, and accountants. To thrive in this new environment, it is important that you go beyond developing your expertise (talent) and master the *winning management* skills described in this book so that you can perform equally well in the project manager or resource provider role.

- Think globally. Globalization is accelerating at a nanosecond pace. For example, the market value of U.S. direct investments overseas increased 35 percent from 1987 to 1992 while foreign investments in the United States more than doubled during the same time period.[6] Another barometer of how much globalization has taken place is the number of international phone calls made to and from the United States, which rose from 500 million in 1981 to about 2.5 billion per year a decade later.[7] To take advantage of globalization, you must dramatically increase your cultural awareness. If you now work in a primarily white, male-dominated organization, I recommend that you seek employment in a multicultural organization before it is too late. Don't know where to start? Get hold of *Fortune*'s latest issue of "America's Most Admired Corporations" (published annually in March), and apply to any of the top ten. In today's global economy you can't sustain the competitive advantage unless you are culturally diverse, so any of the top ten are a very good bet. Equally important: learn a foreign language. If you're not speaking at least one foreign language fluently, plus one more to get by, you are looking for trouble. And put your language skills to work by traveling to foreign countries. You'll really learn to speak well, become culturally sensitive, and will bring back a ton of great ideas that will accelerate your success dramatically.

Mastering languages reminds me of overhearing several business people in a restaurant in Singapore:

Businessman: What do you call an individual who speaks two languages?
Businesswoman: Bilingual.
Businessman: What do you call someone who speaks several languages?
Businesswoman: Multilingual.
Businessman: What do you call an individual who speaks only one language?
Businesswoman: American.

- Think weird. Dramatic future growth in the world will come from the *imagination business*. Consider that by the year 2000 fewer than 3 percent of the U.S work force will be growing food and fewer than 16 percent will be producing things.[8] Mind you, those 19 percent are not only taking care of our needs, but a good portion of the rest of the world. If this upsets you, it shouldn't! It means that, for the most part, the United States is continuing to become incredibly productive, much of it as a result of chip technology. So think different. No, better yet, think weird. Force yourself to color outside of the lines, to look at the same thing as everyone else and see something different. Act crazy. Be weird, just don't be comfortable. Look around you. Look at the people who are the real geniuses of today's age, like Bill Gates of Microsoft, Anita Roddick of Body Shop, and minivan inventor Harold Sperlich. All of them came up with things that they were passionate about and that no customer ever asked for. They swim upstream, ignoring all conventional wisdom. They did things not only different, they did exactly the opposite of what others perceive as rational. Remember, if it were rational, everyone would do it. And being like everyone won't enable you to succeed in this brave new world.

- Become a problem solver. One of the best ways to position yourself for advancement or pay increases is to become a problem solver. In this competitive world, you can no longer simply expect to be compensated for time, only for results and problems solved. So actively look for a problem, focus on one that impacts negatively on the bottom line, put a team together, and solve it. Then, let others know what a great job your team did and how much your team improved the profitability of your organization.

Winning Action Step

Get out your résumé and check for specific outcomes, specific impact on the bottom line, and variety and content of work, projects, and leadership experiences. Are you impressed? Would you hire this person? If so, congratulations.

Think of Yourself As Self-Employed

Seeing yourself working for one company for the rest of your career is, to put it gently, crazy! It is important that you see yourself as being self-employed, even if you "rent" your services out to someone else (your employer). Today's economy is driven by small organizations and the contingency work force, as opposed to giant corporations. Big companies are shrinking faster than a 100 percent cotton shirt. Case in point: In 1985 IBM had about 406,000 employees. By 1996 it was down to 225,000.[9] This phenomenon is so pervasive that today one of every four employees is part of the contingency work force. That number is estimated to swell to 50 percent of all employees by the year 2000.[10] Another component of the contingency work force is the self-employed, which also has risen steadily. In 1970, for example, 7.8 percent of federal income tax returns were filed on Schedule C—non-farm sole proprietorships. In 1992 it had risen to 13.6 percent.[11]

To position yourself in this contingency work force is to begin to behave as if you are self-employed, even if you are not. To get you started, pretend that you are an entrepreneur or a consultant who is selling services to a client (your employer). To make this realistic, compute your daily compensation. Be sure to add your benefits. If you are not sure how much that is, add 30 percent. Then ask yourself: Have I created value today that has exceeded my daily compensation? Repeat that question every day you are at work. You may even find it helpful to place a nice-looking sign on your desk that says: How are you creating $_____ today? The other side of the coin is to keep asking yourself, How have I grown in my job today? To make this happen, think of going to work each day with a briefcase of skills and competencies. At the end of the day, check your briefcase to see if there is more in it than at the beginning of the day. If, day after day, what you bring to work is the same as you take home, it's is time to move on.

Reality Check

The most important question to ask on the job is not "What am I getting?" The most important question to ask is "What am I becoming?"

—Jim Rhon

Make Sure Your Net-Is-Working

One of the most powerful strategies you can develop is to become a highly effective networker, both inside and outside of your organization. It is so important that of all activities managers perform at work, Luthans found that "only networking had a statistically significant relationship with success."[12] To test your networking effectiveness, ask yourself who you have been eating lunch with during the past week. If it is pretty much the same people, you are missing tremendous networking opportunities, opportunities that you won't be able to bring back if you want or need to go in business for yourself tomorrow. So start today to become an effective networker. Also get in the habit of sitting with people you do not know at meetings and to attend conferences that are sponsored by other than your primary reference group.

Check Yourself

To help keep yourself on track, you may want to ask yourself the following diagnostic questions:[13]

- Are you learning? If you are not learning something new all of the time, your value in the marketplace is diminishing rapidly. According to John Kotter, noted Harvard professor of management, "When there's nothing you can learn where you are, you've got to move on, even if they give you promotions."[14]
- Are you being taken advantage of? Your employer is taking advantage of you when you are consistently having to sacrifice your long-term development to put out short-term fires. Don't let your ego get the better of you when you are being told that you are so critical to the organization that "we can't afford to do without you." Hogwash! No one is indispensable. Never get caught in persistent short-term traps at the expense of your long-term development.
- If your job were open, would you get it? It is important that you benchmark your skills all of the time. One way to do that is to look at the want ads to find out what the marketplace is looking for. And if you do not possess the skills that the marketplace is looking for, it's time to invest more in yourself.

- How are you adding value? How long does it take you to answer this question? If you are unable to answer it immediately, in fewer than two or three sentences, you can assume that no one else knows how you contribute value either. In that case, you are a likely target during the next downsizing.
- Are you good at selling? Many managers see no need to become excellent at selling. The reality is that you sell all the time. You sell your vendor on a delivery date, you sell the president or board of directors on a raise, you sell your team members on an idea. In addition, you do the same at home with your spouse, your children, and even your pets. Since it is something you do all of the time, I recommend that you get good at it. No wait—I recommend you get *great* at it! So start looking for a good sales course and attend it this year!
- Are you computer savvy? If you have not made your computer your best friend and learned how to master a wide variety of software, as well as the information superhighway, it's time to start—*now!*
- Are you getting energized by change? If you are still fighting change, you are in trouble. All indications are that change will continue to accelerate at hyperspeed, so you might as well start welcoming it.

Winning Action Step

Go out of your way to find out what your boss does not like to do and volunteer yourself for these tasks and responsibilities. Make every effort to make your boss look good, and give her the credit in front of others. (No, that is not "brown nosing" or devious; she did have the smarts to hire you, didn't she?) Once you have demonstrated your capabilities, your boss will be more likely to assign you more important roles and responsibilities.

Take Action

And now for the *biggie!* This one is more important than all the others. It can best be summarized by ready, fire, aim! (Not a typo.) It's the one skill that when all else fails will determine whether you will thrive in this rapidly changing world. The skill is to take *action!* Action lets you know whether what you've tried works. If it does, do more of it. If it does not, try something else. Start the same process all over again, and soon you'll find yourself succeeding faster than you have ever thought possible. Action gets you away from bemoaning change and mourning the lack of job security. Action will liberate and empower you. Action will get you to grow, change, and adapt. Action will provide you with virtual job security, enable you to achieve the competitive advantage, and assure that you thrive in the game of management.

In short, be a winner, as described in Exhibit 8-1, courtesy of my able executive assistant, Gail Wolfson.

Exhibit 8-1: A Winner

To be a Winner or a Loser—
The choice is plain to see.
Here are a few things
You must *always* do,
So a winner you will be.

A winner knows that team members
Really are the key.
A winner empowers.
A winner *makes* time.
For others, not just for "me."

A winner translates dreams
Into reality.
A winner searches for answers.
A winner finds solutions.
A winner takes responsibility.

A winner says, "I will. I can."
A winner finds the opportunity
To listen to others
And learn from others.
A winner explores every possibility.

To be a Winner or a Loser—
The choice is plain to see.
Make winning choices,
Expect to succeed,
And a winner you *will* be.

I know that if you consistently apply the principles advanced in this book and put the winning action steps to work, you will succeed in the dynamic and challenging field of management, or in any other field to which you choose to apply your unlimited potential. I would like to stress to you one more time that you must *act now*. Because no matter how much you enjoyed reading this book, nothing will come of it unless you *do something*. It is just like reading a physical fitness book. No matter how good the book and no matter how well you know the principles, you just are not going to lose any weight, look any slimmer, or feel any better until you *do something!* So what are you waiting for? Don't just sit there; start traveling the journey! After all, mastering *winning management* is a journey... not a destination, *so* here is your road map to make your travels easier and more enjoyable.

Exhibit 8-2: Roadmap To Practicing *Winning Management*

I hereby commit to:
- **Give** my credit away
- **Listen** more and talk less
- **Create** desire instead of fear
- **Keep** my eye on the long term
- **Treat** *every* employee like a volunteer
- **Speak** from the heart, instead of from the head
- **Tell** team members more than they want to know
- **Focus** more on customer service and less on the bottom line
- **Invest** in team members so they can become the best they can be
- **Share** our mission, vision, and core values at least six times every day
- **Trust** customers and team members until *they* prove me wrong
- **Build** on people's strengths and accept their weaknesses
- **Manage** by appreciation instead of by exception
- **Push** decision making down to the lowest level
- **Catch** others doing things *almost right*
- **Ask** more and assign less
- **Make** work *fun*

Remember: 85 percent of your success comes from your team members, so begin *right now to give your power away!*

If I can help you travel the journey, please contact:

Wolf J. Rinke, PhD, CSP
c/o Achievement Publishers
P.O. Box 350
Clarksville, MD 21029
Phone (410) 531-9280   Fax (410) 531-9282
E-mail wolfrinke@aol.com or 74267.3703@compuserve.com
Or visit my Web site at http://speakers.com/crywolf.html

Keep your life in balance, have fun at whatever you do, nurture a positive attitude in yourself and others, and always keep your eye on your mission, vision, and core values. Most of all, be supremely confident in your ability to become a *winning manager,* and you will build a high-performance organization and achieve dramatic improvements in performance, productivity, and profitability. Until I have the opportunity to meet you at one of my live programs, continue to...

Enjoy practicing winning management!

SUMMARY

- You can achieve and maintain the competitive advantage by:
    - Taking charge of your career
    - Investing more in yourself than in your job
    - Thinking contribution, not position
    - Thinking of yourself as self-employed
    - Becoming an effective networker
    - Continually diagnosing yourself to make sure that you are competitive
    - Taking action

NOTES

1 S. Sherman, "A Brave New Darwinian Workplace," *Fortune* 127, no. 2 (1993): 51.

2. L. S. Smith and E. M. Davies, "Riskiest Industries," *Fortune* 133, no. 6 (1996): 76.

3. W. J. Rinke, *The 6 Success Strategies for Winning at Life, Love and Business* (Deerfield Beach, FL: Health Communications Inc., 1996).

4. B. O'Reilly, "The New Deal: What Companies and Employees Owe One Another," *Fortune* 129, no. 12 (1994): 44.

5. T. A. Stewart, "Planning a Career in a World without Managers," *Fortune* 131, no. 5 (1995): 72–80.

6. T. A. Stewart, "Welcome to the Revolution," *Fortune* 128, no. 15 (1993): 67.

7. Ibid., 76.

8. W. Kiechel, "A Manager's Career in the New Economy," *Fortune* 129, no. 7 (1994): 69.

9. J. Nocera, "Living with Layoffs," *Fortune* 133, no. 6 (1996): 69.

10. J. Fierman, "The Contingency Work Force," *Fortune* 129, no. 2 (1994): 30-36.

11. T.A. Stewart, "Planning a Career in a World without Managers."

12. F. Luthans, "Successful vs. Effective Real Managers," *Academy of Management Executive* 11 (1988): 130.

13. T. A. Stewart, "Planning a Career in a World without Managers."

14. Ibid., 76.

Reality Check

Without action, a terrible thing will happen—nothing!

—Wolf J. Rinke

For Your Continuing Learning...

Here is a list of resources that will help you become a *winning manager* faster:

Bartlett, C. A., and S. Ghoshal. "Changing the Role of Top Management: Beyond Strategy to Purpose," *Harvard Business Review* 72, no. 6 (1994): 79–88.

Batten, J. *Building a Total Quality Culture*. Menlo Park, CA: Crisp Publications, 1992.

Bennis, W., and B. Nanus. *Leaders. The Strategies for Taking Charge*. New York: Harper and Row, 1985.

Bowen, D. E., and E. E. Lawler. "Empowering Service Employees," *Sloan Management Review* 36, no. 4 (Summer 1995): 73-84.

Collins, J. C., and J. I. Porras. *Built to Last: Successful Habits of Visionary Companies*. New York: Harper Business, 1994.

Covey, S. R. *Principle Centered Leadership*. New York: Simon and Schuster, 1992.

DePree, M. *Leadership Is an Art*. New York: Bantam Doubleday Dell, 1989.

Dess, G. G., et al. "The New Corporate Architecture," *Academy of Mangement Executive* 9, no. 3 (1995): 7–20.

Drucker, P. F. *Managing for the Future*. New York: Truman Talley Books/Dutton, 1992.

Farkas, C. M., and S. Wetlander. "The Ways Chief Executive Officers Lead." *Harvard Business Review* 74, no. 3 (1996): 110–122.

Greenleaf, R. K. *Servant Leadership*. New York: Paulist Press, 1977.

Gross, T. S. *Positively Outrageous Service*. New York: Master Media, 1991.

Hamel, G., and C. K. Prahalad. *Competing for the Future*. Boston: Harvard Business School Press, 1994.

Hammer, M., and J. Champy. *Reengineering the Corporation: A Manifesto for a Business Revolution*. New York: Harper Collins Publishers, Inc., 1993.

Handy, C. *The Age of Paradox*. Boston: Harvard Business School Press, 1994.

Jasinowski, J., and R. Hamrin. *Making It in America*. New York: Simon and Schuster, 1995.

Johansen, R., and R. Swigart. *Upsizing the Individual in the Downsized Organization*. Reading, MA: Addison-Wesley Publishing Company, 1995.

Kawasaki, G. *How to Drive the Competition Crazy*. New York: Hyperion, 1995.

Kotter, J. P. *A Force for Change: How Leadership Differs from Management*. New York: The Free Press, 1990.

Kouzes, J. M., and B. Z. Posner. *The Leadership Challenge*. San Francisco: Jossey-Bass Publishers, 1987.

Lawler, E. E. *High-Involvement Management.* San Francisco: Jossey-Bass Publishers, 1986.

Livingston, J. S. "Pygmalion in Management," *Harvard Business Review* 66, no. 5 (1988): 121–130.

Manz, C. C., and H. P. Sims. *Super-Leadership.* New York: Prentice Hall Press, 1989.

Maurer, R. *Beyond the Wall of Resistance.* Austin, TX: Bard Books, Inc., 1996.

Nelson, B. *1001 Ways to Reward Employees.* New York: Workman Publishing, 1994.

Peters, T. J. *Thriving on Chaos.* New York: A. Knopf, 1988.

Peters, T. J. *The Pursuit of Wow!* New York: Vintage Books, 1994.

Pfeffer, J. *Competitive Advantage Through People.* Boston: Harvard Business School Press, 1994.

Reichheld, F. F. *The Loyalty Effect: The Hidden Force Behind Growth, Profits, and Lasting Value.* Boston: Bain and Company, Inc., 1996.

Rinke, W. J. "Empowering Your Team Members," *Supervisory Management* 34, no. 4 (1989): 21–24.

Rinke, W. J. "How to Build a Winning Team," *Food Management* 26, no. 6 (1991): 39.

Rinke, W. J. "How to Develop a Positive Attitude. How to Maintain a Positive Attitude," *Bottom Line Personal* 15, no. 9 (2 May 1994): 9.

Rinke, W. J. "How to Stay Positive in a Changing and Competitive Health Care Environment," *Long-term Care Administrator* 28, no. 7 (1994): 1, 11.

Rinke, W. J. *Make It a Winning Life: Success Strategies for Life, Love and Business.* Clarksville, MD: Achievement Publishers, 1992. (Also available in audio and video format, 1996.)

Rinke, W. J. "Maximizing Management Potential by Building Self-Esteem," *Management Solutions* 33, no. 3 (1988): 11–16.

Rinke, W. J. *The 6 Success Strategies for Winning at Life, Love and Business.* Deerfield Beach, FL: Health Communications Inc., 1996.

Rinke, W. J. "Treat Your People Like Winners," *Restaurants USA* 9, no. 4 (1989): 12–16.

Rinke, W. J. *The Winning Foodservice Manager: Strategies for Doing More with Less,* 2nd ed. Clarksville, MD: Achievement Publishers, division of Wolf Rinke Associates, Inc., 1990.

Rinke, W. J. *"Winning Management:* Doing More With Less," *Supervisory Management* (June 1991): 4.

Rinke, W. J. *"Winning Management:* How to Build a Solid Foundation for Total Quality Management (TQM)," *AFSMI Journal* 17, no. 3 (1992): 49–52.

Rinke, W. J. *Winning Management: How to Empower Your Team and Provide Consistently High Quality.* Clarksville, MD: Wolf Rinke Associates, Inc., 1995 (video training album).

Rinke, W. J. *Winning Management: 6 Fail-Safe Strategies for Building High-Performance Organizations.* Clarksville, MD: Wolf Rinke Associates, Inc., 1997 (audio album).

Rosener, J. B. *America's Competitive Secret: Utilizing Women as a Management Strategy.* New York: Oxford University Press, 1995.

Senge, P. M. "The Leader's New Work: Building Learning Organizations," *Sloan Management Review* (Fall 1990): 7–23.

Simons, R. "Control in an Age of Empowerment," *Harvard Business Review* 73, no. 2 (1995): 80–88.

Smith, D. K. *Taking Charge of Change.* Reading, MA: Addison-Wesley Publishing Company, 1996.

Stayer, R. "How I Learned to Let My Workers Lead," *Harvard Business Review* 68, no. 6 (1990): 66–83.

Sukenick, R. *Networking Your Way to Success.* Dubuque, IA: Kendall Hunt, 1995.

Tannen, D. *Talking from 9 to 5.* New York: Avon Books, 1995.

Tichy, N. M., and S. Sherman. *Control Your Destiny or Someone Else Will.* New York: Doubleday, 1993.

Weiss, A. *Our Emperors Have No Clothes.* Franklin Lakes, NJ: Career Press, 1995.

Winslow, C. D., and W. L. Bramer. *Future Work: Putting Knowledge to Work in the Knowledge Economy.* New York: The Free Press, 1995.

Zenger, J. H., et al. *Leading Teams: Mastering the New Role.* Homewood, IL: Business One Irwin, 1994.

Reality Check

Real learning occurs after you think you know it all.

—Earl Nightingale

Index

About the Author...

Wolf J. Rinke, PhD, RD, CSP, is the founder and president of Wolf Rinke Associates, Inc., a human resources development and management consulting company dedicated to helping *organizations and individuals maximize their potential.*

Dr. Rinke is:
- A dynamic certified speaking professional (CSP*) who is internationally known for his ability to energize, entertain, and empower. (*CSP is a credential earned by fewer than three hundred individuals worldwide.)
- A highly effective management consultant with more than thirty years of hands-on management and leadership experience.
- A widely published author of audio, video, and print media.
- An associate professor with adjunct faculty appointments at the University of Maryland and The Johns Hopkins University.
- A media personality who has been featured on CNN and hundreds of other TV and radio programs.
- A highly decorated retired, Lieutenant Colonel of the U.S. Army Medical Specialist Corps.
- A high achiever who started to work full time on a ship at age fourteen and worked his way to the top.

Wolf holds a Ph.D. from the University of Wisconsin and has been honored for his many accomplishments by various professional organizations and the military. He is a member of four honor societies and has been listed in *Who's Who in the World* and nine other international biographical references.
To get in touch with Dr. Rinke, contact:

Achievement Publishers
P.O. Box 350
Clarksville, MD 21029
Phone (410) 531-9280 Fax (410) 531-9282
E-mail: wolfrinke@aol.com or 74267.3703@compuserve.com
Web site: http://speakers.com/crywolf.html

What Do You Think About This Book?

This is your chance to let me know what you think of this book. You can even become an expert contributor. Please answer the following questions in enough detail so that I have a clear idea of what, why, when, where, and how something did, or did not, work for you. If I incorporate your input in the next edition or in another book, I will send you a personalized copy of the book absolutely *free*.

Wolf, the strategies you described in chapter _____ on pages _____ worked for me.

This is how I applied them:

_____

_____

_____

_____

These are the results I achieved:

_____

_____

_____

_____

Wolf, the strategies you described in chapter _____ on pages _____ did not work for me.

This is how I tried to use them:

_____

_____

_____

_____

These are the results I achieved:

_____

_____

_____

_____

This is how I fixed it:

_____

_____

_____

_____

Wolf, the following pages describe a personal experience related to the topic of your book. Please feel free to use it as you wish.

Your signature _____

Today's date _____

Your name, complete mailing address, and telephone number (please print):

_____

_____

_____

_____

Send to:
Achievement Publishers
P.O. Box 350
Clarksville, MD 21029
Fax (410) 531-9282

Thanks in advance for taking the time to provide me with your feedback!

P.S. If you find any errors—please let us know those, too!

Your group will be...

energized... motivated... empowered!

Wolf J. Rinke, PhD, CSP

America's Business Success Coach

Benefit from high-impact, *customized* presentations:

- Achieving the Competitive Advantage in a Rapidly Changing World
- Winning Management: Six Fail-Safe Strategies for Building High-Performance Organizations
- Exceptional Quality Service (EQS): How to Consistently Exceed Customers' Expectations
- Coaching: How to Achieve Extraordinary Results with Ordinary People
- Creativity and Innovation: How to Out-think, Out-smart, and Out-perform the Competition
- Win-Win Selling: How to Sell More, Faster, by Mastering the Inner Game of Selling

"Dr. Rinke delivers excellence every time."

Consulting Services

Want to build a high-performance organization, improve quality, deliver superior service and *achieve dramatic improvements in performance, productivity, and profitability?* Contact us. We will help you maximize the only resource that has the potential to appreciate: *you* and your *people!*

**To schedule Dr. Rinke to speak at your next event,
CRY WOLF... 1-800-828-WOLF** (9653)

WINNING ORDER FORM

NO	DESCRIPTION	QTY	PRICE	TOTAL
	Books			
B101	Make It a Winning Life: Success Strategies for Life, Love and Business (hard cover)		24.95	
B102	The Winning Foodservice Mgr: Strategies for Doing More with Less, 2nd ed. (hard cover)		32.50	
B103	Winning Mgt: 6 Fail-Safe Strategies for Building High-Performance Organizations (hard cover)		24.95	
	Audiotapes			
A101	Make It a Winning Life: Success Strategies for Life, Love and Business (6 cassette album)		59.95	
A128	Winning Mgt: 6 Fail-Safe Strategies for Building High Performance Organizations (6 cassette album)		59.95	
A126	Make It a Winning Life (40 min audiotape)		14.95	
A127	Winning Management (40 min audiotape)		14.95	
	Training Videos			
V101	Make It a Winning Life Video Album (40 min video, 57 pg workbook, 40 min audiotape)		95.00	
V102	Winning Management Video Album (40 min video, 55 pg leaders guide, 40 min audiotape)		95.00	
	Other Winning Products			
M101	Make It a Winning Life Monthly Mental Stretch Action Pack		6.95	
M102	Make It a Winning Life Monthly Reminder Action Pack		6.95	
M104	111% Gold Tone Lapel Pin		6.95	

Shipping & Handling: Order Amount		
$50 or less add $4.50	$201 to $250 add $14.50	
$51 to $100 add $7.00	$251 to $300 add $17.00	
$101 to $150 add $9.50	$301 to $350 add $19.50	
$151 to $200 add $12.00	$351 to $400 add $22.00	
Canada - S&H x 2	Foreign Overseas - S&H x 4	

Subtotal		
Maryland Residents, add 5% sales tax		
Shipping & Handling (see table)		
International Orders: Credit Card only TOTAL		

For faster service FAX your credit card charge order to (410)531-9282
or call (800)828-9653 or (410)531-9280

> Need more than 6 of anything?
> Call us for bulk discounts!

> **UNCONDITIONAL GUARANTEE:**
> You will be totally satisfied with our products, or
> you may return them and get your money back!

PAYMENT

❑ Check **payable to Wolf Rinke Associates, Inc.**

❑ Please charge $_____ to my MC/Visa/AMEX/DISC

CC# _____

Expiration Date _____ Signature_____

(We need your CC#, the expiration date, and your signature to ship your charge order.)

Please send my order to: (Please print)

Name_____

Tel.# (_____)_____

Address _____

_____

City_____State____ Zip_____

WOLF RINKE ASSOCIATES, INC.
P.O. Box 350 • Clarksville, MD 21029-0350 USA
e-mail: wolfrinke@aol.com or 74267,3703@compuserve.com

Are you tired of slash and burn tactics? Are you fed up with re-engineering, downsizing and other interventions which, at best, only achieve short-term benefits? Or are you ready to build the foundation for a solid high-performance organization... an organization that **unleashes the power of your most underutilized resource: your *people?*** In short, are you ready to achieve a sustainable long-term advantage which will force your competitors to play catch-up?

If so, this book is for YOU! Especially if you are a CEO, president, or owner of a small to midsize company; or a manager who wants to master cutting edge strategies which will get you promoted, *faster!*

In one of the most practical management books ever written, Dr. Rinke provides you with easy to implement, step by step, fail-safe strategies that will enable you to thrive in a rapidly changing, highly competitive, global economy.

More specifically, this book shows you how to:
- **build** a high-performance team
- **reduce** employee turnover
- **empower** without losing control
- **convince** every employee to buy into your vision
- **grow** and retain highly qualified people
- **implement** an effective reward system
- **master** strategies that build trust
- **manage** more like a coach than a "cop"
- **compete** on service not on price
- **overcome** communication barriers
- **attain** dramatic improvements in customer satisfaction
- **build** a highly effective learning organization
- **get** team members to love change
- **achieve** extraordinary results with ordinary people
- **plus much, much more!**